A Companion to the United States Constitution and Its Amendments

Second Edition

A COMPANION TO THE UNITED STATES CONSTITUTION AND ITS AMENDMENTS

Second Edition

John R. Vile

Westport, Connecticut
London

Library of Congress Cataloging-in-Publication Data

Vile, John R.
   A companion to the United States Constitution and its amendments /
John R. Vile.—2nd. ed.
     p.   cm.
   Includes bibliographical references and index.
   ISBN 0-275-95785-3 (alk. paper)
    1. United States—Constitutional law. 2. United States.
Constitution. I. United States. Constitution. II. Title.
KF4550.V55   1997
342.73'02—dc20
[347.3022]   96-33191

British Library Cataloguing in Publication Data is available.

Library of Congress Catalog Card Number: 96-33191
ISBN: 0-275-95785-3

First published in 1997

Praeger Publishers, 88 Post Road West, Westport, CT 06881
An imprint of Greenwood Publishing Group, Inc.

Printed in the United States of America

♾™

The paper used in this book complies with the
Permanent Paper Standard issued by the National
Information Standards Organization (Z39.48–1984).

10 9 8 7 6 5 4 3 2 1

To my wife, Linda Christensen Vile

Contents

The Colonial Setting • The Declaration of Independence •
The Background of the Declaration • The Purpose of the
Document • The Idea of Equality of Human Rights • The
Purpose of Government • The Right of Revolution •
Charges Against the English King • Indictments Against the
King and the Parliament • War Atrocities • Recapitulation
of Earlier Petitions • Conclusion • The Articles of
Confederation • The Background • The Principles and
Structures • The Problems • Prelude to the Constitutional
Convention • The Constitutional Convention • The
Delegates • The Rules • The Virginia Plan • The New
Jersey Plan • Prominent Convention Issues • Ratification
of the Constitution • References and Suggestions for
Further Study

Presidential Appointments • The State of the Union
Address • Power to Convene and Adjourn Congress • The
President as Chief Diplomat • Power to Execute the Laws
and Executive Privilege • Commissioning of Military
Officers • Presidential Impeachment • References and
Suggestions for Further Study

Organization and Guidelines • The U.S. Supreme Court
and Other Inferior Courts • Judicial Tenure • Judicial
Qualifications • Judicial Compensation • The Number of
Justices • Supreme Court Decisions • Jurisdiction •
Cases Based on Subject Matter and Parties to the Suit •
Cases of Original and Appellate Jurisdiction • Limits on
the Judicial Branch • Judicial Powers • Statutory
Interpretation and Judicial Review • Judicial Review in
Practice • Protections • Trial by Jury • Treason • The
Nature of Article III • References and Suggestions for
Further Study

Three Forms of Government • Layer Cake or Marble
Cake? • Obligations of States to One Another • The
Full Faith and Credit Clause • The Privileges and
Immunities Clause • Extradition • The Fugitive Slave
Clause • The Admission of New States • Governing the
Territories • Obligations of the Nation to the States • The
Guarantee Clause • Rejected Doctrines of Federalism •
Interposition • Nullification • Secession • The Status of
Local Governments • References and Suggestions for
Further Study

The Importance of Amendments • Amending Procedures
• The Most Common Route • The Unused Convention
Mechanism • Rescissions • Is the Amending Process
Exclusive? • Unamendable Provisions • The History of
Amendments in the United States • Article VI • The

Continuing Validity of Debts • The Supremacy Clause •
Oaths of Office and Prohibition of Religious Tests • Article
VII • Ratification of the Constitution • The Convention
Resolution • References and Suggestions for Further Study

Background • Application of the Bill of Rights • The Bill
of Rights: A Floor or a Ceiling? • The Idea of Rights •
The Placement of the First Amendment • The
Establishment and Free Exercise Clauses • The Three-Part
Lemon Test and the Wall of Separation • Application of
the Establishment Clause • The Free Exercise Clause and
the Belief/Practice Dichotomy • Application of the Free
Exercise Clause • Justifications for Freedom of Speech •
The Development of Free Speech Tests • Subsidiary
Principles • Obscenity • Symbolic Speech • Fighting
Words • Libel • Commercial Speech • Freedom of the
Press and Prior Restraint • Assembly and Petition • The
Right to Bear Arms • The Prohibition Against Quartering
Troops • References and Suggestions for Further Study

Unreasonable Searches and Seizures • Administrative
Searches • The Exclusionary Rule • Indictment by Grand
Jury • The Double Jeopardy Provision • Protection
Against Self-Incrimination • The Due Process Clause •
The Takings Clause • Right to a Petit Jury • The Rights of
Notification, Confrontation, and Compulsory Process • The
Right to Counsel • Petit Juries in Common Law Cases •
References and Suggestions for Further Study

The Eighth Amendment • The Ninth Amendment and the
Right to Privacy • The Tenth Amendment and States'
Rights • The Eleventh Amendment and Suits Against the

Preface to Second Edition

Almost all Americans know the story of Goldilocks and the three bears. During her visit to the bears' house, Goldilocks discovered that porridge can be too hot or too cold, and chairs and beds can be too hard or too soft. So too, students and citizens find that books can be too long or too short, too ponderous or too breezy. There is, to switch to an Aristotelian analogy, a "golden mean" in regard to good books as well as in respect to conduct and character. This book attempts to strike such a golden mean in regard to a document that is generally conceded to have initiated a new era in human governance. That document is the U.S. Constitution as it has been interpreted and amended over the last two hundred years or so.

One who looks will find no lack of dense scholarly commentaries on the meaning of the Constitution and the latest interpretation to be formulated by the most obscure court or scholar on the Constitution's most controversial provision. The author once heard a colleague comment, with only a hint of hyperbole, that a prominent law professor rewrote the Constitution every time he tried to explain it. In a similar vein, countless books have been published over the past ten years examining principles of constitutional interpretation. To such legal commentaries and hornbooks can be added valuable casebooks, studies of the time and philosophy of the Founding Fathers, and even accounts of the day-to-day proceedings of the Constitutional Convention of 1787. So too, there are airy books that do more to extol the Constitution than to explain it or help a reader understand it. Truly, more has already been written on the subject than can possibly be profitably read by most students and, were the subject not so inherently fascinating and important, readers could be excused had they decided long ago to declare a moratorium on reading new books about the Constitution.

In writing the first edition of this work, the author believed there was room, and, indeed, need for another book. He has been gratified to find that students and professors alike have responded positively to a volume whose author, making no pretensions to having cited every Supreme Court decision or scholarly treatise on each subject, focused instead on how much consensus there is about the meaning of the Constitution. Profiting from further study of this document and perceiving a need for somewhat greater detail than was provided in the first volume, the author has not only updated the second edition but has also expanded the number of prior Supreme Court decisions discussed. In the process, he has attempted to see that the reader's view of the constitutional forest remains unobscured by attention to too many judicial trees. To this end, this edition includes a glossary of key terms and a description of 50 key Supreme Court decisions with which many students will want to familiarize themselves.

This book is quite deliberately referred to as a "companion" to the Constitution. The idea of designating the manuscript as a "guide" seemed overly pretentious, whereas the notion of calling it an "interpretation" seemed too individualistic. The author hopes that this book will be a good companion, or accompanist, to a reading of the Constitution. He has attempted to devote rigorous scholarly attention to the Constitution and to cultivate sufficient empathy with the thoughts of those who have framed, interpreted, and amended the document so that he can introduce readers to it much as he might introduce them to one of his friends. Like one might feel about a friend, the author has great respect for a document that he recognizes to be flawed but believes is still one of the greatest documents of its kind in the world.

If such readers come to understand and appreciate the Constitution better because of this author's efforts, he will be grateful that he has been able to repay part of the immense debt he owes to his teachers (many themselves intimate companions to the Constitution), to his brave and wise forebears who were so committed to establishing and preserving a system of liberty under law, and to those who today still cherish and defend constitutional government.

Acknowledgments

More than any manuscript I have written to date, I am indebted in the writing of this book to my students, especially those who have taken my classes in American government and in constitutional law. In the former class, it has been my practice since I began full-time teaching in 1977 to devote at least a week or two toward explicating the Declaration of Independence and the Constitution section by section, and another similar period to dealing specifically with the Bill of Rights, the post–Civil War Amendments, and those of the Progressive Era. In my constitutional law classes, I have utilized a traditional casebook approach, and, again, I have found the knowledge of certain cases to be central both to an understanding of the meaning of the Constitution itself and to a grasp of its historical development. I have tried to put this knowledge to use in this book, realizing, of course, that an average student or citizen does not have need for the legal complexities that are typically the subject of constitutional law classes and that the Constitution remains superior to many of its interpretations.

In writing both editions of this book, I have been especially influenced by my previous writings and by those who helped with them. Praeger has published four other of my books that deal with the theme of constitutional amendment and change, and I have drawn from each of these in writing this volume. In addition, Peter Lang has published a book of readings that I have selected on the subject, and ABC-CLIO has published an *Encyclopedia of Constitutional Amendment, Proposed Amendments, and Amending Issues, 1789–1995*, that has enabled me, since writing the first edition of this book, to familiarize myself in greater depth with many parts of the Constitution. Since writing the first edition, I have also written an essay for Congressional Quarterly's second edition of its *Guide to the Presidency* that has enabled me to examine this institution, and the constitutional issues surrounding it, in greater detail. I owe special thanks to Mike Nelson and others who helped edit this chapter.

I want therefore to thank all those teachers, students, friends, colleagues, and administrators who have taught, encouraged, and challenged me, and furthered my scholarly endeavors. I would also like to thank those at Middle Tennessee State University who have provided continuing research support. Everyone at City Desktop Productions, Inc., in Racine, Wisconsin, deserves thanks, as does Jim Dunton, the acquisitions editor at Praeger.

All who know me well will understand how indebted I am to my wife Linda and why I have dedicated this book to her. Over twenty years ago, we pledged our lives to God and to one another, and I deeply appreciate the affection, encouragement, support, and faith that she has given to me and to our two daughters, Virginia and Rebekah. I have previously dedicated both my dissertation and the first edition of this book to my wife, and I am pleased to rededicate this volume to her in deepest appreciation for her continuing affection and support.

Chapter 1

The Background of the Constitution

THE COLONIAL SETTING

Americans today often take their freedoms for granted, but such liberties have come at a high cost and depend on a host of factors, not least of which is a commitment to the rule of law embodied in the U.S. Constitution. Long before this document was written, however, the seeds were being planted for a free nation. Already, there was recognition of the distinction between liberty and license, between representative democracy and mob rule.

Before there was a United States of America, there were 13 colonies planted in a newly discovered world an ocean away from Europe. Because of this distance, many colonies had, almost from the beginning, exercised a good deal of self-government. Settlers at Virginia had established a legislative branch, or House of Burgesses, by 1619, and settlers at Plymouth in the next year would draw up a charter of government, or Mayflower Compact, even before they disembarked from their ship. Many indeed came to the New World in search of freedoms denied them in Europe and, while the colonists were not always as good about granting freedom to others as in seeking it for themselves, this goal remained uppermost in many of their minds.

Over time, England came to rule over all 13 of the colonies, but this rule was initially fairly mild and colonial self-governance was encouraged under the British policy of "salutary neglect." The distance was

simply too great, and British obligations elsewhere too many, for the
mother country to pay much attention to the American colonies. Such
at least was the case until the French and Indian War of 1754 through
1763. Actually a worldwide conflict between British and French allies,
the war in America pitted French and Indian interests against colonial
and British ones. At war's end, English leaders thought it only proper
for Britain to collect taxes from the colonies for the troops she had
supplied. For their part, the colonists felt partly like British pawns.
Moreover, they strongly objected to the idea of English taxes.

Despite the fact that they were colonists, most Americans
thought of themselves as British citizens, fully eligible for all
English rights. As far back as the Magna Carta of 1215, which had
been wrested from a reluctant King John by the English noblemen
and which had been gradually given broader application, a critical
right of English citizenship was embodied in the principle of "no
taxation without representation." English leaders claimed that, as
citizens, the colonists were virtually represented in Parliament.
Absent actual representation in Parliament, however, the colonists
denied that this legislature had the authority, or sovereignty, to tax
or legislate for them. They believed that such an unaccountable
power posed a threat not only to their pocketbooks, but also to
their most basic liberties.

Students of American history know that, while there were other
points of controversy, this dispute over parliamentary authority was
a primary cause of the American Revolution of 1776. Students of the
period may further be able to name the various tax plans—the
Stamp Act, the Tea Act, the Townshend Duties, and the like—that
the British unsuccessfully tried to require of the colonists. At least
through the initial controversy, most inhabitants of America continued to insist that they were good English citizens, simply asking for
the rights to which they were entitled. Denying parliamentary sovereignty, most colonists still acknowledged allegiance to the British
king, earlier kings having granted most colonial charters, the
antecedents to later state constitutions. Unfortunately, the British
king of the day, George III, was little more sympathetic to colonial
interests than was the Parliament. As he rebuffed petition after petition of the so-called continental congresses that the colonists had
convened, a permanent split seemed more and more likely. This
split, it is generally agreed, was furthered by a book by English-born
Thomas Paine, *Common Sense*, published in January 1776. Pointing
to all the disadvantages, including war and oppression, that he

believed were inherent in kingship and the notion of hereditary succession by which future monarchs ascended the throne, Paine proposed that the colonists declare their independence and proclaim that the law should be the only king in America.

Fighting between the colonists and the British had continued sporadically since the battles at Lexington and Concord in April 1775, and the colonists were coming closer and closer to Paine's view that the only remedy for their complaints was a firm declaration of independence. Thus, on June 7, 1776, Virginia delegate Richard Henry Lee introduced three resolutions before the Second Continental Congress. The first resolution proclaimed:

That these United Colonies are, and of right ought to be, free and independent States, that they are absolved from all allegiance to the British Crown, and that all political connection between them and the State of Great Britain is, and ought to be, totally dissolved (Solberg, *The Federal Convention and Formation of the Union of the American States*, p. 32).

Other resolutions called for forming military alliances and for creating "a plan of confederation."

THE DECLARATION OF INDEPENDENCE

The Background of the Declaration

Five men were appointed to the committee to write a Declaration of Independence: John Adams, Ben Franklin, Roger Sherman, Robert Livingston, and Thomas Jefferson. Of these, Jefferson turned out to be the most important. It was he who authored the document, later revisions being made by Adams and Franklin and the Continental Congress itself. The American Declaration of Independence, on whose fiftieth anniversary both John Adams and Thomas Jefferson were to die, would be one of three accomplishments for which Jefferson wished to be remembered on his tombstone at Monticello, Virginia (the other two were his authorship of the Virginia Statute for Religious Freedom and his founding of the University of Virginia).

As lucid as any document in American history with the possible exception of Lincoln's Inaugural and Gettysburg Addresses (which themselves drew much of their power from evoking principles implicit in the Declaration), the Declaration of Independence was not intended to be particularly novel. Thus writing to Richard Henry Lee about the Declaration of Independence in 1825, Jefferson said it was designed:

Not to find out new principles, or new arguments, never before thought of, not merely to say things which had never been said before; but to place before mankind the common sense of the subject, in terms so plain and firm as to command their assent. Neither aiming at originality of principles or sentiments, nor yet copied from any particular or previous writing, it was intended to be an expression of the American mind (Becker, *The Declaration of Independence*, pp. 26–27).

The value of this document, then, rests not in its originality but in its expression of American sentiments.

When, in the course of human events, it becomes necessary for one people to dissolve the political bands which have connected them with another, and to assume, among the powers of the earth, the separate and equal station to which the laws of nature and of nature's God entitle them, a decent respect to the opinions of mankind requires that they should declare the causes which impel them to the separation.

The Purpose of the Document

However much the Declaration of Independence might have been directed at mobilizing opinion within the once separate colonies, its opening words indicate its primary purpose was that of explaining to foreign nations why the colonies were declaring their independence. In so doing, Jefferson resorted to common philosophic concepts of his day, referring, for example, to "the laws of nature" and to "nature's God." He further indicated that, whatever the former relations between Great Britain and America, the residents of the two areas were now distinct peoples.

We hold these truths to be self-evident: That all men are created equal; that they are endowed by their Creator with certain unalienable rights; that among these are life, liberty, and the pursuit of happiness;

The Idea of Equality of Human Rights

The most profound words of the Declaration are in the second paragraph. To modern ears, the words may appear sexist, the word "men" being used instead of "human beings." In eighteenth century times, as today's, however, the male pronoun was often used as a way of including both genders. Moreover, although written by a slaveholder—albeit one who was never really comfortable with the nefarious institution—the Declaration did not explicitly limit its coverage to whites, and many blacks and whites, including Abraham Lincoln, Frederick Douglass, and Martin Luther King, Jr., would subsequently use its words as justifications for limiting slavery, granting emancipation, and extending full rights to black Americans. Recognizing that the onetime colonies were now claiming to be independent of Britain, Jefferson now phrased his grievances not in terms of the rights of Englishmen (although Englishmen would be most familiar with the kinds of rights Jefferson cited), but in broader terms of the rights of men.

The notion of human equality is not necessarily as self-evident as Jefferson made it sound. Certainly, individuals vary immensely in their physical and intellectual endowments, so immensely that the great Greek philosopher Plato had declared in one mythical formulation in *The Republic* that individuals could be separated into three groups, those with souls of gold, those with silver, and those with bronze. Jefferson would have none of this. Undoubtedly, he recognized and appreciated human differences; he would himself later refer to the need for an aristocracy of talent and virtue. More importantly, however, he recognized human likenesses. All are born of the same species, and, as human beings made by a common Creator, all are entitled to certain rights. Jefferson designated these rights as "life, liberty, and the pursuit of happiness." The last category is perhaps most interesting for, if Jefferson had completely followed the lead of John Locke, a seventeenth century English theorist who otherwise seems to have exerted a significant influence on the Declaration of Independence, he might have used the word "property" instead. Presumably the pursuit of happiness is a more inclusive term; moreover, it recognizes that although government may provide the conditions for individuals to seek their own happiness, they can rarely, if ever, guarantee its fulfillment.

that, to secure these rights, governments are instituted among men, deriving their just powers from the consent of the governed;

The Purpose of Government

Different regimes have different purposes. For some, the primary goal is to enforce what they believe to be the will of God. Other regimes, detested alike by political theorists and subjects from classical times to the present, have little more purpose than the aggrandizement of the person or persons in power. For Jefferson, by contrast, the true end of government was to serve human beings, and, specifically, to secure their rights. Agreeing with social contract theorists like John Locke, Jefferson declared that governments and governors derive their "just powers," not from the will of God—what James I and other English kings had designated as "the divine right of kings"—or the mandate of the leader, but rather from "the consent of the governed."

that whenever any form of government becomes destructive of these ends, it is the right of the people to alter or to abolish it, and to institute new government, laying its foundation on such principles, and organizing its powers in such form, as to them shall seem most likely to effect their safety and happiness. Prudence, indeed, will dictate that governments long established should not be changed for light and transient causes; and accordingly all experience hath shown that mankind are more disposed to suffer, while evils are sufferable, than to right themselves by abolishing the forms to which they are accustomed. But when a long train of abuses and usurpations, pursuing invariably the same object, evinces a design to reduce them under absolute despotism, it is their right, it is their duty, to throw off such government, and to provide new guards for their future security.

The Right of Revolution

Here Jefferson advances the case for revolution. If government is a human creation designed to secure human happiness, then the people have the right to change or overthrow it when it fails to accomplish its objects.

In proclaiming a right of revolution, Jefferson was following the lead of John Locke and other English theorists. Like them, he faced the problem of how to justify a particular revolution without undermining future governments and creating anarchy. Jefferson's solution was to argue that revolution should not occur on a whim or for what he designated as "light and transient causes" but rather only "when a long train of abuses and usurpations . . . evinces a design to [create] . . . absolute despotism."

Such has been the patient sufferance of these colonies; and such is now the necessity which constrains them to alter their former system of government. The history of the present King of Great Britain is a history of repeated injuries and usurpations, all having in direct object the establishment of an absolute tyranny over these states. To prove this, let facts be submitted to a candid world.

He has refused to assent to laws, the most wholesome and necessary for the public good.

He has forbidden his governors to pass laws of immediate and pressing importance, unless suspended in their operation till his assent should be obtained; and, when so suspended, he has utterly neglected to attend to them.

He has refused to pass other laws for the accommodation of large districts of people, unless those people would relinquish the right of representation in the legislature, a right inestimable to them, and formidable to tyrants only.

He has called together legislative bodies at places unusual, uncomfortable, and distant from the depository of their public records, for the sole purpose of fatiguing them into compliance with his measures.

He has dissolved representative houses repeatedly, for opposing, with manly firmness, his invasions on the rights of the people.

He has refused for a long time, after such dissolutions, to cause others to be elected; whereby the legislative powers, incapable of annihilation, have returned to the people at large for their exercise; the state remaining, in the mean time, exposed to all the dangers of invasions from without and convulsions from within.

He has endeavored to prevent the population of these states; for that purpose obstructing the laws for naturalization of foreigners; refusing to pass others to encourage their migration hither, and raising the conditions of new appropriations of lands.

He has obstructed the administration of justice, by refusing his assent to laws for establishing judiciary powers.

He has made judges dependent on his will alone, for the tenure of their offices, and the amount and payment of their salaries.

He has erected a multitude of new offices, and sent hither swarms of officers to harass our people and eat out their substance.

He has kept among us, in times of peace, standing armies, without the consent of our legislatures.

He has affected to render the military independent of, and superior to, the civil power.

Charges Against the English King

Jefferson devoted the central portion of the Declaration to establishing that George III was the type of tyrant to whom resistance was justified. Most colonists, it may be recalled, had already previously rejected the notion of parliamentary sovereignty, so it was natural that the king, descendant of the monarchs who had granted the original colonial charters, would now be the focus of their complaints.

The 25 or so accusations against the king that follow are designed, much like a legal brief, with a view toward showing a pattern of abuses that evidenced a hostile design on the part of the king toward the colonists. Many relate to abuses of the colonists' rights to self-government and thus point to the type of institutions Americans would have preferred. Thus, for example, Jefferson accused the king of refusing to assent to laws, suspending laws, attempting to bargain with the people for their liberties, calling legislative bodies together "at places unusual and difficult," dissolving legislatures, delaying elections to the legislatures, and so forth.

A number of other indictments by Jefferson demonstrate colonial concerns with the system of justice. Thus, he noted British refusal to agree to a colonial justice system, and British efforts to undercut judicial independence by keeping judges dependent upon the king for their tenure and salaries. So too, Jefferson accused the king of multiplying governmental officials, keeping standing armies in the colonies, and failing to maintain civilian control over the military.

He has combined with others to subject us to a jurisdiction foreign to our constitution, and unacknowledged by our laws, giving his assent to their acts of pretended legislation:

For quartering large bodies of armed troops among us;

For protecting them, by a mock trial, from punishment for any murders which they should commit on the inhabitants of these states;

For cutting off our trade with all parts of the world;

For imposing taxes on us without our consent;

For depriving us, in many cases, of the benefits of trial by jury;

For transporting us beyond seas, to be tried for pretended offenses;

For abolishing the free system of English laws in a neighboring province, establishing therein an arbitrary government, and enlarging its boundaries, so as to render it at once an example and fit instrument for introducing the same absolute rule into these colonies;

For taking away our charters, abolishing our most valuable laws, and altering fundamentally the forms of our governments;

For suspending our own legislatures, and declaring themselves invested with power to legislate for us in all cases whatsoever.

Indictments Against the King and the Parliament

Although unnamed, the Parliament also comes in for blame where Jefferson indicts the king for combining "with others" and for giving assent "to their acts of pretended legislation." Here the charges include grievances connected with troops, trade, taxes ("without our consent"), trials on foreign soil without the protection of juries, alterations of charters, suspension of legislatures, and so forth.

He has abdicated government here, by declaring us out of his protection and waging war against us.

He has plundered our seas, ravaged our coasts, burned our towns, and destroyed the lives of our people.

He is at this time transporting large armies of foreign mercenaries to complete the works of death, desolation, and tyranny already begun with circumstances of cruelty and perfidy scarcely paralleled in the most barbarous ages, and totally unworthy the head of a civilized nation.

He has constrained our fellow-citizens, taken captive on the high seas, to bear arms against their country, to become the executioners of their friends and brethren, or to kill themselves by their hands.

He has excited domestic insurrections among us, and has endeavored to bring on the inhabitants of our frontiers the merciless Indian savages, whose known rule of warfare is an undistinguished destruction of all ages, sexes, and conditions.

War Atrocities

Among the final charges leveled against Britain are those atrocities connected with the start of the armed conflict that had begun the previous April. Jefferson's much longer indictment accusing the king of encouraging slave revolts was shortened by the Continental Congress to, "He has excited domestic insurrections among us," perhaps with recognition that it was problematical both to proclaim human equality and indict a king for encouraging slaves to gain their freedom.

In every stage of these oppressions we have petitioned for redress in the most humble terms; our repeated petitions have been answered only by repeated injury. A prince, whose character is thus marked by every act which may define a tyrant, is unfit to be the ruler of a free people.

Nor have we been wanting in our attentions to our British brethren. We have warned them, from time to time, of attempts by their legislature to extend an unwarrantable jurisdiction over us. We have reminded them of the circumstances of our emigration and settlement here. We have appealed to their native justice and magnanimity; and we have conjured them, by the ties of our common kindred, to disavow these usurpations, which would inevitably interrupt our connections and correspondence. They too, have been deaf to the voice of justice and of consanguinity. We must, therefore, acquiesce in the necessity which denounces our separation, and hold them, as we hold the rest of mankind, enemies in war, in peace friends.

Recapitulation of Earlier Petitions

Jefferson recapitulates the history of colonial petitions to England as a way of establishing his earlier contention that the colonists had been patient and pursued peaceful means of change before resorting to revolution. While the king is again the central focus, Jefferson makes it clear that other people and institutions in England had long been aware of colonial grievances. It is interesting to note that, by Jefferson's theory, the colonists became free by their move to the New World. They, and not their English sponsors, had taken the initiative, and therefore the British Parliament had no continuing authority over them.

We, therefore, the representatives of the United States of America, in General Congress assembled, appealing to the Supreme Judge of the world for the rectitude of our intentions, do, in the name and by the authority of the good people of these colonies, solemnly publish and declare, that these United Colonies are, and of right ought to be, FREE AND INDEPENDENT STATES; that they are absolved from all allegiance to the British crown, and that all political connection between them and the state of Great Britain is, and ought to be, totally dissolved; and that, as free and independent states, they have full power to levy war, conclude peace, contract alliances, establish commerce, and do all other acts and things which independent states may of right do. And for the support of this declaration, with a firm reliance on the protection of Divine Providence, we mutually pledge to each other our lives, our fortunes, and our sacred honor.

Conclusion

Jefferson ends, appealing to God to establish the colonists' good motives and incorporating Richard Henry Lee's resolution for independence. The colonies would now take their independent places among the family of nations, the 56 signatories of the document and delegates from these former colonies mutually affirming their lives, fortunes, and honor.

Jefferson's document was adopted by the Continental Congress on July 4, 1776, just two days after the Congress had voted to accept Richard Henry Lee's resolution for independence. The document was subsequently prepared and signed, not as painters have imagined, on a single day, but during a period of months. But from the adoption of the document, the die had been cast. Benjamin Franklin is reported to have noted that, from here on, the colonists would have to hang together or find themselves hanging separately from the ends of British nooses.

THE ARTICLES OF CONFEDERATION

The Background

On the same day that Richard Henry Lee offered his resolution for independence, he also proposed that plans be made for a new confederation. The initial job of writing such a confederation was given to John Dickinson of Pennsylvania, who submitted his work to the Continental Congress in August 1776. Consideration of this proposal gave way to more pressing matters of war and, when the plan of confederation was reviewed in 1777, the delegates, influenced by Thomas Burke, governor of North Carolina, weakened the central authority of the new government at the expense of the states, each of which had until this time been separate. The Articles were not adopted until 1781, smaller states insisting that large states with western land claims give them up before the smaller states would join the new confederacy.

The Principles and Structures

There are two primary features to remember about the Articles of Confederation. In the first place, it was as much a treaty, or league of friendship, as a central government. Similarly, chief power rested under the Articles of Confederation with the individual states. Thus, Article II of the Constitution of the Articles stated that,

each state retains its sovereignty, freedom, and independence, and every Power, Jurisdiction and right, which is not by this confederation delegated to the United States, in Congress assembled.

Truly the centrifugal forces were to be greater than the centripetal ones.

Under the Articles of Confederation, there was essentially one branch of government, the Congress, and it had only one house or chamber. While states could send from two to seven delegates, each state had a single vote regardless of size. Moreover, representatives were chosen by, and thus accountable to, the state legislatures rather than directly to the people they represented. Congress lacked certain modern powers like control over interstate commerce. Moreover, in most matters, Congress was dependent on the states. If it needed taxes, it could petition, but not coerce, the states for such revenues. If armies needed to be raised, Congress was again dependent upon the states, who often looked jealously at their neighbors before deciding how much to contribute. On most key matters, the vote of nine states was needed before Congress could act; and, because it was essentially a treaty, in order for the Articles of Confederation to be amended, all the state legislatures had to agree to such alterations.

The Problems

Although the Articles of Confederation served as a valuable trial government that was responsible for a number of important political achievements, including passage of the Northwest Ordinance of 1787 specifying how the territories would be governed, the negative results of such a weak alliance were fairly predictable. Economic problems resulted as states began enacting tariffs and other trade restrictions on one another's goods. Currency was not uniform from one state to another. Congress was too weak. On the foreign policy front, the new government found it difficult to enforce or live up to treaties, and American diplomats found themselves treated with disrespect abroad. Politically, the new government lacked adequate power of taxation and defense, and when needed changes were proposed, they were stymied by the rigid requirements to adopt constitutional amendments. States had their own problems. Although many had led the way to constitutional government, many had also patterned their governments on a model similar to that of the Articles, with weak or practically nonexistent executive branches and unstable legislatures torn by factional battles.

PRELUDE TO THE CONSTITUTIONAL CONVENTION

The result was a series of events that led to the Constitutional Convention of 1787. First was a meeting between the states of Virginia and Maryland at George Washington's home, Mount

Vernon, to attempt to work out problems concerning commerce on a mutual waterway, the Potomac River. Subsequently, a convention was called where all the states could deal with such problems. Initially, it appeared as though this Annapolis Convention would be a failure, since delegates from only five of the 13 states attended. Nationalistic delegates like James Madison and Alexander Hamilton decided, however, to use this convention to call for yet another to be held in Philadelphia, the same city in which the Declaration of Independence had been written, and to deal not simply with problems of commerce, but with problems of state and national relations generally.

Initially, it appeared that this new convention would be no more successful than the last. In the winter of 1786–1787, however, many people, particularly those with wealth and influence, were shocked by a debtors' and taxpayers' rebellion in Massachusetts. Designated Shays' Rebellion after its revolutionary leader, Daniel Shays, this rebellion seemed to many to signal the beginning of anarchy and yet another demonstration of the impotency of the Articles. Congress subsequently gave its blessing to the new convention that was to meet in Philadelphia to revise the Articles of Confederation, and twelve of thirteen states eventually sent delegates.

THE CONSTITUTIONAL CONVENTION

The Delegates

Most delegates probably arrived in Philadelphia believing that they were there to revise rather than to scrap the Articles of Confederation. It was soon obvious, however, that the delegates from Virginia, who introduced the first plan discussed at the convention, had come prepared to rethink the entire system of government. Once their plan had been put forward and debated, it set the agenda; it subsequently became difficult to think of the existing Articles of Confederation as much more than a constitutional irrelevance.

Altogether some 55 delegates from twelve states attended the Constitutional Convention. These delegates represented the elite of the colonies, including state governors, men who had been active in writing state constitutions, and 39 present or former members of Congress. Among the best known and most influential delegates were George Washington, James Madison, James Wilson,

Gouverneur Morris, and Alexander Hamilton. John Adams was serving as a diplomat in England and Thomas Jefferson in France, and a few others—most notably Patrick Henry, who, with his strong states' rights views, professed "to smell a rat"—refused to attend, but it would have been difficult to assemble a much better educated or more serious body of men.

Children of the Enlightenment, most believed it was possible to apply the lessons of experience to the creation of a new government; at the same time, most were realists in regard to human nature, recognizing, as Madison argued in *Federalist* No. 51, that human beings were not angels and that government must necessarily guard against some destructive human impulses. The Framers have been variously painted as near demigods and condemned as representatives of narrow social and economic interests. In his book, *Constitution Making*, Calvin Jillson has convincingly argued that the convention delegates attempted both to push for certain constitutional principles and to protect state and regional interests.

The Rules

The convention's first item of business was to choose a president. Two members of the convention, George Washington and Benjamin Franklin, had worldwide reputations, but Franklin, the oldest member, was so frail that he had to be conveyed to the convention in a specially built contraption, and it was he who thus moved that the convention nominate Washington as its president. As the former commander of American forces during the Revolutionary War, Washington was quite mindful of his high place in the public mind, and he had ruminated for months about whether to attend the convention. His decision to do so and to agree to serve as president may well have been decisive in the Constitution's eventual acceptance by the people. Although he said little as president, his presence lent a special gravity to the proceedings that would not have been possible in his absence.

The convention adopted several rules, an understanding of which helps cast light on its deliberations and the intentions of its participants. As in the Articles of Confederation, voting was by states, with each state delegation having a single vote. Thus, votes were not recorded under individual names, and, when members of the convention desired to retake votes, they could do so. The hope was to encourage compromise and allow reason to change delegates' minds. Finally, the convention voted that its proceedings would not be made public. There was great fear that, with publicity, rational deliberation might give way to power politics and perhaps even mob action in the streets of Philadelphia. Delegates were to consider themselves free to propose or discuss anything, knowing that the end result of their deliberations would then be weighed openly by the public.

Fortunately, one delegate, other than the official secretary whose notes were skeletal, took upon himself the responsibility of recording convention votes and debates. This delegate was the physically diminutive James Madison of Virginia, who had spent literally months reading books mailed from Europe by his friend Jefferson and writing essays on needed changes in government. Positioning himself near the front of Washington's chair, Madison kept about as meticulous notes as could be expected in an age before tape recorders. Madison was the last of the convention delegates to die, and his notes of the Constitutional Convention were not released until after his death. Since then, they have served as the best record available of the proceedings.

The Virginia Plan

As noted, the Virginia delegation was the first to present a plan to the convention for consideration. This plan, in the writing of which Madison (often designated as "father" of the Constitution) is believed to have played a major part, dominated the discussion for the first two weeks. The plan called for a much strengthened national government, and, perhaps not surprisingly, its scheme of representation favored populous states like Virginia. The Virginia Plan proposed that three branches of government be established. The legislature was to be bicameral, rather than unicameral, as under the Articles of Confederation. Both houses were to be apportioned according to population, the first chamber to be elected by the people and the second house to be chosen by the first chamber from among members of state legislatures. The executive—probably conceived of as a single individual—was to be chosen by the legislative branch and limited to a single term. So too, the judicial branch was to be chosen by the legislature and to consist of men who would serve during good behavior. The Virginia Plan also proposed a Council of Revision consisting of the executive and members of the national judiciary. Such a council, very much a key part of Madison's scheme, would have had power to veto acts of state and national legislation, subject however to an override by a supermajority. The Virginia Plan also proposed an amending process and had provisions for admitting new states.

The New Jersey Plan

After about two weeks of discussion, an alternative to the Virginia Plan was proposed by the New Jersey delegation and introduced by William Paterson of that state. Despite some evidence to the contrary (most notably its inclusion of the supremacy clause, which will be discussed in a later chapter of this book), the New Jersey Plan seems to have been supported by those who were more fearful of granting increased powers to the national government. More obviously, it favored the interests of the small states.

Because it came after two weeks of discussion and agreement, however, the New Jersey Plan incorporated a number of features of the Virginia Plan. Thus, it accepted the idea that the new government would have three branches. Whereas the Virginia Plan proposed a bicameral legislature, however, the New Jersey Plan wanted to keep a unicameral legislature in which each state would continue to have a single vote. Moreover, the New Jersey Plan favored a plural executive appointed by Congress for a fixed term. The judiciary would be appointed by this executive branch. While the New Jersey Plan made no mention of an amending process or a Council of Revision, it did wisely provide, as had the Virginia Plan, for the admission of new states.

Prominent Convention Issues

Eventually, the convention decided to move ahead with the Virginia Plan, but many of the ideas of the New Jersey Plan were incorporated in the convention's final product. Most notably, in the most difficult issue faced by the members of the convention, the delegates reached a compromise whereby the plan for representation of the Virginia Plan was used for one house of Congress and that of the New Jersey Plan for the second. Other compromises had to be worked out regarding the taxation, representation, and importation of the slaves; selection of the president; state and national relations; powers of the Congress, the president, and the courts; and a host of other issues that divided North and South, small states and large, proponents of a strong nation and defenders of states' rights, and those who trusted and those who feared the people. These compromises will be discussed in subsequent explications of the constitutional text.

When the convention's work was near an end, a Committee of Style was created to put the final touches on the document. The most influential member of the committee appears to have been Gouverneur Morris, the large Pennsylvania delegate with a peg leg. After he and the committee reported the document back to the convention, it was signed on September 17, 1787. Most of the delegates appear to have agreed with Benjamin Franklin, who argued, in a speech prepared for the last day of the convention that, while not perfect, the document was the best distillation of collective wisdom that could be expected under the circumstances. Defenders of the Constitution also pointed out that the new document would be open to changes as problems revealed themselves.

In his notes, Madison recorded that it was Franklin who turned to a colleague as the Constitution was being signed and said he believed that the sun painted on the top slat of the magnificent Chippendale chair on which George Washington was sitting was a rising rather than a setting sun. Truly, there was hope that a new day of freedom, prosperity, and justice would dawn in America once the Constitution was adopted.

RATIFICATION OF THE CONSTITUTION

Almost as soon as the Constitutional Convention finished its work, the country divided into two groups. Proponents of the new Constitution, soon to be designated the Federalists, naturally pushed for its quick adoption, pointing to the clear weaknesses of the Articles of Confederation and the need for change. They touted the new document as a way to maintain liberty while strengthening the national government so that it would be adequate to the crises it faced.

Opponents of the Constitution, the Antifederalists, in turn raised a variety of objections to the new Constitution, some based on unfounded fears of any change and others of a more substantial nature. Certainly, many Antifederalists, relying for primary support on the French philosopher Montesquieu (who was also strongly associated with arguments for separation of powers), argued that a national government over such a large land area would swallow the states and destroy civil liberties. Many Antifederalists thought that the absence of a bill of rights in the new Constitution was confirmation either that its framers were unconcerned with civil liberties or that they did not know how to protect them. Generally, Antifederalists wanted the states to call for yet another convention to resolve such issues before the new Constitution was accepted.

While many Federalists appear to have considered a bill of rights unnecessary and possibly even counterproductive or dangerous (what would happen, for example, if some rights were inadvertently omitted?), they were also concerned about the possibility that another convention would destroy the work of the first, plunge the nation into renewed chaos, and/or further tarnish America's international image. These concerns, probably reinforced by the belief that a bill of rights could serve some productive purposes, led key Federalists to indicate that they would work for a bill of rights, if such a bill were to be introduced *after* the new Constitution went into effect.

Federalists also launched a very successful series of newspaper articles (written by Alexander Hamilton, James Madison, and John Jay under the pen name Publius) eventually collected in *The Federalist Papers*, arguing for the new Constitution. Some essays were directed specifically against Montesquieu's contention that democratic government was unsuited for governments over a large land area. In what is perhaps the most famous of these essays, *Federalist* No. 10, James Madison argued indeed that a large government would be better able to avoid the perennial problem of faction, or injustice caused by self-interests, than would a small one. He pointed out that the new government was not a pure democracy like classic examples of the past, but rather a republic, or indirect democracy. Such a republic would refine the public view through a system of representation and, by its very size and the varied interests that it would therefore embrace, further reduce the possibility that private interest groups could successfully collude against the public interest.

In addition to such arguments, Federalists had a number of advantages in their contest with the Antifederalists. They were, of course, calling for a positive solution to an obvious problem. Federalists were well-organized; many had been working for a new government not only during the long hot summer of 1787, but even earlier. Although the contests were often close in the state ratifying conventions where the acceptance of the Constitution had to be decided upon, the necessary number of states, set by the convention at nine, was soon reached, and George Washington was elected president in 1789, the year that the Constitution went into effect. All 13 states had joined the new union by the end of Washington's first term.

REFERENCES AND SUGGESTIONS FOR FURTHER STUDY

Mortimer J. Adler, *We Hold These Truths: Understanding the Ideas and Ideals of the Constitution* (New York: Macmillan Publishing Company, 1987).

George Anastaplo, *The Constitution of 1787: A Commentary* (Baltimore, MD: The Johns Hopkins University Press, 1989).

Thorton Anderson, *Creating the Constitution: The Convention of 1787 and the First Congress* (University Park: The Pennsylvania State University Press, 1993).

Bernard Bailyn, *The Ideological Origins of the American Revolution* (Cambridge, MA: Harvard University Press, 1967).

Lance Banning, *The Sacred Fire of Liberty: James Madison and the Founding of the Federal Republic* (Ithaca, NY: Cornell University Press, 1995).

Fred Barbash, *The Founding: A Dramatic Account of the Writing of the Constitution* (New York: Simon and Schuster, 1987).

Carl L. Becker, *The Declaration of Independence: A Study in the History of Political Ideas* (New York: Vintage Books, 1970).

Richard Beeman, Stephen Botein, and Edward C. Carter, II, *Beyond Confederation: Origins of the Constitution and American National Identity* (Chapel Hill: University of North Carolina Press, 1987).

Catherine Drinker Bowen, *Miracle at Philadelphia* (Boston: Little, Brown and Company, 1966).

Edward F. Cooke, *A Detailed Analysis of the Constitution*, 5th ed. (Savage, MD: Rowman & Littlefield Publishers, Inc., 1984).

Edward S. Corwin, *The "Higher Law" Background of American Constitutional Law* (Ithaca, NY: Cornell University Press, 1955).

Noble E. Cunningham, Jr., *The Pursuit of Reason: The Life of Thomas Jefferson* (Baton Rouge: Louisiana State University Press, 1987).

James A. Curry, Richard B. Riley, and Richard M. Battistoni, *Constitutional Government: The American Experiment* (St. Paul, MN: West Publishing Company, 1989).

Max Farrand, *The Framing of the Constitution of the United States* (New Haven, CT: Yale University Press, 1913).

Max Farrand, *The Records of the Federal Convention of 1787*, 5 vols. (New Haven, CT: Yale University Press, 1966).

James Thomas Flexner, *Washington: The Indispensable Man* (Boston: Little, Brown and Company, 1974).

George J. Graham, Jr. and Scarlett G. Graham, *Founding Principles of American Government: Two Hundred Years of Democracy on Trial* (Chatham, NJ: Chatham House Publishers, 1984).

Alexander Hamilton, James Madison, and John Jay, *The Federalist Papers*, Clinton Rossiter, ed. (New York: New American Library, 1961).

Robert H. Horowitz, *The Moral Foundations of the American Republic*, 2nd ed. (Charlottesville: University Press of Virginia, 1979).

Harry V. Jaffa, *How to Think About the American Revolution: A Bicentennial Cerebration* (Durham, NC: Carolina Academic Press, 1978).

Thomas Jefferson, *Notes on the State of Virginia* (New York: Harper & Row, 1964).

Merrill Jensen, *The Articles of Confederation* (Madison: University of Wisconsin Press, 1966).

Calvin C. Jillson, *Constitution Making: Conflict and Consensus in the Federal Convention of 1787* (New York: Agathon Press, Inc., 1988).

Michael Kammen, *A Machine That Would Go of Itself: The Constitution in American Culture* (New York: Alfred A. Knopf, 1987).

Joseph T. Kennan, *The Constitution of the United States: An Unfolding Story*, 2nd ed. (Chicago: The Dorsey Press, 1985).

Ralph Ketcham, *Framed For Posterity* (Lawrence: University Press of Kansas, 1993).

Johnny H. Killian, ed., *The Constitution of the United States of America: Analysis and Interpretation* (Washington, DC: U.S. Government Printing Office, 1973).

Philip B. Kurland and Ralph Lerner, *The Founders' Constitution*, 5 vols. (Chicago: The University of Chicago Press, 1987).

Leonard W. Levy, ed., *Essays on the Making of the Constitution* (New York: Oxford University Press, 1969).

John Locke, *Two Treatises of Government*, rev. ed., Peter Laslett, ed. (New York: New American Library, 1963).

Donald S. Lutz, *The Origins of American Constitutionalism* (Baton Rouge: Louisiana State University Press, 1988).

Alpheus T. Mason and Gordon E. Baker, *Free Government in the Making: Readings in American Political Thought*, 4th ed. (New York: Oxford University Press, 1985).

Drew R. McCoy, *The Last of the Fathers: James Madison and the Republican Legacy* (Cambridge, England: Cambridge University Press, 1989).

Forrest McDonald, *Novus Ordo Seclorum: The Intellectual Origins of the Constitution* (Lawrence: The University Press of Kansas, 1985).

Charles H. McIlwain, *Constitutionalism: Ancient and Modern* (Ithaca, NY: Cornell University Press, 1947).

Marvin Meyers, ed., *The Mind of the Founder: Sources of the Political Thought of James Madison* (New York: The Bobbs-Merrill Company, Inc., 1973).

William L. Miller, *The Business of May Next: James Madison and the Founding* (Charlottesville: University Press of Virginia, 1992).

Thomas Paine, *Common Sense and Other Political Writings*, Nelson F. Adkins, ed. (New York: The Liberal Arts Press, 1953).

J.W. Peltason, Corwin and Peltason's *Understanding the Constitution*, 12th ed. (San Diego, CA: Harcourt Brace Jovanovich, 1991).

William Peters, *A More Perfect Union: The Making of the United States Constitution* (New York: Crown Publishers, Inc., 1987).

Jack N. Rakove, *Original Meanings: Politics and Ideas in the Making of the Constitution* (New York: Knopf, 1996).

John P. Reid, *Constitutional History of the American Revolution*, 3 vols. (Madison: The University of Wisconsin Press, 1987–1992).

Neal Riemer, *James Madison: Creating the American Constitution* (Washington, DC: Congressional Quarterly Inc., 1986).

Clinton Rossiter, *1787: The Grand Convention* (New York: W.W. Norton and Company, 1966).

Robert A. Rutland, ed., *James Madison: The Founding Father* (New York: MacMillan, 1987).

R.C. Simmons, ed., *The United States Constitution: The First 200 Years* (Manchester, England: Manchester University Press, 1989).

Shlomo Slonim, ed., *The Constitutional Bases of Political and Social Change in the United States* (New York: Praeger, 1990).

David G. Smith, *The Convention and the Constitution: The Political Ideas of the Founding Fathers* (New York: St. Martin's Press, 1965).

Winton U. Solberg, *The Federal Convention and Formation of the Union of the American States* (New York: The Liberal Arts Press, 1958).

Herbert A. Storing, *What the Anti-Federalists Were For: The Political Thought of the Opponents of the Constitution* (Chicago: The University of Chicago Press, 1981).

This Constitution (Washington, DC: Congressional Quarterly, 1986).

Francis N. Thorpe, ed., *The Federal and State Constitutions, Colonial Charters and Other Organic Laws of the States, Territories, and Colonies Now or Heretofore Forming the United States of America* (Washington, DC: Government Printing Office, 1909).

Robert H. Webking, *The American Revolution and the Politics of Liberty* (Baton Rouge: Louisiana State University Press, 1988).

Morton White, *The Philosophy of the American Revolution* (New York: Oxford University Press, 1978).

Garry Wills, *Inventing America: Jefferson's Declaration of Independence* (New York: Doubleday & Company, Inc., 1978).

Gordon S. Wood, *The Creation of the American Republic: 1776–1787* (Williamsburg: The University of North Carolina Press, 1969).

Gordon S. Wood, *The Radicalism of the American Revolution* (New York: Alfred A. Knopf, 1992).

Chapter 2

The Preamble and Article I: The Legislative Branch

AMERICA'S WRITTEN CONSTITUTION

Many general statements can be made about the U.S. Constitution, but one of the most obvious is that it is a written document, the kind that can be included in a book like this or even carried around in one's pocket. To Americans, indeed, it is difficult to conceive of any other type of constitution. Historically, however, a constitution may either be a single written document like that in America or a set of rules, practices, and principles, only some of which are written. Significantly, the British do not have a written constitution like that in the United States, which is superior to ordinary acts of legislation. Although cultural constraints have prevented drastic changes, in theory at least, the British legislature, the Parliament, is sovereign and can do anything other than that which it is physically impossible to perform. Fearing abuses like those that the colonists had once witnessed on the part of the British, the American founders attempted to give greater security to their liberties by creating a written constitution that would be paramount to, and foundational for, all other laws that would be passed. In this action, the people who met at the Constitutional Convention were following an example that the states had already taken individually in a surge of constitution writing that had accompanied the start of the Revolutionary War.

THE PREAMBLE

We the People of the United States, in Order to form a more perfect Union, establish Justice, insure domestic Tranquility, provide for the common defence, promote the general Welfare, and secure the Blessings of Liberty to ourselves and our Posterity, do ordain and establish this Constitution for the United States of America.

The Purposes of the Constitution

The opening paragraph of the U.S. Constitution is called the Preamble. It is rarely cited in judicial decisions because it grants no specific powers to the national government or to any other. Its primary importance is as a statement of the goals or aspirations of those who wrote and ratified the Constitution. The opening words are some of the most important and far-reaching in the entire document. They assert the origins of the Constitution in "We the People," but also identify this people as those who reside in the United States. On through the Civil War, there were intense controversies as to whether the people of the nation as a whole were sovereign or whether such power, or sovereignty—a word that a delegate to the Constitutional Convention and later Supreme Court justice, James Wilson, would sagely observe in *Chisholm v. Georgia* (1793) was curiously missing from the constitutional text itself—was exercised by the people of the states. As later portions of this book will reveal, even after that war and its repudiation of extreme notions of states' rights, legitimate questions remain as to the relationship between the national government and the states.

The second phrase of the Constitution is one of its clearest references to its own antecedents. The Constitution was established "to form a more perfect Union." Obviously, a less perfect union existed prior to the Constitution. Those who have read the first chapter of this book will know that this union was called the Articles of Confederation. This "Union" was more a treaty, or League of Friendship, than a real government, and the problems—economic, diplomatic, and political—of this union, which had been officially ratified by the last state in 1781, led to the Convention that wrote the current Constitution.

The next provisions of the Preamble refer to the ideas of

establishing Justice, insuring domestic tranquility, providing for the common defence, and promoting the general welfare.

These were precisely the areas of concern that had been so at issue under the Articles of Confederation. Justice had been particularly jeopardized in the sovereign states, where legislative majorities had sometimes ridden roughshod over the rights of minorities. Domestic tranquility had in turn been shattered—most notably in Shays' Rebellion in the winter of 1786–1787—as disputes broke out on taxation and state fiscal policies. Defense had been jeopardized under the Articles by the stipulated dependency of the national government on the states for requesting troops while the internecine warfare over commerce had severely eroded the general welfare.

Ultimately, however, the goal of the Constitution was the establishment of the "Blessings of Liberty," a phrase given meaning in the Revolutionary struggle that had defeated the British and which had been previously articulated in the Declaration of Independence. The founders distinguished liberty from license, recognizing that liberty requires adherence to law. Such liberty was a goal worthy to be passed down to posterity. To rephrase a popular song, the Constitution was to last, not just for an hour, not just for a day, but always. Written in 1787, this document is now over two hundred years old.

Article I, Section 1. All legislative Powers herein granted shall be vested in a Congress of the United States, which shall consist of a Senate and House of Representatives.

THE SEPARATION OF POWERS AND THE STRUCTURE OF THE CONSTITUTION

Almost all descriptions of the philosophy of the Constitution refer to the doctrine of separation of powers, a doctrine not directly articulated in the document but certainly consistent with its structure. The body of the Constitution is divided into seven major divisions, called Articles. The first three articles, called distributing clauses, illustrate the doctrine of separation of powers in that each establishes a separate branch of the central, or national, government. Article I deals with the legislative branch, Article II with the executive branch, and Article III with the judicial branch. This order is purposeful and instructive. As a democratic, or representative, or republican, government that rests for its authority on what the Declaration of Independence called "the consent of the governed" and what the Constitution simply refers to as "We the People," it was logical for the authors of the Constitution to begin with the two branches elected by the people and then proceed to the branch appointed and confirmed by the first two. The legislative branch had, in effect, been the only branch of government under the Articles of Confederation. It was the first to be discussed at any length at the Constitutional Convention, and most of the delegates appear to have assumed that it would continue to be the most powerful. Even this branch, however, would be limited. It would not, like the British Parliament, be entrusted with power to do anything possible (the notion of parliamentary sovereignty), but would be restricted to exercising legislative powers "herein granted." Although we shall observe below that the delegated powers of Congress have been broadly interpreted and supplemented with implied powers, such powers are still effectively balanced by the power of the other two branches.

Because "legislative power" is vested in Congress, however, the powers it may delegate to the other branches are limited. Probably the best example of this limitation occurred in *Schechter Poultry Corporation v. United States* (1935). Here Congress had, under the National Industrial Recovery Act of 1933, allowed individual industries to establish binding codes of fair competition subject only to the approval of the president. The Supreme Court ruled such massive delegation of powers inappropriate. The Supreme Court has generally been more generous in upholding congressional delegations of power in the area of foreign affairs, as with a law in the case of *United States v. Curtiss-Wright* (1936) that permitted the president to declare an arms embargo to a warring region in South America when he thought it was in the nation's best interest to do so.

BICAMERALISM

The first four articles of the Constitution are divided into a number of sections written in paragraph form. Section 1 of Article I indicates that the Congress, entrusted with legislative power, is to consist of two houses, a Senate and a House of Representatives. This is the principle of bicameralism and acts, much like the division of government into three branches, as an internal check on the Congress. There is a story that, when asked by Thomas Jefferson— who had been serving during the Constitutional Convention as an ambassador to France—why there were two houses of Congress, George Washington had poured some coffee into his cup plate and, as was the custom, blown over it to cool the liquid. One house, he indicated, would cool the passions of the other much as his breath had cooled the liquid in his cup plate (Farrand, *The Framing of the Constitution*, p. 74). The British Parliament, the "mother of Parliaments" and the legislative branch with which the colonists would have been most familiar, was bicameral, but certainly significant differences existed between the House of Lords and House of Commons in England, and the Senate and House of Representatives under the U.S. Constitution. Perhaps because of the aristocratic origins and composition of the House of Lords, the colonists had settled in the earlier Articles of Confederation on a single-house legislature.

THE U.S. HOUSE OF REPRESENTATIVES

Article I, Section 2. [1] The House of Representatives shall be composed of Members chosen every second Year by the People of the several States, and the Electors in each State shall have the Qualifications requisite for Electors of the most numerous Branch of the State Legislature.

[2] No person shall be a Representative who shall not have attained to the Age of twenty-five Years, and been seven Years a Citizen of the United States, and who shall not, when elected, be an Inhabitant of that State in which he shall be chosen.

Terms of Office and Qualifications

Section 2 of Article I deals with the House of Representatives, designed to be the most popular, or representative—its name gives a good clue to this fact—house of the most popular branch. Members of the House serve for terms of two years, and all are up for election at once. The intention of this arrangement was to make members of Congress highly responsive to the electorate. Rather than set national voting qualifications at a time when such qualifications varied widely from one state to another, the framers simply specified that a state would utilize the same qualifications as it did for state legislative elections. Such qualifications are now further restricted by a number of constitutional amendments. So too, the qualifications for a representative as outlined in paragraph 2 are minimal. A House member needs only to be 25 years old, seven years a citizen, and an inhabitant of the state from which the member is chosen. Convention appears to dictate that a representative also be from the district that elected him or her, but this is an extra-constitutional development.

Article I, Section 2. [3] *Representatives and direct Taxes shall be apportioned among the several States which may be included within this Union, according to their respective Numbers, which shall be determined by adding to the whole Number of free Persons, including those bound to Service for a Term of Years, and excluding Indians not taxed, three fifths of all other Persons.* The actual Enumeration shall be made within three Years after the first Meeting of the Congress of the United States, and within every subsequent Term of ten Years, in such Manner as they shall by Law direct. The Number of Representatives shall not exceed one for every thirty Thousand, but each State shall have at Least one Representative; and until such enumeration shall be made, the State of New Hampshire shall be entitled to chuse [sic] three, Massachusetts eight, Rhode-Island and Providence Plantations one, Connecticut five, New York six, New Jersey four, Pennsylvania eight, Delaware one, Maryland six, Virginia ten, North Carolina five, South Carolina five, and Georgia three.

Representation and Taxation

Under the Articles of Confederation, states had been represented equally in the national legislature, but when the new Constitution was written, there were hopes of changing this arrangement. As discussed in the previous chapter, the first plan introduced at the Constitutional Convention was the Virginia Plan. Consistent with the interests of the large states like Virginia and with more general conceptions of representational fairness, this plan had proposed that states be represented in both houses of this proposed national legislature according to population and/or tax contributions. While initially decided in Virginia's favor, the issue of representation had been one of the most vexing faced by the convention. In opposition to the Virginia Plan, William Paterson proposed in the New Jersey Plan that states continue to be represented equally in a unicameral, or one house, legislature similar to that under the existing Articles of Confederation. Ultimately, a compromise, generally called the Connecticut, or Great, Compromise, was forged. Under this plan, the new legislature would be bicameral, as the Virginians had proposed. In further accord with the Virginia Plan, the House of Representatives was to be apportioned according to population; in the second house, the Senate, however, states would be represented equally, as in the proposed New Jersey Plan and the Articles of Confederation.

The Three-Fifths Clause

This paragraph of Section 2 also reflects another, less defensible, compromise made at the Constitutional Convention. Whereas the central question of representation was perceived as an issue that divided the large states from the small states, a subsidiary issue involved a conflict between the states of the North and the South, the issue of slavery. It would be a mistake to read northern and southern sentiments in 1787 as though they were the later views of 1860. At the time the Constitution was written, northerners were generally less concerned about the morality of slavery. For their part, southerners were more likely to defend the institution of slavery in 1787 much as people might today defend war or taxes, that is, as necessary evils rather than as one of the positive goods that slavery was later proclaimed by many southern spokesmen, like John C. Calhoun, Hinton Rowan Helper, and George Fitzhugh.

Nonetheless, key differences of interest in the institution of slavery reinforced already diverging views of its morality. The North was eager to see slaves counted when states were assessed taxes, but quite unwilling to see slaves count toward the number of representatives that each state would be apportioned. For their part, southerners wanted as many representatives as they could get, but were reluctant to see states taxed on the numbers of slaves. The compromise, embodied (like other superseded parts of the document throughout this book) in the italicized portion of Article I, Section 2, was to count slaves as three-fifths of a person for both purposes, this odious ratio apparently having being used on previous occasions during the Articles of Confederation. It is difficult to know whether to take some hope in the fact that slaves were at least accorded partial personhood or to decry the fact that they were considered less than full persons. It certainly is significant that the word slave is never used in the Constitution, "all other Persons" instead being contrasted to free persons, Indians, and those who were indentured servants. The omission of the term "slave" in a document designed to secure the blessings of liberty would appear to be significant. Noting this omission, Lincoln said that slavery "is hid away, in the constitution, just as an afflicted man hides away a wen [cyst] or a cancer which he dares not cut out at once, lest he bleed to death" (Kammen, *A Machine That Would Go of Itself*, p. 102). The three-fifths clause was, of course, altered by the Civil War, the Thirteenth Amendment abolishing slavery, and Section 2 of the Fourteenth Amendment now specifying that representation would be on the basis of "the whole number of persons in each State, excluding Indians not taxed."

Initial State Representation

The Constitution was designed to be perpetual and, as such, rarely deals with passing political matters. If a new constitution were to be put into effect, however, some scheme of representation for the existing 13 states had to be established. Accordingly, initial representation figures for the House of Representatives were provided, subject to alteration after enumerations or censuses that would be held within each subsequent decade. Clearly, Virginia, with ten representatives, was believed to be the most populous state and Rhode Island, with one representative, the least. New Jersey, which had so effectively represented the interests of the small states at the Constitutional Convention, was awarded four House seats.

Article I, Section 2. [4] When vacancies happen in the Representation from any State, the Executive Authority thereof shall issue Writs of Election to fill such Vacancies.
[5] The House of Representatives shall chuse [sic] their Speaker and other Officers, and shall have the sole Power of Impeachment.

House Vacancies, the Speaker, and Impeachment

Paragraph 4 specifies that House vacancies will be filled by elections called by the state executive authority. Such elections have not been as significant as the "by-elections" in Britain and other parliamentary democracies for two reasons. First, House terms are so short (two years as compared to a maximum of six years in England) as to minimize the number of such vacancies. Second, even a change in the party composition of one or both Houses of Congress would not bring down the president's government in the same way that a party change and a subsequent "vote of no confidence" would bring down the prime minister in a parliamentary democracy.

The House of Representatives has the prerogative of choosing its own Speaker, a position invariably attained by the majority party in one of the few straight party votes in this body whose members otherwise demonstrate a great deal of independence of party leaders. This means that the House Speaker may be from a different party than the president and/or the Senate majority leader. There have been some very powerful Speakers in House history, particularly Speaker Joe Cannon, who presided from 1903 to 1911. The power of modern Speakers has been undercut by liberal-minded reforms in the 1960s and 1970s that dispersed power more widely within Congress. At least for a time, Georgia Representative Newt Gingrich succeeded in bringing new visibility to this office after mobilizing his Republican colleagues around the Contract With America (a set of proposals that signers agreed to support if elected) in the election of 1994 and subsequently gaining control of the House for his party. Such powers can clearly ebb and flow, with few restrictions imposed by the Constitution.

The Constitution vests the House of Representatives with the power of impeachment. Contrary to popular understanding, the power to impeach is simply the power to bring charges. Impeachment trials are conducted, as will be discussed below, in the Senate, where a two-thirds vote is required for conviction.

THE U.S. SENATE

Article I, Section 3. [1] The Senate of the United States shall be composed of two Senators from each State, *chosen by the Legislature thereof*, for six Years, and each Senator shall have one Vote.

Representation, Voting, and Terms

While Section 2 deals with the lower house, the House of Representatives, Section 3 deals with the upper house, the Senate. Whereas the House of Representatives reflects the scheme of representation in the Virginia Plan, the Senate embodies the plan of representation in the Articles of Confederation and the New Jersey Plan. Regardless of size, each state has two senators, each with a single independent vote. Originally, senators were chosen by members of their respective state legislatures, a constitutional provision changed during the Progressive Era to popular statewide election.

Whereas all members of the House of Representatives stand for election every two years, only one-third of the Senate is elected every two years, since senators serve for terms of six years rather than two. This longer term is designed to give the Senate greater stability so that it can oppose rash legislative measures of the House. Unlike the president who is now, by the terms of the Twenty-Second Amendment, limited to two full terms, there are no restrictions on the number of terms a representative or senator can serve.

Given the high reelection rates of incumbents, particularly members of the House of Representatives, and the career orientation that this has fostered, some current sentiment favors an amendment that would provide such limits and move the nation closer to the ideal of the citizen (rather than career) legislator. Critics argue, however, that this would restrict the people's current power of choice, result in a diminution of the legislature's institutional memory, and might result in some unintended consequences. In recent years, many states attempted to limit the number of terms their representatives could serve. In *U.S. Term Limits v. Thorton* (1995), however, the Supreme Court narrowly decided that existing qualifications in Article I, Section 3 are exclusive. Absent a change of heart by the Court, it would thus appear that, if term limits are to be adopted, they must be instituted by constitutional amendment.

Article I, Section 3. [2] Immediately after they shall be assembled in Consequence of the first Election, they shall be divided as equally as may be into three Classes. The Seats of the Senators of the first Class shall be vacated at the Expiration of the Second Year, of the second Class at the expiration of the fourth Year, and of the third Class at the Expiration of the sixth Year, so that one-third may be chosen every second Year; *and if Vacancies happen by Resignation, or otherwise, during the Recess of the Legislature of any State, the Executive thereof may make temporary Appointments until the next Meeting of the Legislature, which shall then fill such Vacancies.*

Staggered Senate Terms and Vacancies

This provision was necessary to get the first Congress on its feet. All senators needed to be in place, but there was a desire to see that the Senate was a more stable body than the House. Accordingly, the terms of new senators were arranged so that, at the end of the first six years, one-third of the senators would be up for election every two years. State governors were initially allowed to fill Senate vacancies when state legislatures were out of session and may still make such temporary appointments. Under the terms of the

Seventeenth Amendment, however, such vacancies are permanently filled by elections rather than by state legislative appointment.

Article I, Section 3. [3] No person shall be a Senator who shall not have attained to the Age of thirty Years, and been nine Years a Citizen of the United States, and who shall not, when elected, be an Inhabitant of that State for which he shall be chosen.

Qualifications

Requirements for membership in the Senate are hardly onerous, but the age limit—30 years instead of 25—and the citizenship requirement—nine years rather than seven—indicate that the Senate is designed to be a more stable and mature body. Its members are neither, as in the British House of Lords, hereditary, nor do they serve for life; the differences between the U.S. House and Senate flow from differing terms and wider constituencies rather than from special wealth or privilege.

Article I, Section 3. [4] The Vice President of the United States shall be President of the Senate, but shall have no Vote, unless they be equally divided.

The Legislative Role of the Vice President

While the Constitution embodies the theory of separation of powers, no hermetic or airtight relationship was designed to exist among the branches that frequently share powers. Thus, the vice president, a member of the executive branch, is officially designated as president of the Senate, with voting privileges in case of a tie. Because of other extra-constitutional duties that a president often assigns to a vice president, most vice presidents do not spend much time in the Senate, and thus the Constitution also provides for a president pro tempore. Still, the vice president has a right to preside, and, when the president delivers the annual State of the Union Address in full view of the television cameras, the vice president, rather than the Senate majority leader, sits with the Speaker of the House on the rostrum behind the president.

Article I, Section 3. [5] The Senate shall chuse [sic] their other Officers, and also a President pro tempore, in the Absence of the Vice President, or when he shall exercise the Office of President of the United States.

Other Senate Officers

As in the case of the House, the Constitution contains relatively little about the specific responsibilities of officers in the Senate, which is responsible for selecting its own leaders. While the president pro tempore clearly has the task of presiding, other roles and functions can be distributed by the Senate relatively free of constitutional limitations.

Article I, Section 3. [6] The Senate shall have the sole Power to try all Impeachments. When sitting for that Purpose, they shall be on Oath or Affirmation. When the President of the United States is tried, the Chief Justice shall preside: And no Person shall be convicted without the Concurrence of two thirds of the Members Present.

[7] Judgment in Cases of Impeachment shall not extend further than to removal from Office, and disqualification to hold and enjoy any Office of honor, Trust or Profit under the United States: but the Party convicted shall nevertheless be liable and subject to Indictment, Trial, Judgment and Punishment, according to Law.

Trials of Impeachment

Reference was made in Article I, paragraph 5, to the power of the House of Representatives to impeach. This power is further elaborated under the responsibilities of the Senate. Whereas the House of Representatives impeaches, or brings charges against, public officials, the Senate is responsible for trying impeachments. The penalty for conviction, per se, extends no further than removal from office and requires a two-thirds vote of the members present, presumably as a means of limiting convictions to cases of genuine wrongdoing rather than to partisan expressions. A number of federal judges have been impeached and a smaller number have been convicted in American history, and occasionally there are politically motivated efforts at impeachment that never lead to a congressional vote—during Earl Warren's controversial tenure as chief justice of the Supreme Court, right-wing organizations posted numerous roadside signs calling for his impeachment. Only one president, Andrew Johnson, has been impeached, however, and the Senate vote in his case fell one short of the necessary two-thirds needed for conviction. President Richard Nixon would probably have been impeached and convicted had he not resigned before this contingency could occur after the House Judiciary Committee had voted to accept a number of charges against him. In cases where a president is on trial and a vice president might have a vested interest in the outcome, the Constitution specifies that the chief justice of the United States shall preside. In and of itself, conviction on charges of impeachment results simply in removal from office and disqualification from other national offices. A person who is impeached and convicted may, however, be subject to trial and punishment for any crimes committed while in office.

Recent years have witnessed the conviction of three federal judges on impeachment charges. Each conviction was somewhat unusual. Judge Harry F. Claiborne was impeached, convicted, and removed from office after he failed to resign after being convicted of felonies. Judge Alcee Hastings was elected to Congress by his Florida district after having been impeached, convicted, and removed from his judgeship. Judge Walter L. Nixon, like Claiborne, also had refused to resign his office, in Nixon's case after having been convicted of perjury.

Nixon subsequently objected to the proceedings whereby the Senate conducted its initial investigation through a committee rather than in the chamber as a whole. In *Walter L. Nixon v. United States* (1993), the Court subsequently rejected Nixon's challenge. Speaking for the Court, Chief Justice Rehnquist relied heavily on the fact that the language of Article I, Section 3 vested the "sole" power to try impeachments in the Senate rather than in the courts.

OTHER MATTERS INVOLVING CONGRESSIONAL OPERATIONS

Article I, Section 4. The Times, Places and Manner of holding Elections for Senators and Representatives, shall be prescribed in each State by the Legislature thereof; but the Congress may at any time by Law make or alter such Regulations, except as to the Places of chusing [sic] Senators.

The Congress shall assemble at least once in every Year, and such Meeting shall be on the *first Monday in December, unless they shall by Law appoint a different Day.*

Elections for Congress

Section 4 of Article I does not require a great deal of explanation. It is, however, a bit ambiguous, granting state legislatures the power to prescribe "the Times, Places and Manner of holding Elections" for members of Congress but also allowing Congress to "alter such Regulations, except as to the places of chusing [sic] Senators." This section also provides that Congress will assemble at least once yearly, with the first meeting set for the first Monday in December. That provision was later changed by the Twentieth Amendment to January 3, or some other time designated by law.

Article I, Section 5. [1] Each House shall be the Judge of the Elections, Returns and Qualifications of its own Members, and a Majority of each shall constitute a Quorum to do Business; but a smaller Number may adjourn from day to day, and may be authorized to compel the Attendance of absent Members, in such Manner, and under such Penalties as each House may provide.

[2] Each House may determine the Rules of its Proceedings, punish its Members for disorderly Behaviour, and, with the Concurrence of two thirds, expel a Member.

[3] Each House shall keep a Journal of its Proceedings, and from time to time publish the same, excepting such Parts as may in their Judgment require Secrecy; and the Yeas and Nays of the Members of either House on any question shall, at the Desire of one fifth of those Present, be entered on the Journal.

[4] Neither House, during the Session of Congress, shall, without the Consent of the other, adjourn for more than three days, nor to any other Place than that in which the two Houses shall be sitting.

Housekeeping Provisions

While Section 4 discusses the election of members of Congress and when they shall meet, Section 5 basically concerns itself with what might be called routine housekeeping functions of Congress. Each house judges "the Elections, Returns, and Qualifications of its own Members," meaning that this body is the judge of disputed elections. A majority of each house is necessary for a quorum. Lesser numbers may require the attendance of their colleagues. Each house of Congress sets its own rules and can punish its members "for disorderly Behaviour," but a two-thirds vote is required to expel a member. Moreover, in *Powell v. McCormack* (1969), which dealt with representative Adam Clayton Powell of New York, the Supreme Court decided that the Congress was obligated to seat a member who met the minimal qualifications established in the Constitution.

Each house keeps a daily journal now known as the *Congressional Record*, but, because Congress itself controls the content of the

Record, it is often a better guide to what members of Congress wished they had said rather than what they actually did say. According to Section 5, votes must be recorded, hence the designation of "roll-call votes," at the insistence of one-fifth or more of those who are present. Moreover, neither house can adjourn for more than three days without notifying the other, nor can either meet other than in its designated place. Undoubtedly, the Founding Fathers remembered that one of their accusations against King George III in the Declaration of Independence was that he had called the legislature into session at untimely intervals and locations.

The amazing feature of this part of the Constitution is the relative absence of rules to govern the internal structure of each house. There is no mention of the role of congressional committees or their chairs, no requirement that a seniority system be utilized, no mention of the Senate filibuster, no elaboration of the role that political parties will play in either house, no real description of the job of the Speaker of the House or the president pro tempore of the Senate, and no mention of other functionaries like majority and minority leaders and whips. Wisely, it seems, the framers realized that such matters could best be resolved through experience; when changes are needed or desired in these arrangements, they face few constitutional obstacles. Reformers can thus make such changes short of constitutional amendments.

Article I, Section 6. [1] The Senators and Representatives shall receive a Compensation for their Services, to be ascertained by Law, and paid out of the Treasury of the United States. They shall in all Cases, except Treason, Felony and Breach of the Peace, be privileged from Arrest during their Attendance at the Session of their respective Houses, and in going to and returning from the same; and for any Speech or Debate in either House, they shall not be questioned in any other Place.

Congressional Compensation and Privilege

Section 6 provides that members of Congress shall receive a salary from the U.S. Treasury, thus cutting off a source of state control that had sometimes proven embarrassing to national power under the Articles of Confederation. In what might at first appear to be a serious violation of the principle of checks and balances (an understood corollary to the doctrine of separation of powers), members of Congress, at least collectively, set their own salaries. Appearances on this point might be deceiving. Few members of

Congress can expect to vote a pay increase for themselves that is not brought into question when they run for reelection. Such arguments can often be intense, and can indeed sometimes torpedo the chances of an incumbent. Moreover, if the Twenty-Seventh Amendment to the Constitution endures (and its belated ratification will be further discussed in Chapter 12), no new congressional pay raises will be able to go into effect without an intervening election.

The Constitution assures that members of Congress are given certain privileges designed to ensure that they can participate without fear in robust debate. Thus, only in cases of "Treason, Felony, and Breach of the Peace," can members of Congress be arrested while attending or commuting to or from work. This latter clause has, however, been interpreted to include all criminal offenses, leaving this clause only as protection against arrests in civil suits, which are no longer made. More important to understanding current congressional prerogatives is the speech and debate clause that exempts members of Congress from being questioned about "any Speech or Debate" in which they participate in either house. This provision, designed to remedy abuses that had taken place under English Tudor and Stuart monarchs who had attempted to prosecute members of Parliament for positions they took in that body, has been extended at least partially in *Gravel v. United States* (1972) to congressional aides.

Article I, Section 6. [2] No Senator or Representative shall, during the Time for which he was elected, be appointed to any civil Office under the Authority of the United States, which shall have been created, or the Emoluments whereof shall have been encreased during such time; and no Person holding any Office under the United States, shall be a Member of either House during his Continuance in Office.

The Incompatibility Clause

Rarely does the Constitution recognize the existence of a power or privilege without limiting it. It is therefore not surprising that the next paragraph prohibits a member of Congress from being appointed during this term for any office for which the "emoluments," or salary, shall have been increased.

In 1908, President (and later, Chief Justice) William Howard Taft nominated Senator Philander C. Knox to be secretary of state. The salary for this position had been raised from $8,000 to $12,000 during Knox's term of office.

Taft persuaded Congress to roll the secretary's salary back so that Knox could be appointed to the office. The procedure has been repeated a number of subsequent times and is often called the "Saxbe Fix," after Senator William Saxbe who was appointed as attorney general by President Nixon in 1973, in a manner similar to Knox's appointment. Debate has recently resurfaced as to whether the mechanism, which clearly seems to fall outside the literal words of the emoluments clause, meets its spirit (O'Connor, 1995).

Just as they are not to profit by appointments to positions created during their tenures, so too, members of Congress may not simultaneously hold other civil offices. This provision, or "incompatibility clause," as it is sometimes called, furthers the doctrine of separation of powers previously referred to. Whereas in Great Britain and other parliamentary democracies members of the prime minister's cabinet are chosen from the Parliament, where they remain as cabinet officers, if an American president appoints a member of Congress to office, that member must then resign from Congress. When President Jimmy Carter appointed Senator Edmund Muskie as secretary of state, for example, Muskie had to relinquish his Senate seat representing Maine. Similarly, when Representative Jack Kemp of New York accepted a position as secretary of housing and urban development in the Bush administration, he had to resign his seat in the House of Representatives.

Those who prefer parliamentary democracy, or at least this particular aspect of it that might strengthen relations between the legislative and executive branches, have frequently argued for changes in this part of the Constitution. To date at least, no such changes have been made. In addition to those who support the idea of separation of powers, some have persuasively argued that the heads of cabinet departments already have enough to do without also having to represent a district or state constituency.

ARTICLE I, SECTION 7—PROCEDURES FOR PASSING LAWS

Article I, Section 7. [1] All Bills for raising Revenue shall originate in the House of Representatives; but the Senate may propose or concur with Amendments as on other Bills.

Revenue Bills

Sections 7 through 10 of Article I are especially important. The first specifies the procedures whereby bills, or proposals, become laws. First, this section provides that all bills for raising revenue must originate in the House. This restriction has not proven particularly effective, current congressional rules being very generous in the types of amendments, or "riders," including those dealing with revenue, that they allow members of both houses, and particularly Senators, to make. Clearly though, the framers of the Constitution wanted to draw a close connection between taxation and representation; and members of the House of Representatives, who were elected directly and frequently by the people, were the closest connection that could be made. The framers of the Constitution had not forgotten the Revolutionary slogan of "no taxation without representation," a principle dating at least as far back as the English Magna Carta of 1215.

Article I, Section 7. [2] Every Bill which shall have passed the House of Representatives and the Senate, shall, before it becomes a Law, be presented to the President of the United States; If he approve he shall sign it, but if not he shall return it, with his Objections to the House in which it shall have originated, who shall enter the Objections at large on their Journal, and proceed to reconsider it. If after such Reconsideration two thirds of that House shall agree to pass the Bill, it shall be sent, together with the Objections, to the other House, by which it shall likewise be reconsidered, and if approved by two thirds of that House, it shall become a Law. But in all such Cases the Votes of both Houses shall be determined by yeas and Nays, and the Names of the Persons voting for and against the Bill shall be entered on the Journal of each House respectively. If any Bill shall not be returned by the President within ten Days (Sundays excepted) after it shall have been presented to him, the Same shall be a Law, in like Manner as if he had signed it, unless the Congress by their Adjournment prevent its Return, in which Case it shall not be a Law.

Procedures for Lawmaking and Presidential Vetoes

Paragraph 2 of Section 7 comes as close as any provision to demonstrating the founders' commitment to the doctrine of checks and balances. To become laws, all bills must be approved in identical language by majorities in both houses and presented to the president for his approval. If the president signs the bill, it becomes law. If the president does nothing, then again, after ten working days, it becomes law. If the president returns a bill to Congress with his veto, however, this can only be overridden by a two-thirds vote of both houses, with members required to go on record with their votes. Given the supermajorities required, it should not be surprising that approximately 90 percent of presidential vetoes have been successful.

In addition to the president's regular veto power, he may also exercise a pocket veto. This occurs when the president simply fails to sign a bill that Congress passes within ten days of its adjournment. Congress has no way to override such a veto. The pocket veto thus serves as an incentive for Congress to get its most important work done before the last few days of a session.

Some ambiguity remains as to whether a congressional recess can trigger a pocket veto in cases where Congress has designated an officer to receive veto messages. Lower court decisions appear to suggest that such recesses do not give the president occasion to exercise such a veto, but, to date, the Supreme Court has yet to resolve the issue (Nelson, *Guide to the Presidency*, p. 1318).

Under the Constitution, all laws are presented to the president. Exceptions have been made for internal housekeeping matters and for constitutional amendments; the latter, as will be explained in another chapter, already require a vote by two-thirds majorities of each house.

Beginning with Ulysses S. Grant in 1873, a number of presidents have advocated an item, or so-called line-item, veto similar to that exercised by many state governors. Such vetoes allow executives to void individual items within appropriations bills that are presented to them. An item veto would allow presidents to veto nongermane "riders" that are attached to bills and would, according to advocates of such a veto, also help cut federal budget deficits. Although proposed amendments to vest such powers in the president have so far fallen short, Congress did in March of 1996 pass legislation allowing presidents to rescind individual items within appropriations bills, subject to congressional disapproval within 30 days. It seems likely that the courts will review the constitutionality of this mechanism in the near future.

Article I, Section 7. [3] Every Order, Resolution, or Vote to which the Concurrence of the Senate and House of Representatives may be necessary (except on a question of Adjournment) shall be presented to the

President of the United States; and before the Same shall take Effect, shall be approved by him, or being disapproved by him, shall be repassed by two thirds of the Senate and House of Representatives, according to the Rules and Limitations prescribed in the Case of a Bill.

The Presentment Clause

This passage of the Constitution reiterates the importance of the president in the law-making scheme. The intention is to see that the president's veto power is not evaded by calling a law by another name. This provision was a key basis for the Supreme Court's decision in *Immigration and Naturalization Service v. Chadha* (1983) in which it rejected a so-called legislative veto. In this case Congress had delegated power to the attorney general to decide on exceptions to deportation orders, with the provision that a single house of Congress could counter this decision. Chief Justice Warren Burger declared that this legislative veto ran afoul of both the presentment clause and the bicameralism requirement and voided it. Although Congress removed a number of legislative veto provisions from some laws, it has continued to add them to still others. Congress also appears to have substituted informal agreements with various agencies to replace earlier statutory mandates (Nelson, *Guide to the Presidency*, pp. 1319–20). Discussion thus continues over the wisdom and effectiveness of the *Chadha* decision.

ARTICLE I, SECTION 8—POWERS GRANTED TO CONGRESS

Few parts of the Constitution are as important as Sections 8 and 9, because few do more to embody the very notion of what a Constitution is. As the name "constitution" implies, the document exists to help "constitute," or, given the prior role of the Articles of Confederation, to "reconstitute," the polity. This requires that powers be granted and distributed. Yet when Americans think of a constitution, they probably more often think of limits, another important part of a constitution's function. This dichotomy is evident in Article I, Sections 8 and 9. Section 8 provides a list of powers granted to Congress. These powers are often referred to as granted, or enumerated powers, because they are so listed. Section 9, in turn, provides a list of constitutional limits on the powers of Congress. These limits are a kind of internal bill of rights within the

Constitution and indicate that, long before objections were raised as to the omission of such a bill of rights, the founders had sought to assure that certain liberties would be recognized and secured.

Article I, Section 8. The Congress shall have Power
[1] To lay and collect Taxes, Duties, Imposts and Excises, to pay the Debts and provide for the common Defence and general Welfare of the United States; but all Duties, Imposts and Excises shall be uniform throughout the United States;
[2] To borrow money on the credit of the United States;

Taxing, Spending, and Borrowing

Altogether, 18 paragraphs list the powers specifically delegated or granted to Congress—such powers are accordingly designated as delegated or granted powers. The original theory of the Constitution was that Congress, and the national government more generally, would only be able to exercise the powers (at least in domestic affairs) that were specifically enumerated in the Constitution or could be implicated from the grants of power therein. This was, incidentally, the basis on which many Federalists continued their opposition to a bill of rights. If the national government had no powers to regulate freedom of speech, religion, and the like, what need would there be for protections against abuse of such powers? Correctly predicting that many constitutional clauses would be expansively interpreted, Antifederalists continued to insist.

One could argue that their judgment on this point has been confirmed. Aside from restrictions such as those contained in the Bill of Rights and elsewhere in the Constitution, there are few powers indeed that the modern U.S. Congress cannot exercise under the general welfare, commerce, and necessary and proper clauses, and others described in the following.

It is significant that the first power delegated to Congress relates to taxes and duties. Congress is the branch of government entrusted with this important power, often called "the power of the purse." It was this very power of appropriating or withholding money for the kings' wars that initially led to the rise of the Parliament in England. In America, such taxes may be enacted to pay for the debts, provide for defense, and promote the general welfare.

While some like James Madison had argued that congressional spending and taxing powers must be tied to other specific grants of power within Article I, Section 8 and elsewhere, the more expansive view of this phrase that was championed by Alexander Hamilton has since prevailed (*United States v. Butler*, 1936). Accordingly, the taxing and spending clause has come to be viewed as an independent power. Congress has used this clause both as a justification for raising money and for regulatory purposes. Congress may thus use its taxing power to encourage or discourage certain kinds of activities. Moreover, when Congress appropriates money, it usually attaches conditions, giving it increased power. This is especially true of the categorical grants-in-aid programs by which most federal aid has been funneled to the states. Thus, to take a recent example, Congress passed a law withholding a portion of federal highway funds from states that did not raise their legal drinking age to 21. Even in so-called block grants and revenue-sharing programs with fewer strings attached and greater state discretion, Congress usually insists that certain general rules—nondiscrimination, for example— be followed. It should be noted that, under the Constitution, duties must be uniform throughout the nation.

Akin to raising money is the power to borrow; this power is granted in paragraph 2 and has been freely—some think too freely—exercised. Debt limits periodically set by law have been circumvented by new laws with new limits, albeit often after rancorous debate. After years of unsuccessful attempts to limit deficit spending by legislation (the Gramm-Rudman-Hollings law, for example), some believe this objective can only be effected by constitutional amendment. Others, however, question the wisdom of incorporating such an economic policy within the Constitution and raise concerns about whether such an amendment, usually encumbered with a number of reservations to deal with war, recession, and inaccurate revenue projections, could be enforced in the courts.

[The Congress shall have Power]
[3] To regulate Commerce with foreign Nations, and among the several States, and with the Indian Tribes;

Power to Regulate Commerce

Under the Articles of Confederation, the central authority had no power to regulate interstate and foreign commerce. The result was that states that had fought in the Revolutionary War against a common foe now began taxing one another's commerce, thus losing the potential benefit of a common commercial union. The state of New

Jersey was thus once jokingly compared to a cask with a tap at both ends. Paragraph 3 now invests the power over commerce with foreign nations, Indian tribes, and among the states to Congress. There is no stated limitation on this power, but the task of defining the relationship between intrastate matters left to the states and commerce among the states has been an elusive one that has provided continual controversy and generated scores of opinions from the judicial branch.

One of the earliest and most important decisions on the commerce clause, *Gibbons v. Ogden* (1824), showed that the framers' concern over state rivalry had been justified. The state of New York attempted to give a monopoly to steamship owners Robert Fulton and Robert Livingston, who had licensed Ogden to navigate the route between New York and New Jersey, thus precluding from its rivers those like Gibbons who were operating in these waters under authority of a federal piloting license. Chief Justice John Marshall (the fourth chief justice of the U.S. Supreme Court) decided that commerce should be defined broadly as "intercourse" rather than more narrowly as "traffic," and that congressional powers were inclusive enough to protect such commerce against all state legislation that would interfere with it. He thus voided New York's grant of a monopoly.

Subsequent cases have established that certain state laws impeding interstate commerce are illegal even in the absence of congressional legislation. Thus, for example, state regulations of the length of trains (*Southern Pacific Company v. Arizona*, 1945) and laws attempting to prohibit the importation of out-of-state hazardous wastes (*City of Philadelphia v. New Jersey*, 1978) have both been struck down as unconstitutional, even in the absence of specific congressional legislation on the subject. The Court has recognized, most notably in *Cooley v. Board of Wardens* (1852) that, while some areas of commerce require a single uniform national rule, others, in this case rules for navigating in a dangerous harbor, just as necessarily demand accommodation to local circumstances. The courts have played a major role in deciding which circumstances are applicable in a given area.

As the nation industrialized, Congress increasingly turned to the commerce power to justify the exercise of powers over the economy not otherwise delegated by the Constitution. For a time, the Supreme Court attempted to limit congressional controls under the commerce clause to items of commerce like impure foods, colored oleomargarine, lottery tickets, and other items deemed to be in themselves harmful or deceptive. It further struck down some exercises of congressional power as interferences with state police powers. For a time, the Supreme Court thus voided the exercise of congressional power to restrict the shipment of goods produced by child labor in interstate commerce on the basis that such goods were not in and of themselves harmful (*Hammer v. Dagenhart*, 1918). Similarly, when first confronted with a case regulating monopolies under the Sherman Anti-Trust Act of 1890, the Court declared in *United States v. E.C. Knight* (1895) that this was a matter for state control. These extraconstitutional distinctions proved extremely difficult to enforce and were eventually repudiated. Today's courts take a broad view of congressional power over commerce, allowing specific constitutional prohibitions (for example, the First Amendment would trump a law banning the interstate shipment of books) rather than perceptions of harm or states' rights to serve as the primary limitation on the commerce power.

Obviously, the power to regulate commerce has been interpreted very broadly. The first congressional regulatory commission, the Interstate Commerce Commission (ICC), was created in 1887 to deal with railroad rates, an authority later widened to include other forms of transportation. Other commissions established under authority of congressional powers over commerce include the Federal Trade Commission (1915), Federal Power Commission (1920), Federal Communications Commission (1934), Securities and Exchange Commission (1934), National Labor Relations Board (1935), and Civil Aeronautics Board (1938) (Diamond, *Powers of Congress*, p. 115). For reasons that will be partly explained by the chapter on the Post–Civil War Amendments, even the Civil Rights Act of 1964, which prohibits discrimination on the basis of race in places of public accommodations, has been largely justified by recourse to federal powers over interstate commerce. So too, child labor laws and other regulatory legislation passed under the authority of the commerce clause and once struck down by the federal courts during a period roughly dating from 1890 to 1937 have now been upheld on the basis of this same constitutional authority, even though an amendment proposed by Congress to deal with child labor was never ratified by a sufficient number of states.

Recent years have witnessed two cases that have challenged the exercise of federal powers under the commerce clause. In *National League of Cities v. Usery* (1976), the Court interpreted the Tenth

Amendment as a limitation on the power of the national government to prescribe minimum wages for state employees. Although this decision was later overturned in *Garcia v. San Antonio Metropolitan Transit Authority* (1985), in 1995 the Court ruled in *United States v. Lopez* that the national government had exceeded its power under the commerce clause when it sought to prohibit guns within 1,000 feet of a school zone. Scholars will be scrutinizing court cases over the next few years to see whether *Lopez* represents a major shift in policy or whether it was the result of factors largely special to this case.

[The Congress shall have Power]
[4] To establish an uniform Rule of Naturalization, and uniform Laws on the subject of Bankruptcies throughout the United States;

Power over Naturalization and Bankruptcies

The original Constitution is silent on the issue of who is a citizen, a silence that would prove nearly disastrous in the *Dred Scott* decision (1857) that will be discussed in the chapter on the Post–Civil War Amendments. Paragraph 4 of Article I, Section 8, however, provides that Congress may establish "an uniform Rule of Naturalization." Accordingly, a person who today attends such a naturalization ceremony will find that a federal judge acting under the authority of federal laws presides, and the matter of who can become a citizen is governed by national rather than state law. Congress is also empowered to deal with bankruptcies, meaning that such cases will be adjudicated in federal, rather than in state, courts. Congress did not exercise its legislative power under this provision until 1898. Up to this time, the Supreme Court basically allowed states to adopt their own legislation on the subject.

[The Congress shall have Power]
[5] To coin Money, regulate the Value thereof, and of foreign Coin, and fix the Standard of Weights and Measures;
[6] To provide for the Punishment of counterfeiting the Securities and current Coin of the United States;

Coining Money and Establishing Uniform Standards

As in the case of interstate commerce, the coining of money was a real problem under the Articles of Confederation. Without national uniformity, entering another state was somewhat akin to entering a foreign country. Under the Constitution, the national government is accordingly given the power to coin and regulate the value of money, a power closely akin to its authority to establish uniform weights and measures, and to the power, specified in the succeeding paragraph, to punish counterfeiting.

[The Congress shall have Power]
    [7] To Establish Post Offices and post Roads;
    [8] To promote the Progress of Science and useful Arts, by securing for limited Times to Authors and Inventors the exclusive Right to their respective Writings and Discoveries;

Establishing a Post Office and Promoting Scientific Advances

Allied with the authority to regulate interstate commerce is the congressional power to establish a post office. The Constitution also grants Congress the power to promote the Sciences and Arts by establishing laws regulating copyrights and patents, two types of monopoly granted for a number of years for the purpose of encouraging scholarly and scientific advances.

In the *Trade Mark* cases of 1879, the Supreme Court ruled that the power in this section did not extend to the granting of trade marks. Congress has subsequently legislated on the subject in the Lanham Act of 1946 and the Trademark Counterfeiting Act of 1984 under its authority to regulate interstate and foreign commerce.

[The Congress shall have power]
    [9] To constitute Tribunals inferior to the Supreme Court;

Establishing Lower Courts

Paragraph 9 is somewhat redundant with the language of Article III of the Constitution, perhaps as a way of emphasizing congressional authority to create courts inferior to the U.S. Supreme Court. As shall be discussed later, delegates to the Constitutional Convention deferred settling the issue of the precise organization of the federal courts, perhaps because they both found agreement on this point difficult and realized that differing degrees of complexity might be required for different circumstances. Certainly, a nation of three million inhabitants requires less complexity than a nation of more than 260 million.

Members of courts created under authority of Article III, so-called "constitutional courts," serve "during good behavior," and have other constitutionally protected prerogatives. Members of Article I courts, known as "legislative courts," have no such constitutional protections. Such legislative courts—for example, the U.S. Court of Military Appeals—often serve administrative or quasi-legislative duties.

[The Congress shall have Power]
[10] To define and punish Piracies and Felonies committed on the high Seas, and Offenses against the Law of Nations;
[11] To declare War, grant Letters of Marque and Reprisal, and make Rules concerning Captures on Land and Water;
[12] To raise and support Armies, but no Appropriation of Money to that Use shall be for a longer Term than two Years;
[13] To provide and maintain a Navy;
[14] To make Rules for the Government and Regulation of the land and naval Forces;

WAR POWERS

As the Preamble to the Constitution indicates, national defense was a key concern of the framers. Paragraphs 10 through 14 of Article I, Section 8 relate to military powers. The Congress has the right to define and punish piracies and felonies on the high seas where its jurisdiction and international agreements, rather than state laws, prevail. Congress has the power "to declare war," authority that must be balanced against the president's designated power in Article II as commander-in-chief of the armed forces. The power to declare war is one of the most awesome that Congress can exercise, but extended presidential actions in the absence of such declaration, as in Korea (officially designated as a "police action" taken under authority of the United Nations) and in Vietnam (where the Gulf of Tonkin Resolution served as a poor substitute for a declaration of war), can be disastrous. It should be noted, however, that Congress is granted the power to declare war, not to make it; it thus shares war powers with the president.

Letters of marque and reprisal were used in earlier times where the line between piracy and defense of one's country could be a fine one (witness Sir Francis Drake's role in English history and Jean Lafitte's help during the defense of New Orleans in the War of 1812), and thus Congress is granted this power as well. Congress is also empowered to raise and support the army—appropriations limited to two years, perhaps as a way of addressing contemporary republican concerns over the dangers of a "standing army"—and navy. One might question the effectiveness of this provision in an age when orders for major weapons systems may need to be placed a decade in advance. No air force is mentioned in the Constitution, but control over it presumably derives from the same source.

Congressional powers to

make Rules for the Governance and Regulation of the land and naval forces

should be interpreted in conjunction with the Fifth Amendment's exemption of military personnel from grand jury indictment. Given military exigencies, it may not always be possible to accord military personnel the same kinds of due process given in civilian life. Congress has, indeed, set up an entire code, the Code of Military Justice, and a separate court system—albeit one subject to U.S. Supreme Court review—to deal with such personnel.

[The Congress shall have power]
[15] To provide for calling forth the Militia to execute the Laws of the Union, suppress Insurrections and repel Invasions;
[16] To provide for organizing, arming, and disciplining the Militia, and for governing such Part of them as may be employed in the Service of the United States, reserving to the States respectively, the Appointment of the Officers, and the Authority of training the Militia according to the discipline prescribed by Congress;

Calling the Militia

In Article IV of the Constitution, states are guaranteed a republican form of government and promised help against domestic insurrection. Congress is, according to paragraph 15, the source of such protection, although existing laws on the subject have entrusted this role to the president, whose authority to decide whether to send troops was affirmed by the case of *Luther v. Borden* (1849). Finally, Congress is given power over the militia employed in U.S. service, along with the delegated power to determine their officers. This section of the Constitution is the basis for distinguishing state and national guards. The former automatically become members of the latter when so designated in national emergencies. Thus, for example, President Eisenhower nationalized the Arkansas guard when it was called by Arkansas Governor Orval Faubus to resist court-imposed desegregation in Little Rock. Obviously, this can lead to state-federal conflict.

[The Congress shall have Power]
[17] To exercise exclusive Legislation in all Cases whatsoever, over such District (not exceeding ten Miles square) as may, by Cession of particular States, and the acceptance of Congress, become the Seat of the Government of the United States, and to exercise like Authority over all Places purchased by the Consent of the Legislature of the State in which the Same shall be, for the Erection of Forts, Magazines, Arsenals, dock-Yards, and other needed Buildings;

Governing the District of Columbia

Paragraph 17 deals with the governance of what is now the District of Columbia—a district created in one of the earliest cases of congressional vote-swapping or "logrolling." Under the Articles of Confederation, militiamen seeking back pay had once threatened the Congress meeting in Philadelphia. The founders feared that, without federal control over the seat of its own government, the national government might again fall prey to political squabbles and even physical intimidation. The result has been a continuing tutelage over the District criticized by some as antidemocratic. An amendment proposed by the necessary majorities in Congress in 1978 that would have treated the District of Columbia as a state for purposes of representation was rejected by the states, however. While the District now has a "shadow" representative and senator (former presidential candidate Jesse Jackson was the first to be elected to this post), these representatives have no formal rights, and questions remain as to whether continuing federal control is desirable. Some think that as long as some federal enclave is maintained, the rest of the District of Columbia can be made a state by congressional legislation. Alternatively, the inhabited part of the District might be retroceded to Maryland, as other portions were previously returned to Virginia.

Federal control of other facilities, like air and naval bases, is necessarily less controversial than its governance over the District of Columbia.

And [The Congress shall have Power]
[18] To make all Laws which shall be necessary and proper for carrying into Execution the foregoing Powers, and all other Powers vested by this

Constitution in the Government of the United States, or in any
Department or Officer thereof.

Implied Powers

The last paragraph of Article I, Section 8 is at once the most
important, embracive, and controversial. Often called "the elastic"
or "sweeping" clause, it provides that Congress shall have power

to make all Laws which shall be necessary and proper for carrying into
Execution the foregoing Powers, and all other Powers vested by this
Constitution in the Government of the United States.

The most important explanation of this clause came in a case
known as *McCulloch v. Maryland* (1819). There, Chief Justice John
Marshall and his colleagues ruled on the constitutionality of a
national bank, a bank not specifically mentioned in the Constitution
but created in the Washington administration and, after a lapse,
rechartered during the administration of James Madison. Arguing
that the bank was not an end in and of itself but a means to such ends,
Marshall argued that the necessary and proper clause gave Congress
a choice of means as long as the means chosen were consistent with
the powers specifically granted in the Constitution and were not prohibited by it. One of his key arguments was that there were varying
degrees of necessity (the term "absolutely" was not here used, as in
other parts of the Constitution, to modify the word) and that the
desirability of a bank had been established by experience.

Marshall also noted that the elastic clause was found in a section
of the Constitution, that is, Article I, Section 8, that granted, rather
than limited, the powers of Congress. The sum of congressional powers obtained by combining both enumerated and implied powers is
often referred to as resulting powers. Thus, today's Congress may
pass antipollution laws, appropriate funds for building highways, ratify consumer legislation, and regulate a variety of economic activities not specifically mentioned in the Constitution, but justified by
their connection to provisions granting Congress power over interstate commerce, to tax and spend, and over war-making.

Congressional Investigations

One of the most important powers exercised by Congress is its
right to conduct hearings or investigations. Without such investiga-

tive power, Congress would lack information it needs to legislate, oversee the operation of its progress and the conduct of government officials, and obtain necessary information about nominees to federal offices. Although this power is not specifically delineated in the U.S. Constitution, it has thus been justified as an implied power. Congressional hearings have probed into organized crime, health care, environmental issues, the conduct of presidents and their aides in the Watergate scandal and Iran-Contra affair, and the character and qualifications of nominees to the cabinet and the federal courts. Faced with abuses of power during the 1950s, the Supreme Court indicated in *Watkins v. United States* (1957) that Congress could not bring adverse publicity upon individuals simply for the sake of exposing them for unpopular views or past associations, and that its questions would have to be relevant to the subject under investigation. The Court has otherwise been reluctant to limit this very important implied power.

ARTICLE I, SECTION 9—LIMITS ON CONGRESSIONAL POWERS

Whereas Article I, Section 8 of the Constitution grants powers to Congress, Article I, Section 9 indicates that these powers are balanced by limitations. This juxtaposition illustrates the two primary functions of the Basic Law that must create an effective government but limit its potential for abuse.

Article I, Section 9. [1] The Migration or Importation of such Persons as any of the States now existing shall think proper to admit, shall not be prohibited by the Congress prior to the Year one thousand eight hundred and eight, but a tax or duty may be imposed on such Importation, not exceeding ten dollars for each Person.

Slave Importation

The first paragraph of Article I, Section 9 is, fortunately, of no current application. Like the three-fifths clause, this provision emerged from conflict between the North and the South over the issue of slavery. Delegates from some northern states wished to see the importation of slaves ended; some southerners, particularly in states of the deep South, wanted to see the practice continue and thus keep slave prices down. As a compromise, congressional control of the slave trade was delayed for 20 years, a tax of ten dollars per "Person"—and it might be significant that this term is used rather than one merely designating chattel—being the limit of congressional control. Although there was later debate on this subject, congressional power over slave importation would appear to have referred to importation from foreign lands rather than to interstate commerce in slaves, a power that might, however, have been consistent with specific power delegated to Congress under that heading.

Article I, Section 9. [2] The Privilege of the Writ of Habeas Corpus shall not be suspended, unless when in Cases of Rebellion or Invasion the public Safety may require it.

The Writ of Habeas Corpus

The next paragraph of Section 9 outlines another important limitation, namely the protection of the writ of habeas corpus, known in England as "The Great Writ." This Latin term literally means "you have the body." Under this provision, the privilege of defendants to have the charges against them specified as a condition to incarceration cannot be waived except in cases of rebellion or invasion. Without such a clause, those in power could hold opponents in detention without relief. Extended discussions of this clause took place during the Civil War when President Lincoln used his authority as commander-in-chief to detain suspected confederate sympathizers. Whatever is thought of Lincoln's actions, which he considered essential to the preservation of the Union, they clearly would not be constitutional in times of peace.

Article I, Section 9. [3] No Bill of Attainder or ex post facto Law shall be passed.

Bills of Attainder and Ex Post Facto Laws

Bills of attainder and ex post facto laws are also prohibited in Article I, Section 9. Like the writ of habeas corpus, these are technical legal terms, but no less important on that account. A bill of attainder is best understood as a legislative punishment without benefit of a trial. In England, it was not unusual for Parliament to decree a penalty for one of the king's ministers whom members of Parliament believed had committed a wrong. Such a defendant was thus deprived of the normal protections of due process that he would have been accorded in court. The founders hoped to prevent this abuse in America. An early Court decision, *Calder v. Bull* (1798), defined an ex post facto law as a retroactive criminal law, wisely restricting the scope of this provision to criminal, as opposed to mere civil, matters. Thus, an ex post facto law is a law that either makes an action committed in the past a crime for which one can now be punished, or a law that strengthens the penalties for such crimes and applies this penalty retroactively. Again, the founders were aiming for justice or fairness.

Article I, Section 9. [4] No Capitation, or other direct, Tax shall be laid, *unless in Proportion to the Census or Enumeration herein before directed to be taken.*
[5] No Tax or Duty shall be laid on Articles exported from any State.
[6] No Preference shall be given by any Regulation of Commerce or Revenue to the Ports of one State over those of another; nor shall Vessels bound to, or from, one State, be obliged to enter, clear, or pay Duties in another.

Protections for the States

If people today tend to view justice as a matter primarily involving the treatment of discrete individuals, the framers were concerned as well about the rights of individual states that, as will be recalled, had been previously sovereign under the Articles of Confederation. Paragraph 4 limits capitation and direct taxes. The first clause was intended to protect southern slave interests; the second was not clearly defined. An early case, *Hylton v. United States* (1796), ruled that a national tax on carriages was not a direct tax and seemed to indicate that only a few taxes—perhaps only those on persons and land—would fit into the narrow category of prohibited taxes. A much later decision in *Pollock v. Farmers' Loan & Trust Company* (1895) ruled that income taxes were direct taxes and hence unconstitutional. This decision was overturned by the Sixteenth Amendment so that such taxes could not be apportioned on the basis of wealth, or income, rather than population.

Paragraph 5 prohibits export taxes and was considered especially important to the South, which was so dependent on agricultural exports for its income. Paragraph 6 both protects against preference for ports in one part of the country over another and reinforces congressional control over commerce among the states by prohibiting states from enacting duties on vessels entering from other states, as they had sometimes done under the Articles of Confederation.

Article I, Section 9. [7] No Money shall be drawn from the Treasury, but in Consequence of Appropriations made by Law; and a regular Statement and Account of the Receipts and Expenditures of all public Money shall be published from time to time.

The Appropriation of Money

Paragraph 7 stands on its own. It provides that all money spent be appropriated legally, and requires that the government give regular accounts of its receipts and expenditures. Without such accounting, it would be difficult for the people to maintain control over their government.

Despite the forthright language of this provision, the U.S. government does not publish the budget of the Central Intelligence Agency and other such intelligence-gathering operations. Moreover, in *United States v. Richardson* (1974), the Supreme Court denied standing to those who challenged this refusal. Such budgets thus continue as an exception to the general constitutional rule.

Article I, Section 9. [8] No Title of Nobility shall be granted by the United States: And no Person holding any Office of Profit or Trust under them, shall, without the Consent of the Congress, accept of any present, Emolument, Office, or Title, of any kind whatever, from any King, Prince, or foreign State.

Titles of Nobility

In looking at the Senate, it has already been noted that this body is composed of elected officials and not of people who inherit their positions and titles for life, as in the British House of Lords. Paragraph 8 reinforces this distinction by prohibiting the government from issuing titles of nobility and by requiring congressional consent to any titles conferred by foreign nations.

In 1810, Maryland's Senator Philip Reed introduced an amendment that, if adopted, would have added to Article I, Section 9 by specifying that any Americans who accepted titles of nobility from a foreign power would be stripped of their citizenship and be ineligible for any offices. This so-called "phantom amendment" appears to have fallen a single state shy of ratification and to have been prompted by fears that the son of Napolean's brother by an American socialite, Elizabeth Patterson, might one day attempt to set himself up as king (Vile, *Encyclopedia of Constitutional Amendments*, p. 307).

ARTICLE I, SECTION 10—LIMITS ON THE STATES

While Article I, Section 8 grants powers to Congress and Article I, Section 9 limits these powers, Article I, Section 10 goes on to indicate that the states composing the federal system are also subject to restraints. A key reason for a written constitution in a federal system is to delineate the respective relationship between the two levels of government.

Article I, Section 10. [1] No State shall enter into any Treaty, Alliance, or Confederation; grant Letters of Marque and Reprisal; coin Money; emit Bills of Credit; make any Thing but gold and silver Coin a Tender in Payment of Debts; pass any Bill of Attainder, ex post facto Law, or Law impairing the Obligation of Contracts, or grant any Title of Nobility.

Powers Reserved to the National Government

One purpose of a constitution in a federal system, where power is split between a central government and constituent parts that Americans designate as states, is to outline the respective powers of both governments. Article I, Section 10 indicates that a number of powers granted to Congress in Article I, Section 8 are exclusive powers that the states may not exercise concurrently. Thus, treaty-making, matters concerned with war, coining money, and otherwise dealing in currency are prohibited to the states. Like the Congress, states are prohibited from passing bills of attainder and ex post facto laws, or granting titles of nobility.

The Contract Clause

Interestingly, there is an additional restriction that was not similarly applied to the Congress. This restriction is found in the provision prohibiting states from "impairing the obligation of contracts." This provision may be more significant than is generally recognized. Why would such a limitation be placed on the states and not on Congress? The answer is twofold. Historically, one of the problems with state governments under the Articles of Confederation was precisely that certain state legislatures were passing class-based legislation designed to benefit those groups in power. Such a problem was particularly acute in Rhode Island, the single state that refused to send any delegates to the Constitutional Convention. Moreover, in arguing for a continental union, James Madison argued effectively in *Federalist* No. 10 and elsewhere that one of the problems of the states was that, as smaller geographical units with fewer interests, both minority and majority factions, or combinations of individuals out for their own self-interest, were more likely to prevail at the state level than at the national level. Apparently, this is the view that is reflected here. The national government, representing the interests of the whole, was considered less likely to need a constitutional prohibition than were states where self-interested factions were more likely to prevail.

Early in the nation's history, the contract clause was viewed by the courts as an important protection for private property. It was applied in *Fletcher v. Peck* (1810) to prohibit a state from rescinding land grants, even though clear evidence existed that such grants had resulted from political corruption. In the famous case of *Dartmouth College v. Woodward* (1819), the Court applied the contract clause even to contracts entered into prior to the Constitution, in this case to a royal charter that had been granted to Dartmouth College and that the New Hampshire legislature had subsequently sought to revise.

As the nation expanded, there was some concern that an overly strict construction of the contract clause could hinder industrial progress. Thus, in the case of *Charles River Bridge Co. v. Warren River Bridge Co.* (1837), the Court, now headed by Chief Justice Roger Taney, appointed by a president (Andrew Jackson) who was a strong supporter of popular sovereignty, indicated that any ambiguity in the language of a contract would be interpreted to benefit the state. In this case, the Court refused to read an exclusive grant into a contract awarded to a bridge company in the absence of specific language. Again, during the Great Depression of the twentieth century, the Supreme Court upheld a Minnesota mortgage moratorium law in *Home Building & Loan Association v. Blaisdell* (1934) on the basis that this was not a class-based law such as the contract clause had been designed to prevent, but was rather a reasonable effort to preserve the economy, and thus the well-being, of the state as a whole. In *United Trust Co. of New York v. New Jersey* (1977), the Supreme Court indicated that it would look closely at cases where governments attempted to alter their own contracts (thus voiding an impairment of a contract by the New York and New Jersey Port Authority). Generally, however, the twentieth century has witnessed less judicial attention to economic rights, and the justices' treatment of the contract clause is but one indication of this position.

Article I, Section 10. [2] No State shall, without the Consent of the Congress, lay any Imposts or Duties on Imports or Exports, except what may be absolutely necessary for executing its inspection Laws: and the net Produce of all Duties and Imposts, laid by any State on Imports or Exports, shall be for the Use of the Treasury of the United States; and all such Laws shall be subject to the Revision and Controul of the Congress.

[3] No State shall, without the Consent of Congress, lay any Duty of Tonnage, keep Troops, or Ships of War in time of Peace, enter into any Agreement or Compact with another State, or with a foreign Power, or engage in War, unless actually invaded, or in such imminent Danger as will not admit of delay.

Other Limits on the States

Paragraph 2 prohibits state taxes on imports and exports except for what "may be absolutely necessary for executing its inspection laws." (Note the qualifying adjective here that is missing from the elastic clause in the last paragraph of Article I, Section 8.) The same paragraph reaffirms that other import and export taxes are for the national government and not for the states.

Similarly, the third paragraph lists other powers from which states are excluded because of national preemption. Congressional approval is required for states to keep troops, enter into agreements with foreign governments, or agree to compacts among themselves. Provision is made, however, for states to employ force when there is an actual invasion and delay is impossible.

REFERENCES AND SUGGESTIONS FOR FURTHER STUDY

Cases

Calder v. Bull, 3 U.S. 386 (1798).
Charles River Bridge Co. v. Warren Bridge Co., 36 U.S. 420 (1837).
Chisholm v. Georgia, 2 U.S. 419 (1793).

City of Philadelphia v. New Jersey, 437 U.S. 617 (1978).
Cooley v. Board of Wardens, 53 U.S. 299 (1852).
Dartmouth College v. Woodward, 17 U.S. 518 (1819).
Dred Scott v. Sandford, 60 U.S. 393 (1857).
Fletcher v. Peck, 10 U.S. 87 (1810).
Garcia v. San Antonio Metropolitan Transit Authority, 469 U.S. 528 (1985).
Gibbons v. Ogden, 22 U.S. 1 (1824).
Gravel v. United States, 408 U.S. 606 (1972).
Hammer v. Dagenhart, 247 U.S. 251 (1918).
Home Building & Loan Association v. Blaisdell, 290 U.S. 398 (1934).
Hylton v. United States, 3 U.S. 171 (1796).
Immigration and Naturalization Service v. Chadha, 462 U.S. 919 (1983).
Luther v. Borden, 48 U.S. 1 (1849).
McCulloch v. Maryland, 17 U.S. 316 (1819).
National League of Cities v. Usery, 426 U.S. 833 (1976).
Walter L. Nixon v. United States, 113 S. Ct. 732 (1993).
Pollock v. Farmers' Loan & Trust Co., 158 U.S. 601 (1895).
Powell v. McCormack, 395 U.S. 486 (1969).
Schechter Poultry Corporation v. United States, 295 U.S. 495 (1935).
Southern Pacific Company v. Arizona, 325 U.S. 761 (1945).
Trade Mark Cases, 100 U.S. 82 (1879).
U.S. Term Limits v. Thorton, 115 S. Ct. 1842 (1995).
United States Trust Co. of New York v. New Jersey, 431 U.S. 1 (1977).
United States v. Butler, 297 U.S. 1 (1936).
United States v. Curtiss-Wright Corporation, 299 U.S. 304 (1936).
United States v. E.C. Knight, 156 U.S. 1 (1895).
United States v. Lopez, 115 S. Ct. 1624 (1995).
United States v. Richardson, 418 U.S. 166 (1974).
Watkins v. United States, 354 U.S. 178 (1957).

Books

Christopher J. Bailey, *The U.S. Congress* (New York: Basil Blackwell Ltd., 1989).
Sotorios Barber, *The Constitution and the Delegation of Congressional Power* (Chicago: The University of Chicago Press, 1975).
Charles L. Black, Jr., *Perspectives in Constitutional Law* (Englewood Cliffs, NJ: Prentice-Hall, 1970).
Barbara H. Craig, *Chadha: The Story of an Epic Constitutional Struggle* (New York: Oxford University Press, 1988).
Robert A. Diamond, *Powers of Congress* (Washington, DC: Congressional Quarterly Inc., 1976).
John H. Ely, *War and Responsibility: Constitutional Lessons of Vietnam and its Aftermath* (Princeton, NJ: Princeton University Press, 1993).
Max Farrand, *The Framing of the Constitution of the United States* (New Haven, CT: Yale University Press, 1913).
Louis Fisher, *Constitutional Conflicts Between the Congress and the President* (Princeton, NJ: Princeton University Press, 1985).

Louis Fisher, *The Politics of Shared Powers: Congress and the Executive*, 2nd ed. (Washington, DC: Congressional Quarterly Press, 1987).

Felix Frankfurter, *The Commerce Clause Under Marshall, Taney and Waite* (Chapel Hill: University of North Carolina Press, 1937).

Robert A. Goldwin and Art Kaufman, eds., *Separation of Powers—Does It Still Work?* (Washington, DC: American Enterprise Institute for Public Policy Research, 1986).

Alexander Hamilton, James Madison, and John Jay, *The Federalist Papers*, Clinton Rossiter, ed. (New York: New American Library, 1961).

Michael Kammen, *A Machine That Would Go of Itself: The Constitution in American Culture* (New York: Alfred A. Knopf, 1987).

Thomas E. Mann, *A Question of Balance: The President, the Congress and Foreign Policy* (Washington, DC: Brookings, 1989).

John L. Moore, ed., *Guide to U.S. Elections*, 2nd. ed. (Washington, DC: Congressional Quarterly, Inc., 1985).

Michael Nelson, ed., *Guide to the Presidency*, 2nd ed. (Washington, DC: Congressional Quarterly, Inc., 1996).

John F. O'Connor, "The Emoluments Clause: An Anti-Federalist Intruder in a Federal Constitution," *Hofstra Law Review* (Fall 1995), 24:89–178.

William H. Rehnquist, *Grand Inquests: The Historic Impeachments of Justice Samuel Chase and President Andrew Johnson* (New York: William Morrow & Company, 1992).

Randall B. Ripley, *Congress: Process and Policy*, 4th ed. (New York: W.W. Norton & Company, Inc., 1988).

John R. Schmidhauser and Larry L. Berg, *The Supreme Court and Congress: Conflict and Interaction, 1945–1968* (New York: The Free Press, 1972).

Telford Taylor, *The Grand Inquest: The Story of Congressional Investigations* (New York: Simon and Schuster, 1955).

John R. Vile, *Encyclopedia of Constitutional Amendments, Proposed Amendments, and Amending Issues, 1789–1995* (Santa Barbara, CA: ABC-CLIO, 1996).

Michael D. Wormser, *Guide to Congress*, 3rd ed. (Washington, DC: Congressional Quarterly Inc., 1982).

Benjamin F. Wright, *The Contract Clause of the Constitution* (Cambridge, MA: Harvard University Press, 1938).

Chapter 3

Article II: The Executive Branch

A SINGLE EXECUTIVE

Article II, Section 1. The executive Power shall be vested in a President of the United States of America.

While Article I deals with the legislative branch of the national government, Article II deals with the executive branch. Some delegates to the Constitutional Convention, including a number of those associated with the Virginia Plan, favored a single executive; others, generally identified with advocates of the New Jersey Plan, wanted a plural executive. The former group prevailed, and the "executive Power" is vested in a single president who, along with a vice president, serves terms of four years. The difference between the opening sentences of Articles I and II may be significant. Whereas Article I refers to "all powers herein granted," the grant of executive power in Article II reads more expansively. Traditionally, the powers of executives were understood to allow prerogatives and to require greater leeway in operation than those of the legislature. It may be that this more expansive language is intended to indicate this.

Undoubtedly, the power, and what the framers used to call the "energy," of this office were enhanced by the decision to rest the presidency in one individual. As a single individual, the president's words are far more important, and his actions receive far more attention, than if he were but one member of an executive council or committee. The relative attention that the president receives by comparison to a Supreme Court justice might serve as a case in point. The U.S. president is both the head of state and the head of American government. He thus combines the real and symbolic powers that are in England and other constitutional monarchies divided between the prime minister and the king or queen. This combination of powers also works to increase the prestige and symbolic power of the presidency, making this office a unique one for performing both good and ill. Thus, Woodrow Wilson, himself a great president, once noted that "The President is at liberty, both in law and conscience, to be as big a man as he can" (*Constitutional Government in the United States*, p. 70). Certainly, presidents like Washington, Jackson, Lincoln, and the two Roosevelts have shown the accuracy of Wilson's observation. A number of these individuals have radically changed the popular image and expectations of the presidency.

Article II, Section 1. [1] He shall hold his Office during the Term of four Years

THE PRESIDENTIAL TERM

The constitutional specification of a president's term at four years makes his term midway between those provided for members of the House of Representatives and the Senate. The length of the president's term serves to accent constitutional separation of powers. Although all seats in the House of Representatives are up for election in presidential election years, there is no guarantee that a majority will be from the president's own party. Moreover, while no constitutional necessity demands it, the president's party almost invariably loses support in the so-called midterm elections in the House two years later. With only one-third of the senators coming up for election in presidential election years, there is an even greater probability that the Senate will be led by a majority party other than the president's own. Such a split in party dominance is not possible in most parliamentary systems, in which the chief executive, usually designated the prime minister, heads the majority party or coalition. Many scholars have commended the parliamentary system as a desirable substitute for this reason. In favor of such proposals is the fact that it is not altogether clear that the American framers intended for political parties to have the influence they have enjoyed; indeed, strong evidence suggests that they hoped to avoid such party divisions. By the same token, the framers were fairly skeptical about human nature, and many might not have been altogether displeased to have yet another obstacle to dominance by either the ruling executive or legislative power.

After the War for Independence, there was concern about the possibility of executive abuses like those associated with George III. Experience under the Articles of Confederation, as well as a number of state constitutions during this period, had shown the problems connected with weak or nonexistent executive authority. The general belief and hope that George Washington (the chair of the Constitutional Convention) would serve as the nation's first chief executive undoubtedly eased fears and allowed for greater presidential powers.

Article II, Section 1. [1] and, together with the Vice President, chosen for the same Term, be elected, as follows

[2] Each State shall appoint, in such Manner as the Legislature thereof may direct, a Number of Electors, equal to the whole Number of Senators and Representatives to which the State may be entitled in the Congress; but no Senator or Representative, or Person holding an Office of Trust or Profit under the United States, shall be appointed an Elector.

[3] *The Electors shall meet in their respective States, and vote by Ballot for two Persons, of whom one at least shall not be an Inhabitant of the same State with themselves. And they shall make a List of all the Persons voted for, and of the Number of Votes for each; which List they shall sign and certify, and transmit sealed to the Seat of the Government of the United States, directed to the President of the Senate. The President of the Senate shall, in the Presence of the Senate and House of Representatives, open all the Certificates, and the Votes shall then be counted. The Person having the greatest Number of Votes shall be the President, if such Number be a Majority of the whole Number of Electors appointed; and if there be more than one who have such Majority, and have an equal Number of Votes, then the House of Representatives shall immediately chuse* [sic] *by Ballot one of them for President; and if no Person have a Majority, then from the five highest on the List the said House shall in like Manner chuse* [sic] *the President. But in chusing* [sic] *the President, the Votes shall be taken by States, the Representation from each State having one Vote; a quorum for this Purpose shall consist of a Member or Members from two thirds of the States, and a Majority of all the States shall be necessary to a Choice. In every Case, after the Choice of the President, the Person having the greatest Number of Votes of the Electors shall be the Vice President. But if there should remain two or*

more who have equal Votes, the Senate shall chuse [sic] *from them by Ballot
the Vice President.*

[4] The Congress may determine the Time of chusing [sic] the Electors,
and the Day on which they shall give their Votes; which Day shall be the
same throughout the United States.

PRESIDENTIAL SELECTION AND THE ELECTORAL COLLEGE

The problem of presidential selection was not an easy one. If the
president were to be chosen by Congress, as originally proposed in
the Virginia Plan, he could not be subject to reelection without
fear that he might attempt to bargain with, or corrupt, the legislature—a development that the colonists had observed, or thought
they observed, in Great Britain at the time of the American
Revolution. However appealing it may be today, direct election
raised fears about a popular demagogue acquiring prominence as
well as more practical questions, in an age long before computers
and telecommunications, as to how votes could be accurately and
quickly tallied in a nation the size of the new Union. If an indirect
method of election were chosen, questions would immediately
arise—as in the earlier controversy over representation in
Congress—as to how states should be represented. The eventual
response was an electoral college whose original structure is
described in paragraphs 2 and 3. Under this scheme, each state
receives a number of electoral votes equivalent to its total number
of senators and representatives (a minimum of three), thus adopting the Connecticut Compromise not only to the matter of state
representation in Congress, but also to voting for president. Each
state then selects a number of electors who assemble only once to
choose the president and vice president and then dissolve into
oblivion, obviating fears of presidential corruption.

Under the original electoral college scheme, the electors from
each state met separately and cast two ballots, at least one of which
had to go to an out-of-state resident—thus helping to mitigate small
state fears that the largest state would dominate the new system.
These votes were then to be transmitted to the president of the
Senate, who publicly counted the votes, awarding the presidency to
the person getting the highest number, assuming there was a majority, and the vice presidency to the runner-up. In cases where no candidate received a majority or there was a tie (and there is some

evidence that some of the framers thought such occasions would be fairly frequent), the House of Representatives would choose one for president, voting by states from among the top five names; this provision, like other parts of the electoral college, was later modified by the Twelfth Amendment. If the House of Representatives reached a tie vote for vice president, this choice was then to go to the Senate.

Nowhere does the U.S. Constitution mention political parties. It should be apparent from the electoral college arrangement that the founders did not fully anticipate the rise of political parties in the United States and the practice of running on a team-ticket, where ties between the top two candidates would almost be inevitable. This dilemma, fully evident in the election of 1800, brought about one of the nation's first constitutional amendments, the Twelfth, discussed in greater detail in a later chapter.

Article II, Section 1. [5] No Person except a natural born Citizen, or a Citizen of the United States, at the time of the Adoption of this Constitution, shall be eligible to the Office of President; neither shall any person be eligible to that Office who shall not have attained to the Age of thirty five Years, and been fourteen Years a Resident within the United States.

PRESIDENTIAL QUALIFICATIONS

According to these provisions, the presidential office is limited to those who were citizens at the time of the adoption of the Constitution or those who were subsequently natural born. This provision was probably intended to prevent people not thoroughly acculturated to American ideals from running for the office; this requirement would also serve to quash rumors circulating at the time of the Constitutional Convention that the delegates intended to bring in a foreign king. As to the specified minimum age of 35, it is slightly higher than that required for members of the House and Senate but still fairly minimal. Such a person further needs to have been a U.S. resident for a minimum of 14 years, again ostensibly to ensure familiarity with national ideals.

Article II, Section 1. [6] *In Case of the Removal of the President from Office, or of his Death, Resignation, or Inability to discharge the Powers and Duties of the said Office, the Same shall devolve on the Vice President, and the Congress may by Law provide for the Case of Removal, Death, Resignation or Inability, both of the President and Vice President, declaring* *what Officer shall then act as President, and such Officer shall act accordingly, until the Disability be removed, or a President shall be elected.*

THE VICE PRESIDENT AND PRESIDENTIAL DISABILITY

Although the role has become increasingly institutionalized over the past few decades, the Constitution does not list extensive duties for the vice president. Even more than serving as president of the Senate, the vice president's main constitutional responsibility is to serve as a kind of president-in-waiting in case a president dies, resigns, or is disabled. To date, the only president to have resigned is Richard Nixon. Others have, however, died of natural causes or been assassinated. Cases of presidential disability have also occurred, but, absent greater clarification that would come with the ratification of the Twenty-Fifth Amendment (which has modified this section of the Constitution), vice presidents have had little guidance in pressing their claims in such circumstances. Ever since 1841 when John Tyler assumed the reins from William Henry Harrison, who died in office of natural causes, the vice president has served in such cases not as an acting president, but as a president fully endowed with all the prerogatives of his predecessors. The language of paragraph 6 suggests, but does not conclusively prove, that the framers may have anticipated a new election in such circumstances.

Article II, Section 1. [7] The President shall, at stated Times, receive for his Services, a Compensation, which shall neither be increased nor diminished during the Period for which he shall have been elected, and he shall not receive within that Period any other Emolument from the United States, or any of them.

THE PRESIDENTIAL SALARY

Collectively at least, members of Congress determine their own salaries (in a provision since modified by the Twenty-Seventh Amendment). If Congress were given discretion to raise or lower the salary of the president, this power might be used in a partisan fashion and undercut executive independence. The Constitution accordingly prohibits presidential pay from being raised or lowered during a president's term in office. Similarly, he is prevented from accepting any other "Emolument[s]" from the nation or the states, a provision that has done nothing to keep former presidents from "cashing in" on their offices by accepting lucrative speaking and/or publication fees after leaving office.

Article II, Section 1. [8] Before he enter on the Execution of his Office, he shall take the following Oath or Affirmation:—"I do solemnly swear (or affirm) that I will faithfully execute the Office of President of the United States, and will to the best of my Ability, preserve, protect and defend the Constitution of the United States."

THE PRESIDENTIAL OATH

Americans have come to consider the members of the judicial branch as the primary defenders of the Constitution, but the presidential oath puts this responsibility in some perspective. In addition to pledging to execute the office of president, the chief executive also pledges to "preserve, protect and defend the Constitution of the United States," a pledge that has led some presidents, Andrew Jackson for example, to defend their own constitutional views against rival interpretations by the judicial branch. The president may either swear or affirm this pledge, in apparent deference to those with religious convictions against swearing and with a sensitivity to religious beliefs that will later receive renewed emphasis in the First Amendment. The words "so help me God," which are usually added to the presidential oath, are not required by the Constitution.

PRESIDENTIAL DUTIES

Article II, Section 2. [1] The President shall be Commander in Chief of the Army and Navy of the United States, and of the Militia of the several States, when called into the actual Service of the United States;

Commander-in-Chief

Presidential duties are listed in Section 2 of Article II. The first duty, actually an office rather than a function, may well be the most important and is sometimes referred to as the power of the sword. It provides that the president is commander-in-chief of the army and navy, and of state militia called into national service. Thus, the Constitution embodies the principle of civilian control of the mili-

tary that Jefferson cited in the Declaration of Independence. While
a number of generals, like Washington, Harrison, and Eisenhower,
have resided in the Oval Office, a president is the nation's highest
military official regardless of prior military training and service or
lack of it. Thus, the nation has successfully avoided the bloody
coups that have marked the history of many other nations, a number of them in the western hemisphere. Conflicts have sometimes
occurred between the president and the military brass—the controversy between President Harry Truman and General Douglas
MacArthur during the Korean War being a good example—but the
contest is weighted beforehand, as it undoubtedly should be, on the
side of the president.

Conflicts between the president and Congress in the area of foreign affairs are necessarily more complex since this is one of those
areas in which power is divided, with Congress declaring war and
authorizing appropriations for it and the president waging it. A help-
ful concurring opinion by Justice Jackson in *Youngstown Sheet &
Tube Co. v. Sawyer* (1952) thus once explained that presidential war
powers are strongest when exercised in pursuit of congressional
policies, weakest when in direct conflict with these policies, and
somewhere in between when his actions are neither sanctioned nor
condemned by congressional action.

Given the almost perpetual state of cold war that has existed from
the end of World War II to the fall of the Iron Curtain, there has
been concern that presidential powers could result in significant
diminution of civil liberties. An example occurred when the
Supreme Court in *Korematsu v. United States* (1944) sanctioned the
incarceration of over 100,000 Japanese Americans without trial during World War II on the basis of an executive order based on a perceived threat to national security. Fortunately, this decision has itself
been reconsidered and overturned by the Court, and other decisions—often, however, coming after wartime emergencies are
over—have clearly limited executive powers. A decision rendered
after the Civil War, *Ex Parte Milligan* (1866), thus invalidated the
trial of a civilian by a military court in Indiana when the regular
courts were in operation, while a previously referenced ruling during the Korean War (*Youngstown Sheet & Tube Co. v. Sawyer*, 1952)
invalidated an attempted presidential seizure of U.S. steel mills in
order to avoid a threatened strike.

After widespread complaints about presidential abuses of power
during the Vietnam War, Congress passed the War Powers Reso-

lution of 1973, a law that survived President Nixon's veto. The law required presidential consultation with Congress and notification within 48 hours that he was engaging American troops in hostile actions. It also provided that troops could be committed for only 60 days—with a 30 day extension possible—in cases where the president did not receive subsequent congressional approval. John Hart Ely has noted that implementation of the War Powers Resolution has been complicated by "presidential defiance, congressional irresolution, and judicial abstention" (Ely, *War and Responsibility*, p. 49). Not only does the law contain a legislative veto mechanism like that invalidated in the *Chadha* case, but the consultation and reporting provisions of the law are so ambiguous that presidents can sometimes bypass the law by refusing to submit a report that will trigger the 60-day limit. Although presidents have thus sometimes evaded the law, it has probably served to heighten their awareness of the need to seek congressional support when undertaking foreign policy initiatives. Thus, President Bush sought and received support from Congress for his attack on Iraqi troops that had invaded Kuwait. Under congressional pressure, President Clinton subsequently established deadlines for troops committed to peace-keeping assignments in Somalia (an action initiated by Bush), Haiti, and Bosnia.

Article II, Section 2. [1] he may require the Opinion, in writing, of the principal Officer in each of the executive Departments, upon any Subject relating to the Duties of their respective Offices,

Getting Advice from the Cabinet

In addition to personal staffers who have grown (like corresponding congressional staffs) largely outside the constitutional structure, as president the chief executive leads what is known as a cabinet consisting of the heads of various governmental agencies. The president has authority to call upon these heads for written advice connected with their duties. In an early example, President Washington asked his secretary of treasury, Alexander Hamilton; his secretary of state, Thomas Jefferson; and his attorney general, Edmund Randolph, for their opinions on the constitutionality of the bank. As often happens in such cases, he received conflicting opinions. A president is not legally obligated to take votes in cabinet meetings or accept the judgment of his cabinet even in cases where it is unanimous. Cabinet officers serve at the president's pleasure. Only he is elected to office, and only he can assume the responsibility for executing the powers of his office.

Article II, Section 2. [1] and he shall have Power to grant Reprieves and Pardons for Offenses against the United States, except in Cases of Impeachment.

Power to Pardon and Reprieve

As one who executes the laws, there is a certain logic in giving the president power to mitigate the application of the law in cases where he thinks national security or considerations of justice require it. The Constitution thus grants power to issue reprieves and pardons for offenses committed against the United States, a power mirroring that given to most state governors. The president's pardon power is broad, but it neither extends to offenses against individual states nor does it allow for presidential intervention in civil suits. The Supreme Court has ruled that the president can issue pardons to individuals convicted of contempt of Congress (*Ex Parte Grossman*, 1925). The power to pardon has been interpreted to involve the power to issue general amnesties, such as the one President Jimmy Carter extended to Vietnam era draft evaders.

Although the Supreme Court once ruled that a pardon was not valid unless it was accepted, in *Biddle v. Perovich* (1927) Justice Holmes ruled otherwise. He decided that a pardon was "not a private act of grace from an individual happening to possess power" but "a part of the Constitutional scheme." Accordingly, Holmes said that a pardon, like the original punishment, could "be imposed without regard to the prisoner's consent and in the teeth of his will, whether he liked it or not, [since] the public welfare, not his [a prisoner's] consent, determines what shall be done (*Biddle v. Perovich*, 1927, p. 486)." In *Schick v. Reed* (1974), the Court accepted the president's power to issue a conditional pardon.

Shortly after assuming his office, President Gerald Ford decided to pardon former President Richard Nixon—who had resigned after the Watergate scandal—for all crimes he may have committed while in office. Ford hoped this pardon would help heal the wounds of Watergate and allow the nation to move on to other matters, but his pardon was met by intense criticism and probably worked against his reelection. In *Murphy v. Ford* (1975), however, a district court ruled that the pardon was constitutional.

Article II, Section 2. [2] He shall have Power, by and with the Advice and Consent of the Senate, to Make Treaties, provided two thirds of the Senators present concur;

Negotiation and Ratification of Treaties

As commander-in-chief of the armed forces of the United States, the president also serves as the nation's chief diplomat. Specifically, he is responsible for making, or negotiating, treaties. Such treaties do not, however, become law of the land, as recognized under Article VI of the Constitution, until approved by a two-thirds vote of the Senate. This can put the president at a disadvantage in reaching agreement with heads of nations whose actions require no such approval. At least since Woodrow Wilson failed to get Senate approval for the League of Nations that he had advocated, there have been proposals to reduce the majority needed for such affirmation in the Senate (some such proposals would, however, involve the House of Representatives in such a vote). No such proposals have been adopted, however, and presidents have continued to worry about Senate approval—President Jimmy Carter thus proved unable to get approval for the SALT (Strategic Arms Limitation Talks) Treaty that he had negotiated with the Soviet Union. Presidents have sometimes made agreements with foreign governments, often called executive agreements, that deal with matters, particularly of a routine nature, not thought to require formal treaties.

In a number of cases, the Supreme Court has upheld the validity of such executive agreements. In *United States v. Belmont* (1937), for example, the Court upheld an executive agreement under which President Franklin Roosevelt had recognized the government of the Soviet Union. Similarly, in *Dames & Moore v. Regan* (1981), the Court upheld an executive agreement with Iran issued by President Reagan that effectively ratified an earlier order whereby President Carter had frozen Iranian assets and transferred them to the Federal Reserve Bank of New York, pending negotiations to settle differences between the two nations.

The question of agreements with foreign countries is complicated still further by the fact that Congress will sometimes authorize through joint congressional resolution what the Senate might otherwise accomplish through a treaty. This is how the United States entered the agreement with Canada to build the St. Lawrence Seaway. It was also the method used to adopt the controversial

North American Free Trade Agreement (NAFTA) with Canada and Mexico that President Clinton signed in 1994.

The Constitution does not indicate who has the power to terminate treaties. Quite obviously, adoption of a new conflicting law or treaty can void an earlier one. Moreover, when he was president, Jimmy Carter terminated a defense treaty with Taiwan on his own authority. In *Goldwater v. Carter* (1979), a majority of the Supreme Court subsequently sidestepped the issue of his authority by declaring that the issue was not "ripe" for review, but a number of justices indicated their belief that the president had authority to take this action.

Article II, Section 2. [2] and he shall nominate, and by and with the Advice and Consent of the Senate, shall appoint Ambassadors, other public Ministers and Consuls, Judges of the supreme Court, and all other Officers of the United States, whose Appointments are not herein otherwise provided for, and which shall be established by Law: but the Congress may by Law vest the Appointment of such inferior Officers, as they think proper, in the President alone, in the Courts of Law, or in the Heads of Departments.

Presidential Appointment and Removal Powers

Next to his power as commander-in-chief, the president's power of appointment may be his most important. This power, subject to the "Advice and Consent" or approval of the Senate, extends to ambassadors, ministers, judges, and other officers established under the Constitution. The president's role in appointing ambassadors reaffirms his role as the nation's chief diplomat. Because appointments to the judicial branch are for life terms, these are also especially important. The current method of appointment and confirmation is a compromise between two proposals at the Constitutional Convention. Under the Virginia Plan, judges would have been appointed by Congress; under the New Jersey Plan, such appointments would have been made by the executive branch. The resulting compromise includes both parties, giving the president the power of initiative and the Senate the power of veto.

Throughout American history, both powers have been taken seriously. This method of selection almost ensures that most appointees will have a "political" dimension. Presidents have found, however, that, particularly in the case of judges whom they cannot subsequently remove, they cannot always predict accurately how the judges will rule. Thus, while many scholars would not agree with his assessment, President Eisenhower said that his "two biggest mistakes" (a reference to Earl Warren and William Brennan) were "both on the Supreme Court" (Abraham, *Justices and Presidents*, p. 7). President Nixon later found that all three of the justices he had appointed who participated in *United States v. Nixon* (1974), where Nixon's claim of executive privilege was rejected, voted with the other justices against his claim. For its part, the Senate has taken its role of advice and consent seriously, not infrequently rejecting presidential nominees and sometimes delaying the inauguration of nominees in cases where the Senate does not have the votes to deny a presidential choice outright. Confirmation fights can be extremely partisan, but they fulfill an essential role, especially in the case of office-holders who will be in their positions for life.

The Constitution is silent on the removal of officers who do not serve life terms. Some politicians attempted to argue that, in areas where Senate consent was required for appointment, it should also be required for dismissal. This position was argued in, albeit not adopted by, the first Congress and upheld by the Reconstruction Congress, but has not subsequently prevailed. As the chief executive responsible for the execution of laws, it was eventually decided that the president alone should have such removal power. This position was affirmed by former President, then Chief Justice, William Howard Taft, in a Court decision in *Myers v. United States* (1926), and only later slightly modified in *Humphrey's Executor v. United States* (1935) and *Wiener v. United States* (1958) to take care of instances where an appointee was in a quasi-judicial position requiring independence, rather than in an executive position where the will of the president needed to be implemented and responsibility for executive action ultimately rested.

Inferior offices not specifically mentioned in the Constitution are appointed, according to congressional designation, by the president, the Courts, or department heads. Apart from limited cases in which Congress appoints its own officers, it cannot make appointments. Thus in a contemporary case, *Buckley v. Valeo* (1976), the Supreme Court invalidated a scheme whereby some members of a Federal Election Commission, designed to bring about campaign reform, were appointed by key officers of Congress rather than by the president.

In *Bowsher v. Synar* (1986), the Supreme Court decided that the comptroller general of the United States, who is appointed by the president from a list of names submitted by Congress, which body retains the power to remove the comptroller, could not be considered an executive officer. The Court therefore ruled that the comptroller had no authority to recommend budget cuts to the president under the Balanced Budget and Emergency Deficit Control Act, or Gramm-Rudman-Hollings law.

More recently, the Supreme Court in *Morrison v. Olson* (1988) upheld the appointment of a special prosecutor (an executive official) by members of the judicial branch, despite Justice Antonin Scalia's argument that the appointment within the executive branch of such an officer violated the doctrine of separation of powers. Chief Justice William Rehnquist said that the special prosecutor was an "inferior" officer who did not have to be appointed directly by the president and that the law permitted the attorney general sufficient control over the office so that the president could continue to exercise his constitutional duties. Similarly, in *Mistretta v. United States* (1989), the Supreme Court ruled that a U.S. Sentencing Commission, set up to establish binding sentencing guidelines, was constitutional. The Commission consisted of seven members, three of whom were judges appointed by the president from a list supplied by the Judicial Conference of the United States, and removable by the president only for cause. Evoking the little used doctrine of excessive delegation of legislative power, in his dissenting opinion Justice Scalia compared the commission to "a sort of 'junior varsity' Congress" that, unlike Congress itself, was not directly accountable to the people (*Mistretta v. United States*, 1989, p. 427).

Article II, Section 2. [3] The President shall have Power to fill up all Vacancies that may happen during the Recess of the Senate, by granting Commissions which shall expire at the End of their next Session.

Interim Presidential Appointments

It should be noted that, in cases where the Senate is in recess, presidents have the power to issue commissions that will end, unless confirmed, at the end of the next Senate session. This was an important power when Congress met for only a few months of the year and is accordingly less important in an age where Congress meets for most of the year.

Article II, Section 3. He shall from time to time give to the Congress Information of the State of the Union, and recommend to their Consideration such Measures as he shall judge necessary and expedient;

The State of the Union Address

Few Americans have not seen or heard broadcasts of one of the annual State of the Union messages that the president delivers in January. The constitutional basis of this address is found in the first paragraph of Section 3. Traditionally, presidents now deliver these speeches in person, but the Constitution does not require this. The practice did not begin until Woodrow Wilson, who was especially concerned with the potentially beneficial effects of presidential rhetoric, initiated it.

While Congress has the responsibility for making the laws, presidents, especially in modern times, have made major legislative initiatives that often serve as key parts of their election platform. Because of the visibility of their office, presidents have a unique ability to focus on legislative items that are particularly dear to them. The presidential veto further assures that, on most issues at least, the president's wishes will be given great weight by the legislature.

Article II, Section 3. he may, on extraordinary Occasions, convene both Houses, or either of them, and in Case of Disagreement between them, with Respect to the Time of Adjournment, he may adjourn them to such Time as he shall think proper;

Power to Convene and Adjourn Congress

The president has the power to convene one or both houses of Congress in special session, a power not likely to be exercised frequently since Congress now meets most of the year. Fortunately, the president's power to reconcile differences between the two branches of Congress over times of adjournment is not one American presidents have ever found necessary to exercise.

Article II, Section 3. [1] he shall receive Ambassadors and other public Ministers;

The President as Chief Diplomat

As the nation's chief diplomat responsible for appointing ambassadors, the president also receives ambassadors and public ministers from abroad. Perhaps here more than anywhere else, the president's roles as head of government and head of state are merged. The president serves as both the actual and symbolic head of the executive branch. In England, by contrast, the prime minister is the head of government while the king or queen is the symbolic head of state.

Article II, Section 3. he shall take Care that the Laws be faithfully executed

Power to Execute the Laws and Executive Privilege

Consistent with the idea of separation of powers, political scientists often say that Congress makes the laws, the president enforces the laws, and the judges and justices interpret the laws. Certainly, an important presidential duty is to see "that the Laws be faithfully executed." Obviously, this duty requires a balance of deference to legislative decisions and discrimination as to how best to achieve legislative goals.

As in the case of congressional powers, this clause may indicate that the president has certain implied powers necessary to help him in his tasks. Thus, in the case of *In Re Neagle* (1890), for example, the Court upheld the president's authority to assign a U.S. Marshal to the defense of a U.S. Supreme Court justice despite no specific statutory authority to do so.

Given the nature of presidential powers, and particularly their application to foreign affairs, it may not be surprising that presidents have argued that they should also be able to exercise certain inherent powers, that is, powers not specifically stated or implied in the Constitution but thought to derive from, or inhere in, the nature of their office. Even some proponents of strict constitutional construction have exercised expansive powers once in office. Thus, Thomas Jefferson construed his powers broadly in declaring an embargo on goods to Great Britain and in purchasing the Louisiana Territory from France without specific constitutional authorization for doing so. In addition to a wide array of claims that have been made in foreign affairs or during wartime, some presidents have asserted claims of "executive privilege" under which they have attempted to withhold certain sensitive information from congressional committees or from other investigatory bodies.

The boldest claim of executive privilege was made by President Nixon, who attempted to withhold certain of the Watergate tape recordings that he had made of conversations in the Oval Office from a special prosecutor, Leon Jaworski, who had been appointed to investigate possible legal violations by the president and his subordinates. Officially recognizing for the first time that a president has a special need for maintaining the confidentiality of conversations with his subordinates, in *United States v. Nixon* (1974) a unanimous Supreme Court nonetheless rejected Nixon's claim. The Court pointed out that it was particularly critical for a grand jury to hear evidence in cases involving possible criminal wrongdoing and that, in this case, there were no matters of national security that the president was trying to protect. Thus, at one and the same time, the Court acknowledged and limited executive privilege in a decision that helped provide the evidence that would drive Nixon from office.

As the most visible public figures in America, presidents subject to lawsuits tied to their official duties could be easily hamstrung. In *Nixon v. Fitzgerald* (1982), the Supreme Court accordingly extended immunity to presidents in connection with lawsuits resulting from their official acts, in this case former President Nixon's concurrence in the dismissal of a whistle-blowing civilian employee of the Air Force. Presidents may be summoned to testify in trials— as Clinton did in the 1996 Whitewater trial involving former business associates, Jim and Susan McDougal—but, as in this case, courts generally accommodate presidents' schedules and allow them to testify via videotape.

To date, the Supreme Court has not issued a decision as to whether presidential privileges should insulate a sitting president against criminal indictments, but Special Prosecutor Leon Jaworski was uncertain enough that he asked the jury in the Watergate case to name President Nixon as an "*unindicted* co-conspirator." A civil suit, brought in 1994 by Paula Jones against President Clinton for allegedly denying her a position when he was governor of Arkansas after she reportedly refused his sexual advances, raises further questions (which could soon be decided by the Supreme Court) as to whether such civil suits can proceed during a president's tenure in office.

Decisions from the Nixon era restricted the president's growing use of "impoundment," whereby he refused to spend money appropriated by Congress for certain purposes. Legislation on this subject, most notably the Congressional Budget and Impoundment Control Act of 1974, has since distinguished rescissions, or outright refusals to spend monies, from deferrals, or mere delays. After lower courts voided this law because of a legislative veto mechanism, Congress subsequently limited such deferrals to what Louis Fisher has described as "routine managerial actions" (*The Politics of Shared Power*, p. 68).

Article II, Section 3. and shall Commission all the Officers of the United States.

Commissioning of Military Officers

Finally, Section 3 entrusts the president with authority to commission all officers of the United States. As the president is also commander-in-chief, this duty obviously extends to military officials. Whereas officers in some dictatorships pledge personal allegiance to their leaders, American officers, like the president himself, pledge first and foremost to uphold the Constitution of the United States. In this way, the rule of law is affirmed to be more important than the rule of a human leader.

Article II, Section 4. The President, Vice President and all civil Officers of the United States, shall be removed from Office on Impeachment for, and Conviction of, Treason, Bribery, or other high Crimes and Misdemeanors.

PRESIDENTIAL IMPEACHMENT

Section 4 indicates that the president must, like other governmental officials, act within the law; he is thus subject, with other officeholders, to the check of impeachment and conviction. Lest this tool be used in a merely partisan fashion, the grounds of impeachment are specified and limited to cases of "Treason, Bribery and other high Crimes and Misdemeanors." The first two terms have a fairly precise meaning—treason is indeed defined within the Constitution itself (Article III, Section 3). The expression "high Crimes and Misdemeanors" is more ambiguous, but clearly encompasses more than an unpopular stance on a political issue. A committee created to investigate this phrase thus noted:

[T]hat Congress may properly impeach and remove a President only for conduct amounting to a gross breach or serious abuse of power, and only if it would be prepared to take the same action against any President who engaged in comparable conduct in similar circumstances (Committee on Federal Legislation, *The Law of Presidential Impeachment*, p. 6).

Thus, the charges finally accepted by the House Judiciary Committee against President Nixon included obstructing justice, abuse of power, and contempt of Congress.

Just as there are no provisions in the U.S. Constitution for congressional elections other than at the end of fixed terms or to fill vacancies, so too there is no provision, as in the British and most other parliamentary systems, for a "vote of no confidence" by which a new presidential election can be forced or the executive can call an election prior to the end of a president's regular four-year term. This guarantee of presidential tenure assures the president greater independence of Congress than he might otherwise have and thus enhances presidential power. It also arguably reduces presidential responsiveness to national moods and can leave the nation, as it probably has been at times, to be governed by an unpopular individual in whom it no longer has confidence. This is indeed one of the central objections to periodically advanced proposals that would allow the U.S. president to serve for a single six-year term.

REFERENCES AND SUGGESTIONS FOR FURTHER STUDY

Cases

Biddle v. Perovich, 274 U.S. 480 (1927).
Bowsher v. Synar, 478 U.S. 714 (1986).
Buckley v. Valeo, 424 U.S. 1 (1976).
Dames & Moore v. Regan, 453 U.S. 654 (1981).
Ex Parte Grossman, 267 U.S. 87 (1925).
Ex Parte Milligan, 71 U.S. 2 (1866).
Goldwater v. Carter, 444 U.S. 996 (1979).
Humphrey's Executor v. United States, 295 U.S. 602 (1935).
Immigration and Naturalization Service v. Chadha, 462 U.S. 919 (1983).
In Re Neagle, 135 U.S. 1 (1890).
Korematsu v. United States, 323 U.S. 214 (1944).
Mistretta v. United States, 488 U.S. 361 (1989).
Morrison v. Olson, 487 U.S. 654 (1988).
Murphy v. Ford, 390 F. Supp. 1372 (1975).
Myers v. United States, 272 U.S. 52 (1926).
Nixon v. Fitzgerald, 457 U.S. 731 (1982).
Schick v. Reed, 419 U.S. 256 (1974).
Trade Mark Cases, 100 U.S. 82 (1879)
United States v. Belmont, 301 U.S. 324 (1937).
United States v. Nixon, 418 U.S. 683 (1974).
U.S. Term Limits v. Thorton, 115 S. Ct. 1842 (1995).
Walter L. Nixon v. United States, 113 S. Ct. 732 (1993).
Wiener v. United States, 357 U.S. 349 (1958).
Youngstown Sheet & Tube Co. v. Sawyer, 343 U.S. 579 (1952).

Books

Henry J. Abraham, *Justices and Presidents: A Political History of Appointments to the Supreme Court*, 3rd ed. (New York: Oxford University Press, 1992).

Raoul Berger, *Executive Privilege: A Constitutional Myth* (Cambridge, MA: Harvard University Press, 1974).

Raoul Berger, *Impeachment: The Constitutional Problem* (Cambridge, MA: Harvard University Press, 1973).

Robert E. Di Clerico, ed., *Analyzing the Presidency*, 2nd ed. (Guilford, CT: The Dushkin Publishing Group, Inc., 1990).

Committee on Federal Legislation, *The Law of Presidential Impeachment* (New York: Harper & Row, n.d.).

Edward S. Corwin, *The President, Office and Powers* (New York: New York University Press, 1940).

John Hart Ely, *War and Responsibility: Constitutional Lessons of Vietnam and Its Aftermath* (Princeton, NJ: Princeton University Press, 1993).

Louis Fisher, *The Politics of Shared Power: Congress and the Executive*, 3rd ed. (Washington, DC: CQ Press, 1993).

Richard Hofstader, *The Idea of a Party System: The Rise of Legitimate Opposition in the United States, 1780–1840* (Berkeley: University of California Press, 1972).

Charles O. Jones, *The Presidency in a Separated System* (Washington, DC: The Brookings Institution, 1994).

Barbara Kellerman and Ryan J. Barilleaux, *The President as World Leader* (New York: St. Martin's Press, 1991).

Louis W. Koenig, *The Chief Executive*, 4th ed. (New York: Harcourt Brace Jovanovich, 1980).

Harvey C. Mansfield, Jr., *Taming the Prince: The Ambivalence of Modern Executive Power* (New York: The Free Press, 1989).

Christopher N. May, *In the Name of War: Judicial Review and the War Powers Since 1918* (Cambridge, MA: Harvard University Press, 1989).

Forrest McDonald, *The American Presidency: An Intellectual History* (Lawrence: University Press of Kansas, 1994).

Michael Nelson, ed., *Guide to the Presidency*, 2nd ed., 2 vols. (Washington, DC: Congressional Quarterly, 1996).

Michael Nelson, ed., *The Presidency: A History of the Office of the President of the United States from 1789 to the Present* (New York: Smithmark, 1996).

Richard E. Neustadt, *Presidential Power* (New York: Wiley, 1980).

Benjamin I. Page and Mark P. Petracca, *The American Presidency* (New York: McGraw-Hill Book Company, 1983).

Clinton Rossiter, *The American Presidency* (New York: Harcourt, Brace and World, rev. ed. 1960).

Clinton Rossiter expanded with additional text by Richard P. Longaker, *The Supreme Court and the Commander in Chief* (Ithaca, NY: Cornell University Press, 1976).

Mark J. Rozell, *Executive Privilege: The Dilemma of Secrecy and Democratic Accountability* (Baltimore, MD: The Johns Hopkins University Press, 1994).

Robert Scigliano, *The Supreme Court and the Presidency* (New York: The Free Press, 1971).

Jean E. Smith, *The Constitution and American Foreign Policy* (St. Paul, MN: West Publishing Company, 1989).

Robert J. Spitzer, *The Presidential Veto: Touchstone of the American Presidency* (Albany: State University of New York Press, 1988).

Jeffrey K. Tulis, *The Rhetorical Presidency* (Princeton, NJ: Princeton University Press, 1987).

Woodrow Wilson, *Constitutional Government in the United States* (New York: Columbia University Press, 1961).

Donald Young, *American Roulette: The History and Dilemma of the Vice Presidency* (New York: The Viking Press, 1974).

Chapter 4

Article III: The Judicial Branch

ORGANIZATION AND GUIDELINES

Article III, Section 1. The judicial Power of the United States, shall be vested in one supreme Court, and in such inferior Courts as the Congress may from time to time ordain and establish.

The U.S. Supreme Court and Other Inferior Courts

Whereas the first two articles of the Constitution deal with the elected branches, Article III deals with an appointed branch, the judiciary. Article III is the briefest of the first three articles, simply establishing "the judicial power" (a matter discussed in greater detail in a subsequent section of this chapter entitled "Limits on the Judicial Power") in a Supreme Court and in such other courts as Congress shall establish, and leaving most details of judicial organization to be decided later.

Currently, the federal constitutional courts are divided into three tiers, each with distinct functions. The district courts, of which there are currently 94, are trial courts where cases are tried and juries are impaneled. Each state has at least one such court. Above the district courts are 13 circuit courts of appeal (eleven numbered circuits covering distinct geographical regions, and a District of Columbia and Federal Circuit Court, both located in the nation's capital), which hear appeals from the district courts. At the top of this hierarchy is the U.S. Supreme Court, mentioned in Article III. In addition to overseeing the U.S. District and Circuit Courts, the Supreme Court can, where substantial federal issues are involved, hear appeals from state court systems, which are usually structured much like the national court system and are typically headed by their own supreme court or equivalent. It is thus more accurate to refer to the 51 judicial systems in the United States than to one.

Article III, Section 1. The Judges, both of the supreme and inferior Courts, shall hold their Offices during good Behaviour,

Judicial Tenure

Whereas some states provide for the election of judges to fixed terms of office, members of all federal constitutional courts are nominated and appointed by the president with the advice and consent of the Senate (Article II, Section 2 [2]) and hold their offices "during good Behaviour." In effect, this means that judges serve for life rather than at the pleasure of the people or the other elected branches—recall how in the Declaration of Independence Jefferson had accused the king of keeping judges dependent upon his power. The only way that judges leave office is thus through death, resignation, or retirement, or, in rarer cases, impeachment and conviction following constitutional guidelines. Clearly, judges were intended to be insulated from day-to-day political pressures, giving them independence to decide legal cases without fear or favor. In 1980, Congress did adopt the Judicial Councils Reform and Judicial Conduct and Disability Act, which was designed to allow for the disciplining, albeit not the removal, of lower court judges engaged in conduct short of impeachable offenses (Abraham, *The Judicial Process*, p. 42).

Judicial Qualifications

In contrast to members of the legislative and executive branches, no formal constitutional qualifications exist for judges. Perhaps the founders thought there would be less cause to fear that incompetent people would be appointed than elected. Alternatively, they probably expected that legal education would screen out those who were unfit for office. It is also possible that they expected Congress to establish formal judicial qualifications, although it has never done so. Presidents increasingly appear to consider the race, gender, religion, and geographical origins of judges and justices, but they are not required to do so, and some scholars argue that objective merit should be a president's only concern. "Senatorial courtesy," an unwritten convention, rather than a constitutional mandate, permits a senator from a president's party to block the nomination of a judge from his state to which the senator objects and about which the president had not first consulted the senator.

Article III, Section 1. and shall, at stated Times, receive for their Services, a Compensation, which shall not be diminished during their Continuance in Office.

Judicial Compensation

Subject to restrictions recently adopted in the Twenty-Seventh Amendment, members of Congress collectively set their own salaries, and presidential pay may not be increased or decreased during the executive's term. The provision for judges and justices is a bit different. Such judges' pay may be raised but not lowered during their tenure. The framers wished to insulate judges from partisan-based reductions in salary. They further realized that, at least in inflationary times, most judges could not remain in office without raises. By preventing cuts and permitting raises, they hoped to provide adequate salaries while minimizing excessive partisanship in the determination of such salaries.

The Number of Justices

The number of judges and justices is not specified in the U.S. Constitution, theoretically giving Congress power to make needed alterations. This power has been exercised freely in regard to appointing additional judges to lower courts. For the last hundred years or so, however, the number of Supreme Court justices has been fixed at nine, with eight associate justices and one designated, as the Constitution specifies, as the chief justice. The last serious effort to change this number was Franklin D. Roosevelt's so-called court-packing plan of 1937, which would have added one justice for every sitting justice over age 70 up to a total of 15. This proposal was rightly viewed as a partisan maneuver designed to change the decisions of a

Court that, until that time, had ruled negatively on most New Deal programs, and it was rejected as such. Another president proposing such a change would be hard-pressed to demonstrate that his proposals were in the nation's best interest and not a grab for partisan advantage. The number nine has thus almost come to be an unwritten constitutional rule unlikely to be changed except under the most extraordinary circumstances.

Supreme Court Decisions

The Constitution does not require judicial unanimity, enabling justices to make decisions by majority vote, sometimes deciding important cases by a five to four margin. Usually such majority opinions are signed, but sometimes the Court will issue an unsigned *per curiam* opinion. In addition to the majority opinion, it is not uncommon to see concurring and dissenting opinions being filed. In the former, a justice or justices will vote with the majority, but add their own explanations and/or qualifications of their votes. In the latter, justices indicate why they cannot vote with the majority and make their appeal, as it were, to history. By custom, the chief justice of the Supreme Court writes or assigns opinions when he votes on the side of the majority; otherwise, this responsibility rests with the ranking member of the majority.

JURISDICTION

Article III, Section 2. [1] The judicial Power shall extend to all Cases, in Law and Equity, arising under this Constitution, the Laws of the United States, and Treaties made, or which shall be made, under their Authority;—to all Cases affecting Ambassadors, other public Ministers and Consuls;—to all Cases of admiralty and maritime Jurisdiction;—to Controversies to which the United States shall be a Party;—to Controversies between two or more States;—*between a State and Citizens of another State*;—between Citizens of different States;—between Citizens of the same State claiming Lands under Grants of different States, *and between a State, or the Citizens thereof, and foreign States, Citizens or Subjects.*

Cases Based on Subject Matter and Parties to the Suit

Americans justly pride themselves in having a written constitution. Perhaps nowhere is such a constitution more important than in consideration of the judicial branch that hears all cases that arise under the Constitution and thus provides a unity of interpretation throughout the nation. Section 2 of the Constitution delineates the cases that the federal courts hear. These may be divided into two groups, cases that the courts accept because of their subject matter and those that they hear based on the parties to the case. In the first category are cases in law and equity (two branches of English law, the first utilizing traditional judicial remedies and the second designed as a supplement with more flexible remedies, which are combined in the U.S. scheme) arising: (1) under the Constitution; from (2) federal laws; and (3) federal treaties; and (4) in admiralty and maritime law. Such cases, at least those involving a substantial federal question, will thus be heard by federal rather than state courts.

In the second category—based on parties to the suit—are: (1) cases affecting ambassadors, public ministers, and consuls; (2) controversies involving the United States; (3) cases involving two or more states (boundary disputes, for example); (4) cases involving a state and citizens of another state; (5) cases between citizens of different states (so-called diversity of citizenship cases where Congress has once again delegated minor cases to the state judiciaries); (6) controversies between state citizens who claim land under land grants from other states; and (7) cases that arise between a state and its citizens and citizens of foreign states. The Eleventh Amendment caused a slight alteration in this jurisdiction (in cases of disputes instituted against a state by citizens of another state or of a foreign nation), but it is otherwise unchanged from the time the Constitution was written to the present.

It needs to be noted that in a number of these cases, state and federal courts exercise concurrent jurisdiction. That is, Congress has specified that in certain instances, diversity of citizenship cases below a certain minimum monetary amount, for example, cases may be pursued in either state or federal courts. Parties and their attorneys thus sometimes can control in which set of courts they will pursue their case. Generally, the Supreme Court will not review cases in which state judicial judgments rest solely on interpretations of the state constitution. Where important federal issues are involved, however, there are writs (for example, the writ of habeas corpus) by which cases may be transferred from a state court—usually the state's highest, or supreme, court—to the U.S. Supreme Court for review. Because ours is a federal system, courts attempt to adhere to principles of comity, or mutual restraint, deference, and respect, to ease problems that might otherwise develop in such a system. More deferential to state judgments, especially in the area of criminal procedures, than some previous Courts, the Rehnquist Court has significantly tightened restrictions on which cases it will accept for review from the states. This development has been particularly pronounced in its review of death penalty cases in which numerous appeals are filed, especially as the day of execution nears.

Article III, Section 2. [2] In all Cases affecting Ambassadors, other public Ministers and Counsuls, and those in which a State shall be Party, the supreme Court shall have original Jurisdiction. In all the other Cases before mentioned, the supreme Court shall have appellate Jurisdiction, both as to Law and Fact, with such Exceptions, and under such Regulations as the Congress shall make.

Cases of Original and Appellate Jurisdiction

Just as the jurisdiction of the courts may be divided between those based on subject matter and those dependent on the parties to the suit, so too, may cases that reach the Supreme Court be divided into those of original and appellate jurisdiction. The first category refers to cases that both begin and end in the Supreme Court. Such cases are limited to those involving ambassadors and public ministers, as well as cases in which the states are parties. Even in these cases, the Constitution does not require that such jurisdiction be exclusive. In other cases specified earlier, in the large majority of cases reaching the Supreme Court, it has appellate jurisdiction; that is, it hears cases on appeal from the lower courts or from state supreme courts. The Supreme Court's primary concern in such cases is the state of the law and not the lower court's finding of fact.

Limits on the Judicial Branch

The focus of Article III on cases is quite significant because, in important ways, the courts are limited in a fashion that the two other branches of government are not. In defending the judicial branch in *Federalist* No. 78, Alexander Hamilton argued that it would have neither the power of the purse nor the sword, "neither FORCE nor WILL," but, as he put it, would have to rely solely on the power of "judgment" (*The Federalist Papers*, No. 78, p. 465). He might further have added that whereas the legislative and executive branches can take the initiative in seeking legislation and making other changes in governmental practices, the judicial branch has a more passive role, waiting for cases to come before it. Parties before the courts must establish what is known as "standing," that is, a clear stake in the outcome, and the case must be "justiciable," or subject to judicial resolution. Typically, American courts refuse to hear "friendly" suits where there is no real controversy between the parties involved. Moreover, the Supreme Court does not, by long-standing practice based on the Article III "case or controversy" requirement, issue so-called "advisory opinions," or opinions about what it might do in hypothetical cases. In addition, while Congress has granted the Supreme Court wide discretion in choosing the cases it will review, it must still accept cases the way they are, and not necessarily the way the courts themselves would like to frame them. It is inappropriate for interest groups to lobby courts, unlike other institutions of government, except through the formal mechanism of *amicus curiae*, or friend of the court, briefs. In choosing which of the writs of certiorari (as such petitions for review of lower court judgments are called) it will accept, the Supreme Court currently operates by "the rule of four," accepting no cases unless four justices agree to do so. Given the litigious nature of American society, the courts may not have long to wait until they are approached to decide most major issues.

Given their inability to frame cases as they might want to hear them, however, there is still a difference in degree, and arguably in kind, between the role of the elected branches in initiating policy and the more restricted role of the judicial branch in reacting to such policies. Moreover, a keynote of most judicial decision-making is the doctrine of *stare decisis*, according to which courts seek to preserve legal stability by generally adhering to past precedents. Although courts sometimes deviate from this doctrine, most of their decisions bring about only incremental changes.

JUDICIAL POWERS

Statutory Interpretation and Judicial Review

Much of what the courts do is interpret the laws. This important power is called the power of statutory construction; such judgments may, in turn, be reversed by laws more clearly designating congressional intentions. Thus, for example, Congress overturned the Supreme Court's decision in *Tennessee Valley Authority v. Hill* (1978) in which the Court enjoined construction of the Tellico Dam on the Little Tennessee River on the basis that Congress had, in the Endangered Species Act of 1973, intended to stop the construction even of ongoing projects in cases where species were threatened (here the species in question being a three-inch relative of the perch known as a snail-darter). In another case, *Flood v. Kuhn* (1972), which has not been overturned by Congress (despite consideration of the question during the 1995 baseball strike) the Court decided that baseball, unlike other major league sports, was exempt from provisions of the Sherman Anti-Trust Act.

A power even more important and controversial than statutory construction is that of judicial review. This power is not specifically stated in Article III, but may be inferred from it and other parts of the Constitution. Judicial review, which has made American courts among the most powerful in the world, is the power of courts, when confronted with a law or executive action specifically applicable to cases before them, to declare such a law or action to be unconstitutional and hence void. This power was exercised soon after ratification of the Constitution in regard to state laws. Although review of state laws might be considered a necessary adjunct to federalism, the power to void federal laws is perhaps more controversial in a democracy in which every judicial invalidation means rejection of the judgment of the people's elected representatives. In *Marbury v. Madison* (1803), Chief Justice John Marshall cogently argued that the power of judicial review was implicit in the nature of a written constitution serving as a fundamental expression of the will of the people, and in the power granted by the Constitution to the Court to decide cases and controversies that arose under the Constitution. How else could the Constitution be enforced than by a body that neither made nor enforced the law?

Marbury v. Madison was one of the most important and interesting cases to come before the Supreme Court in its early years. At issue was an appointment as a justice of the peace given to Marbury by the outgoing Federalist administration of John Adams, which was attempting to stack the judiciary prior to the Democratic Republicans under Jefferson taking control. When Jefferson and his secretary of state, James Madison, arrived in their offices, they found that, while signed and sealed, Marbury's commission had not been delivered by the outgoing secretary of state, who just happened to be John Marshall himself. Marshall, now chief justice of the U.S. Supreme Court, knew that if he ordered Jefferson and Madison to act, they might expose the weakness of the Court by simply disregarding his order; at the same time, Marshall hoped to strengthen the judicial branch with its strong cohort of Federalists.

Noting that Marbury had brought his case directly to the Supreme Court, rather than on appeal, Marshall further observed that the Constitution did not provide for original jurisdiction in cases such as this and that the law, a section of the Judiciary Act of 1789, purporting to give such original jurisdiction was unconstitutional. Thus, while he castigated Madison and Jefferson for failure to do their duty, he also indicated that he had no power to issue the so-called writ of mandamus that Marbury had requested compelling them to do their duty in this case, because the law that purported to give authority to the Courts in such cases was in violation of Article III's allocation of jurisdiction.

Marshall's decision in *Marbury v. Madison* still stands, and nearly two hundred years of practice have confirmed the Court's exercise of judicial review. Vigorous debate that still rages, concerning how wide judicial interpretations should be, often spills over into confirmation hearings for judges and justices. Sometimes this debate is phrased in terms of those who advocate judicial activism, that is, vigorous assertions of judicial power, versus those who favor judicial restraint, or deference to legislative judgments. At other times, the debate is framed as one between interpretivists, who insist that judicial decisions should be firmly based on the constitutional text and/or on the intentions of the framers and ratifiers of that document, and noninterpretivists, who would permit recourse to more general natural law principles or the spirit of the Constitution as a whole. Advocates of each of the above perspectives can point to arguments and judicial decisions to justify their views.

Judicial Review in Practice

Moreover, courts have emphasized different kinds of issues and diverse principles of interpretation in successive periods of American history. Throughout the first hundred years or so, the Court was most frequently engaged in decisions involving the relationship between state and national powers, and the respective powers of each branch of government. The Court also emphasized property rights, switching focus from its early attention to the contract clause to an emphasis on the due process clauses of the Fifth and Fourteenth Amendments in the period after the Civil War until about 1937. The Court argued that, in addition to their protections of procedure, both clauses had a substantive dimension (the notion of "substantive due process") limiting or prohibiting governmental interferences with the natural laws of the market place. In *Lochner v. New York* (1905), for example, the Supreme Court used this ground to strike down a New York regulation of the hours of bakers.

After Franklin D. Roosevelt's court-packing plan, the Court made a turnabout in *West Coast Hotel v. Parrish* (1937) and in *N.L.R.B. v. Jones & Laughlin Steel Corporation* (1937) that is often called "the switch in time that saved nine." Shortly thereafter, Justice Stone authored a famous footnote—number four—in an otherwise obscure case (*United States v. Carolene Products Company*, 1938) in which he suggested an agenda that has occupied much of the Court's attention to this day. Identified as of central concern to the Court were three areas. The first consisted of enforcement of explicit prohibitions as were found in the Bill of Rights and the Fourteenth Amendment. The second area dealt with legislation that "restricts those political processes which can ordinarily be expected to bring about repeal of undesirable legislation." The third area concerned the protection of racial, religious, and other minorities who might not otherwise be protected by the political process. These three areas of concern have indeed encompassed most cases heard by the Court over the past 50 or 60 years, although in recent years the Court has devoted renewed attention to issues of federalism and separation of powers.

Over time the Court has articulated its differential review by formulating three basic standards. In examining most laws, especially those that deal with the kind of economic regulation that so occupied the Court's attention before the New Deal, the Court now applies the "rational basis" test under which it upholds those laws that are passed in pursuit of a legitimate state interest and that are reasonably related to such interests. When dealing with so-called "suspect classes" (like race, alienage, and national origin) or with fundamental rights (like voting rights and freedom of speech), the Court applies the "compelling state interest" test, under which the burden on the state is much greater. Finally, the Court has developed an intermediate test, requiring "heightened scrutiny," albeit not a compelling state interest. As will be discussed in the chapter on the Fourteenth Amendment, this test is most frequently employed in the area of gender discrimination (Stephens & Scheb, *American Constitutional Law*, pp. 1045-47).

Judicial review has often brought the judiciary into conflict with the elected branches of government. At times this conflict is eased when the courts reverse or modify their own judgments, sometimes in the wake of political pressures. On at least four occasions—the Eleventh, Fourteenth, Sixteenth, and Twenty-Sixth Amendments—Supreme Court decisions have been overturned or modified by constitutional amendments. Usually, though, Supreme Court interpretations of the Constitution stand, sometimes with dramatic consequences.

Given the difficulty of the amending process, it is not surprising that some have sought a short cut to reversing judicial judgments. The possibility of such a short cut seems implicit in the statement in paragraph 2 that grants jurisdiction to the Supreme Court

with such Exceptions, and under such Regulations as the Congress shall make.

Scholarly opinion and judicial decisions—compare, for example, *Ex Parte McCardle* (1869) and *United States v. Klein* (1872)—differ sharply over the extent of this congressional power, and the issue has not yet been conclusively resolved. There have been numerous congressional calls from the 1950s to the present to withdraw controversial issues like school busing, prayer in schools, and abortion from the Court's agenda. A major difficulty in pursuing such an avenue is that, in addition to threatening the rights of those over whom judicial jurisdiction was denied, withdrawing jurisdiction from the Supreme Court might also result in a cacophony of opinions in the lower courts.

PROTECTIONS

Article III, Section 2. [3] The Trial of all Crimes, except in Cases of Impeachment, shall be by Jury; and such Trial shall be held in the State where the said Crimes shall have been committed; but when not committed within any State, the Trial shall be at such Place or Places as the Congress may by Law have directed.

Trial by Jury

The third paragraph of Section 2 provides another indication that the Founding Fathers were sympathetic to human rights even before the Bill of Rights was added to the Constitution. Thus, this paragraph specifies that the trial of all crimes other than impeachment shall be by jury and that such trials shall take place within the state where the crime was committed. The origins of a jury trial go far back into English law, and the suspension of such rights was one of the charges leveled against George III in the Declaration of Independence. Crimes committed outside the states are subject, by this same provision, to direction by federal law.

Article III, Section 3. Treason against the United States, shall consist only in levying War against them, or in adhering to their Enemies, giving them Aid and Comfort. No Person shall be convicted of Treason unless on the Testimony of two Witnesses to the same overt Act, or on Confession in open Court.

The Congress shall have Power to declare the Punishment of Treason, but no Attainder of Treason shall work Corruption of Blood, or Forfeiture except during the Life of the Person attainted.

Treason

One of the stated reasons for which members of Congress may be arrested to and from work, and one of the three grounds specified for impeachment, is treason. Without limitations, this term could be given a meaning so all-embracing as to interfere with legitimate opposition in a democracy. Thus it is that treason is narrowly defined in the Constitution as "levying War" against the United States, or "in adhering to their Enemies, giving them Aid and Comfort." With a similar desire to restrain excessive prosecutions under this clause, no person may be convicted of treason without his own confession or that of two witnesses "to the same overt Act." This requirement eventually led to the acquittal of Aaron Burr during the Jefferson Administration.

Congress is granted the power to decide on the punishment for treason, but this power is subject to limits. The Constitution provides that there shall be no

Corruption of Blood, or Forfeiture except during the Life of the Person attainted.

In short, the sins of fathers and mothers shall not be passed down by law to their children, as had been the odious practice in England and some other European nations.

THE NATURE OF ARTICLE III

In reviewing Article III, it is surprising to see how much power can be granted or surmised from so few paragraphs. More than in the case of the other two branches, the framers were apparently content to provide an outline and allow structures and powers to develop as necessity seemed to demand. Although assured a great deal of independence from day-to-day political pressures, judges are from the time they are appointed to the time they leave office hardly free from contact with the outside world, and from the kinds of checks and balances within which the other branches have to operate.

REFERENCES AND SUGGESTIONS FOR FURTHER STUDY

Cases

Ex Parte McCardle, 71 U.S. 2 (1869).
Flood v. Kuhn, 407 U.S. 258 (1972).
Garcia v. San Antonio Metropolitan Transit Authority, 469 U.S. 528 (1985).
Lochner v. New York, 198 U.S. 45 (1905).
Marbury v. Madison, 5 U.S. 137 (1803).
N.L.R.B. v. Jones & Laughlin Steel Corp., 301 U.S. 1 (1937).
National League of Cities v. Usery, 426 U.S. 833 (1976).
Tennessee Valley Authority v. Hill, 437 U.S. 153 (1978).
United States v. Carolene Products Co., 304 U.S. 144 (1938).
United States v. Klein, 80 U.S. 128 (1872).
United States v. Lopez, 115 S. Ct. 1624 (1995).
West Coast Hotel v. Parrish, 300 U.S. 379 (1937).

Books

Henry J. Abraham, *The Judicial Process: An Introductory Analysis of the Courts of the United States, England, and France*, 6th ed. (New York: Oxford University Press, 1993).

Henry J. Abraham, *The Judiciary: The Supreme Court in the Governmental Process*, 8th ed. (Dubuque, IA: Wm C. Brown Publishers, 1991).

Henry J. Abraham, *Justices and Presidents: A Political History of Appointments to the Supreme Court*, 3rd ed. (New York: Oxford University Press, 1992).

Alice F. Bartee, *Cases Lost, Causes Won: The Supreme Court and the Judicial Process* (New York: St. Martin's Press, 1984).

Lawrence Baum, *American Courts: Process and Policy*, 2nd ed. (Boston: Houghton Mifflin Company, 1990).

Alexander M. Bickel, *The Least Dangerous Branch: The Supreme Court at the Bar of Politics*, 2nd ed. (New Haven, CT: Yale University Press, 1968).

Benjamin N. Cardozo, *The Nature of the Judicial Process* (New Haven, CT: Yale University Press, 1949).

Robert L. Clinton, *Marbury v. Madison and Judicial Review* (Lawrence: University Press of Kansas, 1989).

Phillip Cooper and Howard Ball, *The United States Supreme Court: From the Inside Out* (Upper Saddle River, NJ: Prentice Hall, 1996).

Archibald Cox, *The Court and the Constitution* (Boston: Houghton Mifflin Company, 1987).

Peter G. Fish, *The Office of Chief Justice of the United States: Into the Federal Judiciary's Bicentennial Decade* (Charlottesville, VA: White Burkett Miller Center of Public Affairs, 1984).

Fred W. Friendly and Martha J.H. Elliott, *The Constitution, That Delicate Balance: Landmark Cases That Shaped the Constitution* (New York: Random House, 1984).

Richard Y. Funston, *Constitutional Counter-Revolution? The Warren Court and the Burger Court: Judicial Policy Making in Modern America* (Cambridge, MA: Schenkman Publishing Company, Inc., 1977).

John A. Garraty, ed., *Quarrels That Have Shaped the Constitution*, rev. ed. (New York: Harper & Row, Publishers, 1987).

Leslie G. Goldstein, *In Defense of the Text: Democracy and Constitutional Theory* (Savage, MD: Rowman & Littlefield Publishers, Inc., 1991).

Kermit Hall, ed., *The Oxford Companion to the Supreme Court of the United States* (New York: Oxford University Press, 1992).

Stephen C. Halpern and Charles M. Lamb, *Supreme Court Activism and Restraint* (Lexington, MA: Lexington Books, 1982).

Alexander Hamilton, James Madison, and John Jay, *The Federalist Papers*, Clinton Rossiter, ed., (New York: New American Library, 1961).

Eugene W. Hickok and Gary L. McDowell, *Justice vs. Law: Courts and Politics in American Society* (New York: The Free Press, 1993).

J. Woodford Howard, Jr., *Courts of Appeals in the Federal Judicial System: A History of the Second, Fifth, and District of Columbia Circuits* (Princeton, NJ: Princeton University Press, 1981).

Peter Irons, *The Courage of Their Convictions: Sixteen Americans Who Fought Their Way to the Supreme Court* (New York: Penguin Books, 1990).

Peter Irons and Stephanie Guitton, eds., *May It Please the Court* (New York: The New Press, 1993).

Herbert Jacob, *Justice in America: Courts, Lawyers, and the Judicial Process* (Boston: Little, Brown and Company, 1984).

Paul Kens, *Judicial Power and Reform Politics: The Anatomy of Lochner v. New York* (Lawrence: University Press of Kansas, 1990).

Edward Keynes with Randall Miller, *The Court vs. Congress: Prayer, Busing, and Abortion* (Durham, NC: Duke University Press, 1989).

Jethro K. Lieberman, *The Evolving Constitution: How the Supreme Court Has Ruled on Issues from Abortion to Zoning* (New York: Random House, 1992).

Alpheus T. Mason, *The Supreme Court from Taft to Burger*, 3rd ed. (Baton Rouge: Louisiana University Press, 1979).

Alpheus T. Mason and Donald G. Stephenson, Jr., *American Constitutional Law: Introductory Essays and Selected Cases* (Englewood Cliffs, NJ: Prentice-Hall, Inc., 1987).

John Massaro, *Supremely Political: The Role of Ideology and Presidential Management in Unsuccessful Supreme Court Nominations* (Albany: State University of New York Press, 1990).

Robert G. McCloskey, *The American Supreme Court*, 2nd ed. (Chicago: The University of Chicago Press, 1994).

Daniel J. Meador, *American Courts* (St. Paul, MN: West Publishing Co., 1991).

Walter F. Murphy, *Congress and the Court* (Chicago: University of Chicago Press, 1962).

Walter F. Murphy and C. Herman Pritchett, *Courts, Judges, and Politics: An Introduction to the Judicial Process*, 4th ed. (New York: Random House, 1986).

R. Kent Newmyer, *The Supreme Court Under Marshall and Taney* (New York: Thomas Y. Crowell Company, 1968).

David M. O'Brien, *Storm Center: The Supreme Court in American Politics*, 2nd ed. (New York: W.W. Norton & Company, 1990).

C. Herman Pritchett, *Congress Versus the Supreme Court, 1957–1960* (Minneapolis: University of Minnesota Press, 1961).

C. Herman Pritchett, *Constitutional Law of the Federal System* (Englewood Cliffs, NJ: Prentice-Hall, 1984).

Jeremy Rabkin, *Judicial Compulsions: How Public Law Distorts Public Policy* (New York: Basic Books, Inc., 1989).

William H. Rehnquist, *The Supreme Court: How It Was, How It Is* (New York: William Morrow and Company, Inc., 1987).

Ralph A. Rossum and G. Alan Tarr, *American Constitutional Law: Cases and Interpretation*, 3rd ed. (New York: St. Martin's Press, 1991).

David G. Savage, *Turning Right: The Making of the Rehnquist Court* (New York: John Wiley & Sons, Inc., 1992).

John R. Schmidhauser, *Judges and Justices: The Federal Appellate Judiciary* (Boston: Little, Brown and Company, 1979).

Bernard Schwartz, *Decision: How the Supreme Court Decides Cases* (New York: Oxford University Press, 1996).

Otis H. Stephens, Jr., and John M. Scheb, II, *American Constitutional Law* (Minneapolis/St. Paul, MN: West Publishing Company, 1993).

Stephen L. Wasby, *The Supreme Court in the Federal Judicial System*, 3rd ed. (Chicago: Nelson-Hall Publishers, 1988).

William M. Wiecek, *Liberty Under Law: The Supreme Court in American Life* (Baltimore, MD: The Johns Hopkins University Press, 1988).

Elder Witt, *A Different Justice: Reagan and the Supreme Court* (Washington, DC: Congressional Quarterly, Inc., 1986).

Elder Witt, ed., *Guide to the U.S. Supreme Court*, 2nd ed. (Washington, DC: Congressional Quarterly, Inc., 1990).

Christopher Wolfe, *Judicial Activism: Bulwark of Freedom or Precarious Security?* (Pacific Grove, CA: Brooks/Cole Publishing Company, 1991).

Chapter 5

Article IV: The Federal System

Whereas the first three articles of the Constitution distribute powers horizontally among the three branches, Article IV deals with the vertical distribution between the central or national government (often somewhat inaccurately called the federal government) and the states. As representatives of states that had previously been governed separately and were practically sovereign under the Articles of Confederation, most delegates to the Constitutional Convention were quite jealous of state powers. It was almost inconceivable for most of them to imagine a system in which states did not maintain their separate existence. Moreover, a government that split powers between two sets of governments appeared to them to be most likely to preserve liberty and provide for regional diversity in such a large nation. At the same time, many delegates to the Constitutional Convention realized that state powers had been pushed to an extreme under the Articles with consequences that few desired to perpetuate.

THREE FORMS OF GOVERNMENT

Political scientists commonly speak of three forms of government. The form of government under the Articles of Confederation, like that of the later Confederate States of America, is called confederal. In such a system, states retain their own existence, and the central government must operate—as in allocating taxes and raising troops—through these sovereign states. Under a unitary government, like that of Britain or France, states are simply eliminated as permanent, or sovereign, subunits, and all political subdivisions may be created or destroyed at the central government's will.

The government of the Constitution fits into a third category, which was, for all practical purposes, a unique creation that has since been imitated by other nations such as Canada, Mexico, Switzerland, India, and Australia. This type of government is a federal government and blends elements of the two other forms. Like a confederal system, a federal government maintains states that are sovereign in the sense that they cannot be destroyed by the national government. As in a unitary system, however, the national government in a federal system has the power to operate directly on the individual, as in taxation, for example. One key purpose of a written constitution in a federal system is to outline the division of power between the national government and the states, and the responsibilities that such governments owe one another. This is the central purpose of Article IV of the Constitution, although federal features of the Constitution are also evident in the assignment of congressional representatives; specification of congressional powers and limitations on state powers in Article I, Sections 8 and 10; the electoral college; the Supremacy Clause in Article VI of the Constitution; the Tenth Amendment; and elsewhere.

LAYER CAKE OR MARBLE CAKE?

The traditional view of the relationship among national, state, and local governments in the United States, which may be furthered by the seemingly clear lines of constitutional authority, has been likened to that of a layer cake in which each layer is distinct from the other and in which each government has distinctive rights and powers. Court decisions prior to the New Deal were often based on such a conception, generally designated as dual federalism. It has been argued that the reality of modern federalism is considerably more complex—what political scientist Morton Grodzins has likened to a marble cake and what others have designated as cooperative federalism. Frequently, state and national governments share powers rather than divide them clearly between themselves. As a practical matter, the time is long past when certain problems could be definitively characterized as purely state and local issues. While clear occasions for federal–state conflict exist, on many more occasions both governments work for the common good on projects as diverse as education, highways, and health and safety regulations.

OBLIGATIONS OF STATES TO ONE ANOTHER

Article IV, Section 1. Full Faith and Credit shall be given in each State to the public Acts, Records, and judicial Proceedings of every other State; And the Congress may by general Laws prescribe the Manner in which such Acts, Records and Proceedings shall be proved, and the Effect thereof.

The Full Faith and Credit Clause

Section 1 of Article IV begins by defining an obligation that states owe to one another to recognize, or give "Full Faith and Credit" to "public Acts, Records, and judicial Proceedings" of other states, subject to regulation by Congress. Such a provision means that states will recognize marriages, contracts, wills, legal awards, and other transactions that took place in other states. Because the United States does not have a uniform civil code, questions sometimes arise as to the validity of divorces recognized in some states but not in others. More recently, questions have arisen about what will happen if Hawaii courts follow through on indications that they may strike that state's ban on same-sex marriages. Anticipating such a decision, a number of states have passed laws indicating that they would not recognize such unions. In 1996, Congress, which is given power under the second half of the first sentence in Article IV, Section 1 to pass general laws relative to such matters, has given sanction to their decision. Whether the states' interests in this matter and federal concurrence will prove weighty enough to overbalance the full faith and credit clause and/or any potential conflict with the equal protection clause remains still to be seen.

Article IV, Section 2. [1] The Citizens of each State shall be entitled to all Privileges and Immunities of Citizens in the several States.

The Privileges and Immunities Clause

Additional obligations that states owe to one another follow in Article IV, Section 2. The first provision sounds ambiguous but, whatever legal refinements one might choose to make, this "Privileges and Immunities" clause basically requires that states treat visitors from other states as they do their own residents. This provision has also been interpreted to prevent states from denying employment opportunities to outsiders or preventing outsiders from making property purchases. Some might regret that such provisions have not been considered as requiring that states charge the same college tuition or license fees to out-of-state residents (who have probably not been paying taxes in the state to support schools and public lands) or to extend the right to vote in state elections to non-residents. However, a state that attempted to enforce one set of criminal laws for in-state residents and another for out-of-state residents would soon find itself taken to court on this basis.

Article IV, Section 2. [2] A Person charged in any State with Treason, Felony, or other Crime, who shall flee from Justice, and be found in another State, shall on Demand of the executive Authority of the State from which he fled, be delivered up, to be removed to the State having Jurisdiction of the Crime.

Extradition

The second paragraph of Section 2 deals with a process known in legal jargon as extradition. Under this provision, if a person accused of a crime in one state flees to another, that person will be returned at the request of the governor of the state from which the fugitive fled. Such a request is directed to the state governor. Until fairly recently, this was understood to be a moral, rather than a legally enforceable duty, thus permitting some governors to evade their responsibility. After the Supreme Court's decision in *Puerto Rico v. Branstad* (1987), however, judges may now direct an order requiring a governor to fulfill this duty.

Article IV, Section 2. [3] *No Person held to Service or Labour in one State, under the Laws thereof, escaping into another, shall, in Consequence of any Law or Regulation therein, be discharged from such Service or Labour, but shall be delivered up on Claim of the Party to whom such Service or Labour may be due.*

The Fugitive Slave Clause

The next paragraph is the third in the body of the Constitution to deal with an issue related to slavery. Again, this odious institution is not mentioned by name. Rather the paragraph asserts that persons "held to Service or Labour" in one state and escaping to another shall be returned upon presentment of a claim by "the Party to whom such Service or Labour may be due." This provision was an increasingly bitter source of controversy in the years prior to the Civil War, northerners having moral compunctions about returning slaves into captivity and southerners in search of runaways not always being scrupulous about the rights of free blacks. With the Thirteenth Amendment's abolition of slavery, this clause is, happily, only of historic interest.

Article IV, Section 3. [1] New States may be admitted by the Congress into this Union; but no new State shall be formed or erected within the Jurisdiction of any other State; nor any State be formed by the Junction of two or more States, or Parts of States, without the Consent of the Legislatures of the States concerned as well as of the Congress.

THE ADMISSION OF NEW STATES

Section 3 might be considered one of the most far-sighted provisions of the Constitution. It provides for the admission of new states into the Union, a provision without which wide expanses of the West might have become perpetual colonies. In *Coyle v. Smith* (1911), which upheld Oklahoma's decision to move its state capital once that territory had been granted statehood, the Supreme Court wisely ruled that new states enter the Union on an equal basis with the old, thus assuring that they will not be states in name and colonies in fact. Neither may new states be carved from existing states without their consent, nor may parts of separate states join without the consent of all parties. Vermont, Maine, Kentucky, and Tennessee were all formed from previous states that gave their consent; West Virginia was formed in a more irregular procedure during the Civil War and validated only after the war's end (Witt, *Guide to the U.S. Supreme Court*, p. 135).

Article IV, Section 3. [2] The Congress shall have Power to dispose of and make all needful Rules and Regulations respecting the Territory or other Property belonging to the United States; and nothing in this Constitution shall be so construed as to Prejudice any Claims of the United States, or of any particular State.

GOVERNING THE TERRITORIES

Prior to becoming states, many areas of the nation were territories. Section 3 grants Congress the power to govern such territories;

on most occasions, this power has been interpreted broadly. The extent of this power was, however, a key issue prior to the Civil War. As early as the Northwest Ordinance of 1787, which was enacted while the Articles of Confederation were still in force, and continuing through the Missouri Compromise of 1820 and beyond, the national government had sought to prohibit slavery in some of the territories. In the notorious *Dred Scott* decision of 1857, the Court attempted to invalidate this exercise of power as a violation of the due process clause of the Fifth Amendment. Chief Justice Roger Taney ruled that slaves were chattels, or property, rather than persons; therefore, slave owners should not be deprived of this property without due process of law.

In the twentieth century, Article IV, Section 3 has provided authority for the national government to establish and maintain a system of national parks.

OBLIGATIONS OF THE NATION
TO THE STATES

Article IV, Section 4. The United States shall guarantee to every State in this Union a Republican Form of Government, and shall protect each of them against Invasion; and on Application of the Legislature, or of the Executive (when the Legislature cannot be convened) against domestic Violence.

The Guarantee Clause

While Section 1 of Article IV focuses on the obligations of the states to one another, Section 4, the final section, focuses on obligations owed by the national government to the states. There are actually two separate provisions, but they are sometimes interpreted together. First, the national government is supposed to guarantee a "Republican Form of Government" to each state. Many clever and persuasive interpretations of what might qualify a government as republican have been offered, but it is basically agreed that a republican government is a representative government. It should be added that in guaranteeing only a republican "form" of government to the states, the national Constitution left them free to make changes in or even to adopt completely new constitutions as long as these were consistent with "republican" principles; many states have responded by altering or completely changing their constitutions quite frequently. Generally, it is recognized that a state government is republican if Congress seats its members. In the

1840s, a conflict known as Dorr's Rebellion in Rhode Island pitted two rival governments against one another for a time. In resolving the case of *Luther v. Borden* (1849), which resulted when agents of one government entered the house of a member of the other and were subsequently sued, the Court designated the issue of whether a state government is republican as a "political question" best resolved by the other two branches. This precedent is still accepted as good law today.

Clearly related to, albeit arguably separate from, the guarantee clause is the provision that the national government shall protect the states against invasion or domestic violence. In the latter case, a request for help is properly lodged by the legislative or executive branches. Presumably, the Congress, or the president acting under congressional authority, has a responsibility to provide help in such circumstances. No doubt the example of Shays' Rebellion was prominent in the minds of those who agreed to this provision.

REJECTED DOCTRINES OF FEDERALISM

Few doctrines have been more difficult to practice than the doctrine of federalism. However much the writers of the Constitution attempted to formalize and clarify this complex relationship, controversy has erupted about such issues through most of American history. Rarely has an important matter of public policy not eventually been tied to questions of federalism.

Interposition

An early dispute arose over the passage of the Alien and Sedition Acts in 1798. Designed by the ruling Federalists, who feared the rising popularity of Jefferson's Democratic Republican Party that would oust them from office in the fateful election of 1800, the first of these laws made it more difficult for immigrants—who seemed disproportionately to side with Jefferson—to become citizens. The Sedition Act, in turn, made it a crime to criticize the government or the president, then John Adams, a Federalist, albeit not himself a wholehearted supporter of the new laws.

In opposing these laws, the second of which was in rather clear violation of the First Amendment, the Democratic Republicans had to formulate a strategy that would consider existing Federalist dominance in Congress. Their solution was to introduce the Virginia and Kentucky resolutions (secretly authored by James

Madison and Thomas Jefferson respectively) in the two state legislatures, calling for other states to "interpose" themselves against
this act. However much many citizens of the other states agreed as
to the obnoxiousness of the Federalist legislation in question, others refused to heed Virginia and Kentucky's plea for interposition,
whatever that might mean. With Jefferson's election in 1800 and
the termination of the Sedition Act, this specific controversy came
to an end.

Nullification

In time, however, the doctrine of interposition would bear fruit
that Jefferson arguably and Madison certainly would regret. The
most dramatic development came with the tariff controversies of
the 1820s and 1830s. Northern representatives tended to favor
high tariffs that would protect the nascent industries in their
region from foreign competition. Southerners, who exported agricultural goods and imported manufacturing products, generally
opposed such tariffs, which were nonetheless levied over their
protests. In defending their economic interests, leading southerners—most notably Vice President, and later Senator, John C.
Calhoun of South Carolina—developed the doctrine of nullification. By this theory, states confronted with what they believed to
be unconstitutional laws had the right to "nullify" such laws
within their jurisdiction and appeal to other states for a constitutional convention; federal powers would in the meantime remain
in abeyance unless ratified by the number of states necessary to
amend the national Constitution. Such a theory would have
nearly prostrated national powers at the feet of a small minority
of states. As against Calhoun's views that "the Union" was "next
to our liberty [that is, to states' rights] most dear," President
Andrew Jackson affirmed that "Our Union . . . must be preserved"
(Paul M. Angle, *By These Words*, p. 166). Fortunately, the standoff
between these two men and the views they represented was
resolved in a compromise tariff, but seeds had been sown for the
even more radical doctrine of secession.

Secession

According to this doctrine of secession, which came to full flower
with the Civil War, the Constitution had created a voluntary com-

pact among the states who were free, singly or in a group, to leave the government when they felt it was no longer serving their interests or when the national government assumed powers—by amendment or otherwise—that the states considered inappropriate. The southern states that joined the Confederacy resurrected a number of the features of the earlier Articles of Confederation and attempted to put the doctrine of secession into practice after the election of Abraham Lincoln. Lincoln denied their legal authority to do so and, like Jackson, believed that preservation of the Union was his primary presidential duty. After the war saw the defeat of the seceding states, the Supreme Court affirmed in *Texas v. White* (1869) that the United States Constitution "looks to an indestructible Union, composed of indestructible states." While the war and this decision put nails in the coffins of doctrines like interposition, nullification, and secession, conflicts between state and national powers have continued, as those who recall the action of southern governors like George Wallace and Orval Faubus during the civil rights controversies of the 1950s and 1960s will know.

THE STATUS OF LOCAL GOVERNMENTS

Neither Article IV nor any other provision of the Constitution deals specifically with local governments. This omission was probably intentional. While Americans often value local governments, these governments get their status from state governments rather than from the national Constitution. For legal purposes, local governments are treated as state subdivisions, subject to their governance and control. Given the ever-changing dynamics of population growth and industrialization, it is undoubtedly a blessing that changes in the boundaries of cities and counties do not require changes in the national Constitution.

REFERENCES AND SUGGESTIONS FOR FURTHER STUDY

Cases

Coyle v. Smith, 221 U.S. 559 (1911).
Dred Scott v. Sandford, 60 U.S. 393 (1857).
Luther v. Borden, 48 U.S. 1 (1849).
Puerto Rico v. Branstad, 483 U.S. 219 (1987).
Texas v. White, 74 U.S. 700 (1869).

Books

Paul M. Angle, *By These Words: Great Documents of American Liberty Selected and Placed in Their Contemporary Setting* (New York: Rand McNally & Company, 1954).

Samuel H. Beer, *To Make a Nation: The Rediscovery of American Federalism* (Cambridge, MA: Belknap Press, 1993).

The Book of the States: 1992–1993 Edition (Lexington, KY: Council of State Governments, 1992).

John C. Calhoun, *A Disquisition on Government and Selections From the Discourses*, C. Gordon Post, ed. (Indianapolis, IN: The Bobbs-Merrill Company, Inc., 1953).

David J. Elazar, *American Federalism: A View From the States* (New York: Thomas Y. Crowell, 1966).

Robert A. Goldwin, ed., *A Nation of States*, 2nd ed. (Chicago: Rand McNally & Company, 1974).

Morton Grodzins, *The American System: A New View of Government in the United States* (Chicago: Rand McNally & Company, 1966).

Alpheus T. Mason, *The States Rights Debate: Antifederalism and the Constitution*, 2nd ed. (New York: Oxford University Press, 1972).

David C. Nice, *Federalism: The Politics of Intergovernmental Relations* (New York: St. Martin's Press, 1987).

Laurence J. O'Toole, Jr., ed., *American Intergovernmental Relations: Foundations, Perspectives, and Issues* (Washington, DC: Congressional Quarterly, Inc., 1985).

John R. Schmidhauser, *The Supreme Court as Final Arbiter in Federal-State Relations, 1789–1957* (Chapel Hill: The University of North Carolina Press, 1958).

Lindsay Swith, ed., *The Great Debate Between Robert Young Hayne of South Carolina and Daniel Webster of Massachusetts* (Boston: Houghton Mifflin Company, 1898).

M.J.C. Vile, *The Structure of American Federalism* (Plymouth, England: Oxford University Press, 1961).

Leonard D. White, *The States and the Nation* (Baton Rouge: Louisiana University Press, 1956).

William M. Wiecek, *The Guarantee Clause of the U.S. Constitution* (Ithaca, NY: Cornell University Press, 1972).

Elder Witt, *Guide to the U.S. Supreme Court*, 2nd ed. (Washington, DC: Congressional Quarterly, 1990).

Deil S. Wright, *Understanding Intergovernmental Relations: Public Policy and Participants' Perspectives in Local, State, and National Governments* (North Scituate, MA: Duxbury Press, 1978).

Joseph F. Zimmerman, *Contemporary American Federalism* (New York: Praeger, 1992).

Chapter 6

Articles V–VII: The Amending Provision and Miscellaneous Matters

THE IMPORTANCE OF AMENDMENTS

It is conceivable that the American Revolution might have been avoided had there been a recognized way for Americans to alter their constitutional arrangement with Great Britain, but, absent such channels, the colonists felt they had little choice but to revolt. Similarly, the difficulty of amending the Articles of Confederation, which had required the consent of all 13 state legislatures, was generally conceded to be a critical weakness, and yet a written constitution that could be amended at will would hardly be a constitution at all. Indeed, it can be plausibly argued that what makes the U.S. Constitution different from that in Great Britain is not so much that the U.S. Constitution is written, but that what is written in the U.S. Constitution is enforceable in the courts and unchangeable by ordinary legislative means. An attempt to design an amendable, yet stable, constitution was the primary goal of those who wrote Article V.

Article V. The Congress, whenever two thirds of both Houses shall deem it necessary, shall propose Amendments to this Constitution, or, on the Application of the Legislatures of two thirds of the several States, shall call a Convention for proposing Amendments, which, in either Case, shall be valid to all Intents and Purposes, as Part of this Constitution, when ratified by the Legislatures of three fourths of the several States, or by Conventions in three fourths thereof, as the one or the other Mode of Ratification may be proposed by the Congress;

AMENDING PROCEDURES

The Most Common Route

In *Federalist* No. 43, James Madison praised the amending process as guarding "equally against that extreme facility, which would render the Constitution too mutable; and that extreme difficulty, which might perpetuate its discovered faults" (p. 278). The framers thus created two mechanisms whereby amendments could be introduced and two mechanisms whereby they could be ratified.

Contrary to the hopes of Thomas Jefferson, there are no provisions in the U.S. Constitution requiring amendments at fixed intervals, every generation for example. Rather, pressure first has to build for amendments, and they require extraordinary majorities to be adopted. The first step in the amending process is the proposal. To date all such successful proposals have been made by two-thirds majorities in both houses of Congress (no presidential signature is mentioned, and in *Hollingsworth v. Virginia*, 1798, the Supreme Court ruled that it was unnecessary). All but one of the amendments has been subsequently ratified by three-fourths of the state legislatures.

There are alternatives both for proposing and ratifying amendments, however. To turn first to the alternate ratification mechanism, which has been used only once in the case of the Twenty-First Amendment repealing prohibition, Congress may designate that amendments be ratified by special conventions called within each state. Arguably, and contrary to practice, this should be the preferred method of ratification both because such conventions would be elected on the basis of a single issue and because such ratification would be in line with the way the original document was approved. A number of other nations require such a plebiscite before amendments can be added.

The Unused Convention Mechanism

Of great fascination for those who like to imagine new scenarios is the alternate method of proposing amendments. This method, which was included in the Constitution in an attempt to prevent

Congress from monopolizing the amending process, requires that Congress call a convention for proposing such amendments when it receives petitions from two-thirds of the states to this end. While many more than that number of states have so applied to Congress for conventions, it does not appear that two-thirds of the states have submitted petitions on similar or identical issues in a time span that could be considered to represent the kind of contemporary consensus that the Court has deemed desirable in other matters involving amendments. Calls for a convention to reverse the Supreme Court decisions on state legislative apportionment in the 1960s and, more recently, to propose a balanced budget amendment appear to have approached the required number, but the validity of some state petitions has been disputed.

Such disputes are furthered by the fact that, although such legislation has been proposed, no federal law has been passed to regulate the calling of such a convention, and many issues related to such a convention are necessarily speculative until such a convention is called. A key question would be whether the convention could act independently of restrictions sought to be imposed by Congress or the states. How states would be represented would be another issue, with dispute among those who favor equal state representation, support a scheme based solely on population, and advocate a compromise solution similar to that embodied in the Connecticut Compromise and the electoral college. Debate also exists as to whether the agenda of a convention could be limited beforehand (and, if so, by which governmental institution or institutions) or whether it would have authority to propose any amendments it chose and possibly even rewrite the Constitution itself.

RESCISSIONS

While the Constitution speaks of ratification of amendments, it nowhere specifies whether states can rescind ratifications already voted on but not yet ratified by the necessary majority of the states (currently, however, states are permitted to ratify amendments that they have previously rejected). The Constitution also does not specify the time limit in which amendments may be ratified. While the Court has indicated in *Dillon v. Gloss* (1921) that such ratifications need to reflect a contemporary consensus, it has in *Coleman v. Miller* (1939) and other controversial cases decided that the judgment of such consensus is a "political question" best left to the judgment of Congress.

Some amendments have clauses specifically designating the ratification time. Although Congress extended the seven-year ratification time for the proposed Equal Rights Amendment—which was contained in the congressional authorizing resolution rather than in the text of the proposed amendment itself—by three years and three months, in a controversial vote, the amendment still fell short of the necessary number of state approvals necessary for ratification, and the constitutionality of this extension was thus never conclusively settled. More recently, Congress voted to accept ratification of the Congressional Pay Amendment almost 203 years after it was first proposed by James Madison.

IS THE AMENDING PROCESS EXCLUSIVE?

Are there other ways of amending the Constitution besides those spelled out in Article V? In one sense, the answer is obvious. Every time the Supreme Court issues a decision, it interprets, and to some extent, thus "amends" the Constitution. Over time, congressional and presidential practices also give life to the document. However implicit such interpretations and practices may be, it would seem odd to list them at the end of the Constitution along with the 27 other formal amendments.

In recent years, two students of the Constitution, both from Yale University, have argued that we need to expand our understanding of constitutional amendments by giving more recognition to other means of change. Akil Reed Amar has suggested that Article V only limits agencies of government in proposing and ratifying amendments and suggests that the people could propose and/or ratify amendments through popular vote. Similarly, Bruce Ackerman has suggested that major "constitutional moments" in American history, most notably the writing of the Constitution, the period following the Civil War, and the New Deal period, all departed from strict constitutional procedures. He says that periods of "higher lawmaking" typically involve four steps—a signaling phase, a proposal, mobilized popular deliberation, and a period during which the Supreme Court codifies the new understandings (Ackerman, *We the People*, pp. 266–67). Scholars argue vigorously over whether Ackerman's description is accurate or whether changes brought about in such an extraconstitutional fashion really qualify as amendments.

Article V. Provided that no Amendment which may be made prior to the Year One thousand eight hundred and eight shall in any Manner affect the first and fourth Clauses in the Ninth Section of the first Article; and that no State, without its Consent, shall be deprived of its equal Suffrage in the Senate.

UNAMENDABLE PROVISIONS

The amending provision contains two entrenchment clauses, or unamendable provisions. The first was designed to guarantee the compromise reached in regard to slave importation and direct taxes, and was insisted on by the same interests that had requested that provision. The second restriction is practically, if not theoretically, unalterable because it provides that no state shall lose its equal representation in the Senate without its consent. The clause further demonstrates both the importance of the Connecticut Compromise and the irrevocable commitment of delegates to the Constitutional Convention to maintain the continuing integrity and viability of the states.

Scholars have speculated as to the existence of any implied limitations on the constitutional amending process. Thus, early in this century conservative legal commentators and lawyers argued that such implicit limitations invalidated Amendments 15 through 19. The Supreme Court chose to dismiss such arguments, perhaps believing that, even if such limits could be defined precisely, it would be nearly impossible to enforce them against the kinds of majorities that would be mobilized to propose and ratify amendments. More recently, some scholars of more liberal persuasion have argued that certain rights like freedom of speech or equal protection of the laws might also be unamendable. This view seeks to extend yet another level of protection to the nation's most cherished freedoms. Critics fear, however, that such a view might have the effect of transferring power, or sovereignty, from the people acting under authority of Article V, to the unelected judicial branch.

THE HISTORY OF AMENDMENTS IN THE UNITED STATES

While state constitutions have come and gone—Louisiana has had eleven, for example—and been amended numerous times, the U.S. Constitution remains as it was in 1787, albeit with 27 additions. The remaining chapters of this book will deal with the various amendments that have been added to the Constitution. In accord with a decision reached over James Madison's objections during debates at the first session of Congress, these amendments have been appended to the end of the Constitution rather than integrated into its text, a practice that makes constitutional history much easier to trace. To date, more than 11,000 amendments—many, of course, being redundant—have been proposed in Congress. Still, Congress has itself been the central hurdle for amendments to overcome. It has thus voted to propose only 33 of these by the necessary two-thirds majorities. Of these, 27 have been ratified by the required three-fourths of the states.

The first ten of these amendments—known as the Bill of Rights—were adopted as a group so close to constitutional ratification that a Supreme Court justice commented in *The Slaughterhouse Cases* (1873) that "they were practically contemporaneous with the adoption of the original." Two other amendments—the Eighteenth and the Twenty-First, respectively mandating and repealing national alcoholic prohibition—negate one another. Amendments 13 through 15 were adopted within a relatively short time period, as were amendments 16 through 19. The last amendment to be ratified—the Twenty-Seventh—was approved in 1992.

Clearly, the amending process, while not as wooden as that under the Articles of Confederation, has proven extremely resistant to change. This resistance to formal constitutional change has probably increased pressures on the courts and other institutions of government to adapt the Constitution to changing times; but, no matter how creative many such attempts have been, some changes can still be brought about or firmly secured only by constitutional amendment.

ARTICLE VI

In turning to Article VI, it is difficult to provide a label that will as succinctly characterize its subject matter as in the case of other articles. It is reasonable to assume that this Article ultimately served as a repository for those provisions that did not quite seem to fit into other parts of the Constitution.

Article VI. [1] All Debts contracted and Engagements entered into, before the Adoption of this Constitution, shall be as valid against the United States under this Constitution, as under the Confederation.

The Continuing Validity of Debts

Paragraph 1 is about a housekeeping matter for the new government, asserting that it assumes any debts owed by the Confederation. This is the only direct reference to the Confederation in the Constitution. No doubt such a provision would allay fears of those persons to whom the previous government might have owed debts. This provision did not, however, eliminate subsequent partisan controversy as to whether monies should be paid—as Jeffersonian Republicans would argue—to original bond holders or—as Federalists would contend—to those to whom bonds had subsequently been sold, often at a substantial discount; on this dispute, the Federalist position prevailed.

Article VI. [2] This Constitution, and the Laws of the United States which shall be made in Pursuance thereof; and all Treaties made, or which shall be made, under the Authority of the United States, shall be the supreme Law of the Land; and the Judges in every State shall be bound thereby, any Thing in the Constitution of Laws of any State to the Contrary notwithstanding.

The Supremacy Clause

Paragraph 2 is a very important part of the Constitution usually designated as the Supremacy Clause. This clause originated in the New Jersey Plan and showed how far the new Constitution had come from the notion of sovereign states embodied in the Articles of Confederation. The Supremacy Clause provides that the Constitution and federal laws and treaties will be "the supreme Law of the Land." It further specifies that state judges shall be bound to the U.S. Constitution, "any Thing in the Constitution or Laws of any State to the Contrary notwithstanding."

This clause has served as a key support for judicial review, especially of state legislation and for federal preemption in cases where national laws conflict with those of the states. If the Constitution is to be supreme, it is logical that a branch of government should be designed to enforce this supremacy. If state judges take an oath to support the federal Constitution, they must clearly give it superiority to any contrary provisions within their own states' constitutions. A federal system is thus further distinguished from confederal systems where the states are sovereign.

Serious questions have been raised about the status of federal treaties under the supremacy clause. The language—as well as the opinion of at least one Supreme Court decision, *Missouri v. Holland* (1920), dealing with the status of a migratory bird treaty with Great Britain—appears to suggest that, whereas laws must be made in pursuance of the Constitution to be valid, treaties must merely be made "under the Authority of the United States." By such logic, the U.S. government might try to suppress freedom of speech or religion, as guaranteed in the First Amendment, by entering into a treaty with another government knowing that it could not do this merely by passing a law. More recent court decisions have, however, indicated that the peculiar language of Article VI relative to treaties was not written to exclude them from the reach of the Constitution, but rather to affirm the validity of existing treaties, such as the treaty that ended the Revolutionary War and had been approved under the Articles of Confederation. Accordingly, approved treaties can no more be in violation of the written Constitution than can other laws. Thus, in the case of *Reid v. Covert* (1957), the Court ruled as invalid a law that would have permitted the trial of civilian dependents of American service persons abroad by court martial in violation of constitutional guarantees of trial by jury.

Article VI. [3] The Senators and Representatives before mentioned, and the Members of the several State Legislatures, and all executive and judicial Officers, both of the United States and of the several States, shall be bound by Oath or Affirmation, to support this Constitution; but no religious Test shall ever be required as a Qualification to any Office or public Trust under the United States.

Oaths of Office and Prohibition of Religious Tests

The federal nature of the Union is further evident in the last paragraph of Article VI, which provides that all members of Congress, state legislators, and all other state and federal officials are to be bound by oath or affirmation to support the Constitution. By this paragraph, religious tests are also prohibited as a qualification for office. This provision indicates that the founders opposed an establishment of religion and favored its free exercise even before they ratified the First Amendment.

In *Torasco v. Watkins* (1961), the Supreme Court used the free exercise clause of the First Amendment to extend this ban on religious tests to the states. In this case, it voided a Maryland law requiring all officeholders to declare that they believed in God.

ARTICLE VII

Article VII. The Ratification of the Conventions of nine States, shall be sufficient for the Establishment of this Constitution between the States so ratifying the Same.

Ratification of the Constitution

One of the weaknesses of the Articles of Confederation was that amendments required the consent of all 13 states. Not surprisingly, no such amendments had been ratified up to the time of the Constitutional Convention. Given that one state, Rhode Island, had refused even to send delegates to this gathering, it seemed unlikely that unanimous consent would be immediately forthcoming. Accordingly, the convention provided that the new Constitution would go into effect—albeit only among ratifying states—when nine states joined. This extra-legal, or even illegal, provision proved successful. Once nine states signed, the others feared the consequences of staying outside the new Union.

It is notable too that the new Union was to be ratified by state conventions rather than by state legislatures as the Articles of Confederation had specified and as would come to be the common practice under Article V of the new Constitution. There are two plausible reasons for this change. First, many people probably thought that state legislatures would be more reluctant to give up their status as representatives of sovereign states than would delegates to conventions who had no such personal interests. It therefore made good sense to vest ratification of the document in those more likely to give it. Second, at the time the Constitution was written, many people, influenced by the successful examples of state conventions, had come to regard popular conventions with a degree of deference sometimes reserved for the sovereign people themselves.

A Constitution grounded in such a ratification would surely be likely to prove far more enduring than one resting upon mere legislative approval by bodies not specifically elected for the purpose of ratifying the document. Ratification by special convention thus seemed a way of affirming the commitment to "We the People" that had been asserted in the opening words of the Constitution's preamble.

[D]one in Convention by the Unanimous Consent of the States present the Seventeenth Day of September in the Year of our Lord one thousand seven hundred and Eighty seven and of the Independence of the United States of America the Twelfth In witness whereof We have hereunto subscribed our Names.

The Convention Resolution

It is at this point that some versions of the U.S. Constitution append the resolution by which the Constitution was adopted at the Constitutional Convention. It indicates that the document was signed on September 17 of 1787, twelve years from the nation's independence that the delegates obviously believed they were furthering. The resolution further indicates that the document was adopted in convention "by the Unanimous Consent of the States present." This resolution is followed by the names of 39 men from twelve states who signed the Document.

The resolution, introduced at the convention by Benjamin Franklin, while technically accurate, was designed to conceal two facts. First, as discussed in an earlier chapter, only twelve of the 13 states were present, Rhode Island having refused to send delegates. Second, while there was indeed a majority from each state's delegation willing to agree to the new Constitution, and thus the states present can be said to have consented unanimously, the delegates were not themselves unanimous. Of the 55 men who had been present during convention proceedings, only 42 remained by September 17 (some had, of course, left because of business and personal reasons rather than because of disagreement with the way that proceedings were going). Of those who remained, three delegates, Elbridge Gerry of Massachusetts, and Edmund Randolph and George Mason of Virginia, refused to sign. Their concerns about states' rights and the absence of a bill of rights helped fuel the debate that would follow as the nation decided whether to accept this new charter of government.

REFERENCES AND SUGGESTIONS FOR FURTHER STUDY

Cases

Coleman v. Miller, 307 U.S. 433 (1939).
Dillon v. Gloss, 256 U.S. 368 (1921).

Hollingsworth v. Virginia, 3 U.S. 379 (1798).
Missouri v. Holland, 252 U.S. 416 (1920).
Reid v. Covert, 354 U.S. 1 (1957).
Slaughterhouse Cases (*Butchers' Benevolent Ass'n v. Crescent City Live-Stock Landing and Slaughter-House Co.*), 16 Wallace 36 (1873).
Torasco v. Watkins, 367 U.S. 488 (1961).

Books

Bruce Ackerman, *We the People: Foundations* (Cambridge, MA: The Belknap Press of Harvard University Press, 1991).

American Bar Association, Special Constitutional Convention Study Committee, *Amendment of the Constitution by the Convention Method Under Article V* (Chicago: American Bar Association, Public Service Division, 1979).

Herman Ames, *The Proposed Amendments to the Constitution of the United States During the First Century of its History* (New York: Burt Franklin, 1970; reprint of 1896 edition).

George Anastaplo, *The Amendments to the Constitution: A Commentary* (Baltimore, MD: The Johns Hopkins University Press, 1995).

Richard B. Bernstein with Jerome Agel, *Amending America* (New York: Times Books, 1993).

Mary Frances Berry, *Why ERA Failed: Politics, Women's Rights, and the Amending Process of the Constitution* (Bloomington: Indiana University Press, 1986).

Steven R. Boyd, *Alternative Constitutions for the United States: A Documentary History* (Westport, CT: Greenwood Press, 1992).

Russell L. Caplan, *Constitutional Brinkmanship: Amending the Constitution by National Convention* (New York: Oxford University Press, 1988).

Patrick T. Conley and John P. Kaminski, eds., *The Constitution and the States: The Role of the Original Thirteen in the Framing and Adoption of the Federal Constitution* (Madison, WI: Madison House, 1988).

Wilbur Edel, *A Constitutional Convention: Threat or Challenge?* (New York: Praeger Publishers, 1981).

Jonathon Elliott, ed., *The Debates in the Several State Conventions on the Adoption of the Federal Constitution*, 5 vols., 2nd ed. (Philadelphia, PA: J.B. Lippincott, 1861–63).

Michael Allen Gillespie and Michael Lienesch, eds., *Ratifying the Constitution* (Lawrence: University Press of Kansas, 1989).

Alan P. Grimes, *Democracy and the Amendments to the Constitution* (Lexington, MA.: Lexington Books, 1978).

Kermit L. Hall, Harold M. Hyman, and Leon V. Sigal, *The Constitutional Convention as an Amending Device* (Washington, DC: American Historical Association and American Political Science Association, 1981).

Alexander Hamilton, James Madison, and John Jay, *The Federalist Papers*, Clinton Rossiter, ed. (New York: New American Library, 1961).

John J. Jameson, *A Treatise on Constitutional Conventions: Their History, Powers, and Modes of Proceedings* (New York: Da Capo Press, 1972, Reprint of 1887 edition).

Sanford Levinson, ed., *Responding to Imperfection: The Theory and Practice of Constitutional Amendment* (Princeton, NJ: Princeton University Press, 1995).

Jane J. Mansbridge, *Why We Lost the ERA* (Chicago: University of Chicago Press, 1986).

Lester B. Orfield, *The Amending of the Federal Constitution* (Ann Arbor: The University of Michigan Press, 1942).

Donald L. Robinson, *Reforming American Government: The Bicentennial Papers of the Committee on the Constitutional System* (Boulder, CO: Westview Press, 1985).

U.S. Senate, Subcommittee on the Constitution, Committee on the Judiciary, *Amendments to the Constitution: A Brief Legislative History* (Washington, DC: U.S. Government Printing Office, 1985).

John R. Vile, *The Constitutional Amending Process in American Political Thought* (New York: Praeger, 1992).

John R. Vile, *Constitutional Change in the United States* (Westport, CT: Praeger, 1994).

John R. Vile, *Contemporary Questions Surrounding the Constitutional Amending Process* (Westport, CT: Praeger, 1993).

John R. Vile, *Encyclopedia of Constitutional Amendments: Amendments, Proposed Amendments, and Amending Issues, 1789–1995* (Santa Barbara, CA: ABC-CLIO, 1996).

John R. Vile, *Rewriting the United States Constitution: An Examination of Proposals From Reconstruction to the Present* (New York: Praeger, 1991).

John R. Vile, *The Theory and Practice of Constitutional Change in America: A Collection of Original Source Materials* (New York: Peter Lang, 1993).

Clement Vose, *Constitutional Change: Amendment Politics and Supreme Court Litigation Since 1900* (Lexington, MA: DC Heath, 1972).

Paul J. Weber and Barbara A. Perry, *Unfounded Fears: Myths and Realities of a Constitutional Convention* (New York: Praeger, 1989).

Chapter 7

The Bill of Rights—The First
Three Amendments

BACKGROUND

The first ten amendments to the Constitution were ratified collectively and are called the Bill of Rights. This section is often considered one of the most important parts of the Constitution. Its history gives further insight into the Constitution and the controversies surrounding its ratification.

Almost as soon as the convention reported its work, the nation split into two camps—the Federalists, who supported the new Constitution, and the Antifederalists who opposed it. Antifederalists were particularly concerned about the strength of the new national government, and, despite the elaborate structural features designed to limit this government, widespread fear that it might abuse personal rights still existed. Federalists argued that the national government would not act in an oppressive fashion and that, as a government of enumerated powers, it could only exercise the powers delegated to it. Despite such assurances, Antifederalists continued to insist upon the necessity of binding the new national government, as they had their own state governments, by additional written restraints.

Eventually, prominent Federalists, including James Madison (who was influenced at least partly on this matter by correspondence he received on the subject from Thomas Jefferson), agreed that if the Constitution were ratified, they would ask for the adoption of a Bill of Rights that would be legally enforceable in the courts. Because of his prominent role in shaping the Bill of Rights and getting it through the first Congress, where he served as a congressman from Virginia in the House of Representatives, it is more accurate to refer to Madison as father of the Bill of Rights than father of the Constitution itself. One of Madison's objectives was to see that the Bill of Rights guaranteed individual rights without otherwise altering the strength of the new national government on which he and others had worked so hard. Clearly, many Antifederalists were far more concerned with the rights of the states in the new Union than with the rights of individuals, which had served as a kind of public smoke screen for their cause.

APPLICATION OF THE BILL OF RIGHTS

The provisions of the Bill of Rights originally applied to the national government rather than to the states. A clue to this fact is found in the opening word of the First Amendment, which limits "Congress," or a branch of the national government. At the time the Constitution was ratified, most states already had their own bill of rights. While some individuals like Madison realized that states, with smaller land areas and hence a greater likelihood of domination by a single faction or group of factions, were far more likely to restrict rights than was the national government, the central concern of the Antifederalists, which the Bill of Rights was designed to placate, stemmed from fears of actions of the national government. Indeed, in the same Congress that had proposed the Bill of Rights, Madison had proposed an amendment that would have limited the states, but Congress rejected this idea.

Altogether, twelve amendments were sent on to the states for ratification. Two failed to be ratified—one related to representation and another provided that an election would have to ensue before congressional pay raises could be implemented (an amendment since ratified in 1992). In *Barron v. Baltimore* (1833), his last major decision from the bench, Chief Justice Marshall affirmed that the Bill of Rights applied only to the national government, a situation that remained unchanged until the ratification of the Fourteenth Amendment in 1868.

Among other provisions, this amendment contained a clause prohibiting any state from denying a person's "life, liberty, or property" without "due process of law." There were some who proposed this language, apparently hoping or believing that it would overturn *Barron v. Baltimore* and make the guarantees in the Bill of Rights applicable to the states. Initially, at least, the courts did not accept this interpretation. In *Hurtado v. California* (1884), for example, the Supreme Court refused to read the Fifth Amendment requirement for a grand jury indictment into the due process clause of the Fourteenth Amendment, pointing out that, if the due process clause of the Fourteenth Amendment were so interpreted, then the identical clause in the Fifth Amendment would be redundant.

In *Chicago, Burlington & Quincy Railroad Co. v. Chicago* (1897), however, a property-minded Court indicated that states would be governed, through the Fourteenth Amendment, by the takings clause of the Fifth Amendment; and, in *Gitlow v. New York* (1925), the Court applied free speech guarantees to the states and began increasingly to look to the Bill of Rights for guidance as to the meaning of due process. By 1937, it had "incorporated" or "absorbed" a number of these rights into the due process clause, leaving some to hope that the Court might soon reverse *Hurtado* and simply apply all these guarantees to the states. In *Palko v. Connecticut* (1937), however, Justice Benjamin Cardozo indicated that the Court would not accept such "total incorporation" (the position later most forcefully and consistently advocated by Justice Hugo Black), but that it would selectively apply only those provisions of the Bill of Rights that it considered most fundamental; in the instant case, it decided that the Fifth Amendment provision against double jeopardy was not so fundamental.

Later advocates of total incorporation such as Justice Black would effectively lose the central battle but win the war. By 1969, the last date when another provision of the Bill of Rights was incorporated, all but five such guarantees (the Second Amendment right to bear arms, the Third Amendment provision against quartering troops, the Fifth Amendment grand jury requirement, the Seventh Amendment right to a petit jury in civil cases, and the Eighth Amendment prohibitions against excessive bail and fines) had been so applied to the states. Indeed, some justices had gone even beyond Justice Black's view by arguing that, in addition to specific guarantees in the Bill of Rights, the due process clause incorporated other rights as well—a view often designated "incorporation plus."

THE BILL OF RIGHTS: A FLOOR
OR A CEILING?

However liberal judicial interpretations of the Bill of Rights have sometimes been, not all interpretations, particularly since the retirement of Chief Justice Earl Warren, have expanded individual rights against the government. When Supreme Court decisions were almost invariably more liberal than those of comparable state courts, they were especially regarded by civil libertarians as a benchmark, or ceiling, beyond which it would be difficult to advance. As some state constitutions now contain language protecting individual liberties that is more embracive or has been interpreted more expansively than comparable provisions in the U.S. Constitution, the judicial interpretations of the guarantees in the Bill of Rights and elsewhere in the Constitution have been increasingly viewed as a floor rather than as a ceiling. In short, in some states lawyers may have better success arguing for individual rights on the basis of the state rather than the national constitution.

As ironic as this development may at first seem, it serves as a reminder that most of the guarantees in the Bill of Rights were originally borrowed from declarations or bills of rights within the state constitutions. Moreover, the increased attention to state constitutions shows that, however some states may have lagged behind federal standards in the past, federalism can also enhance human rights, serving as what Justice Louis Brandeis once referred to as individual "laboratories" where new ideas might be tried.

THE IDEA OF RIGHTS

The designation of the first ten amendments as the Bill of Rights requires some comment, for few ideas have been more clearly tied to the American polity than the notion of individual rights. As indicated in the first chapter of this book, Americans had claimed their rights against England in the controversies that led to the War for Independence. When the colonies declared their independence, they had justified their actions on the basis of preserving more universal rights to "life, liberty, and the pursuit of happiness," for which protection they contended that governments were created to provide.

Rights are perhaps best defined as legitimate moral claims, or entitlements. The rights of "life, liberty, and the pursuit of happiness" asserted in the Declaration of Independence can be called human rights because they were asserted to apply to individuals as human beings, endowed with a special dignity by their Creator. When such rights are granted by law against the government, they are usually referred to as civil, or legal, rights; thus, freedom from taxation without representation was considered an essential right of Englishmen.

Obviously, some countries do not recognize rights that most Americans would consider essential to human dignity. Perhaps less obviously, the government can create certain legal entitlements—for example, the right to receive royalty money from oil drilled on public lands within a state—that might go beyond that to which human beings are entitled simply by reason of their personhood. Many nations fail to honor basic human rights. Recognition and protection of rights is a hallmark of a government that respects its citizens. Americans are justly proud that the first amendments to their Constitution were made in an attempt to expand recognition to and protection of such rights.

It is generally agreed that rights imply duties. The U.S. Constitution is surprisingly silent about such responsibilities, but they are at least implicit in its provisions. At a minimum, one who wants such rights as freedom of speech and religion, for example, should be able to see that these rights require a negative duty not to interfere with such rights for others. Quite beyond this, one could argue that a right to a jury trial might entail an obligation to serve on a jury, and a right to due process would imply the duty to be guided in one's actions by the rule of law.

Most rights in the first ten amendments are phrased in fairly broad terms, but it should take little reflection to see that few if any important rights—the right to believe, as long as it is internal, might be a noteworthy exception—are absolute, because rights exercised beyond a certain limit often end up placing individuals in conflict with others. An old adage states that one's right to shadow box ends where another's nose begins. As will be further evident in the following, the right to free speech would not necessarily protect an individual who caused a riot or panic by one's words, nor would the freedom of religion allow the sacrifice of one's own child, much less that of another.

The 27 different rights guaranteed in the first ten amendments to the Constitution are political rights. The twentieth century has seen increased attention to social and economic rights. Some constitutions, those of Mexico and the former Soviet Union, for example, have reflected this emphasis by granting such rights as a minimum wage, the right to an education, and guaranteed paid vacations. With these guarantees, such constitutions tend to be significantly longer than that of the United States. A convincing case can certainly be made that political rights will mean little to people who are starving or otherwise suffering severe economic deprivation, or who lack adequate education. At the same time, written guarantees of such economic rights mean little if the society offering them does not have the wherewithal to finance them; thus, some have argued that such rights, which are often not enforced, do not properly belong in the fundamental law of the land.

THE PLACEMENT OF THE FIRST AMENDMENT

With the possible exception of the Fourteenth, no amendment has been more praised than the First Amendment. Only through an accident—the failure to ratify the first two proposals—is the First Amendment placed first in the Constitution, but this very priority has come to have an important symbolic, almost mystical, value in the popular mind. The Court itself has sometimes referred to the guarantees in this amendment as enjoying what it called a "preferred position."

Amendment I. Congress shall make no law respecting an establishment of religion, or prohibiting the free exercise thereof;

THE ESTABLISHMENT AND FREE EXERCISE CLAUSES

Although He is mentioned several times in the Declaration of Independence, God is not mentioned in the U.S. Constitution unless one counts mention of "the Year of our Lord" in the convention's authorizing resolution that is sometimes appended to the document. Still, Americans are a highly religious people, and the first two provisions of the First Amendment both relate to religion.

The first prohibits Congress from making laws "respecting an establishment of religion." Although it might be more accurate to call this the disestablishment, or nonestablishment, clause, it is usually referred to as the establishment clause. The second, or free exercise clause, forbids Congress from prohibiting "the free exercise of religion." Whatever myriad controversies these two clauses have generated, including the difficulty of defining religion itself, their central aims should be clear. There is no state church in the United States as there was in England and as there had once been in some of the colonies, and persons are to be given wide freedom to practice their religious beliefs.

Debate continues about the relationship between the establishment and free exercise clauses and which should be given priority in cases of apparent conflict. Some argue that both are primarily designed to ensure religious liberty and this goal should be kept paramount. Others think the main danger comes from entanglements between church and state, and accordingly emphasize the establishment clause.

The Three-Part Lemon Test and the Wall of Separation

In interpreting the establishment clause, the Supreme Court has developed a three-pronged test known as the Lemon Test because it was first articulated in the case of *Lemon v. Kurtzman* (1971). This test, which continues to be the subject of intense debate, requires that, to be constitutional, laws related to religion must: (1) have a clear secular, or nonreligious, legislative purpose; (2) have a primary, or central, effect that neither advances nor inhibits religion; and (3) avoid excessive entanglement between church and state. It was primarily on the basis of the second of these three tests that the Supreme Court in *Wallace v. Jaffree* (1985) struck down an amended Alabama law newly specifying that a one-minute moment of silence at the beginning of the public school day could be used for prayer. The third prong on the Lemon Test was in turn used in *Walz v. Tax Commission* (1970) to justify a state's decision to continue to exempt church property from taxation.

Also controversial is an analogy once coined by Thomas Jefferson (a strong advocate of disestablishment within his own state of Virginia and a confidant of James Madison, "father" of the Bill of Rights) and frequently cited by the Supreme Court that refers to a wall of separation between church and state. Some think this analogy useful in understanding the relationship between church and state in the United States, and in warning against support of the former by the latter. Others, including William Rehnquist, the current chief justice of the U.S. Supreme Court, believe this analogy has impeded clear thinking on the subject.

Rehnquist, whose views on church and state are accommodationistic, has argued that the establishment clause is violated only when the government officially establishes a national religion or when it favors one religion over another; he does not think it should preclude either general governmental benefits to religion or require state neutrality between religion and irreligion. Others believe that the clause should be interpreted to provide just such neutrality. Whatever view is accepted, Americans can be glad that their politics have been largely insulated from the acute religious controversies that have plagued so many other countries and have sometimes led to intense warfare.

Application of the Establishment Clause

On the basis of the establishment clause, the Supreme Court ruled in *Engel v. Vitale* (1962) that the states may not compose prayers for children in public schools, and in *Abington School District v. Schempp* (1963) that such schools cannot have devotional exercises consisting of Bible reading and prayer. In a closely divided decision written by Justice Anthony Kennedy in *Lee v. Weisman* (1992), the Court further extended its ban on public prayer to primary and secondary school graduation exercises. The Supreme Court has also declared that religious instruction may not take place on the grounds of public schools. It has denied most forms of state aid to parochial schools, making some exceptions for bus transportation and the provision of secular textbooks under the so-called "child benefit theory" and, more recently, for tax write-offs that apply to school expenses as long as such write-offs apply to parents of children in both public and parochial schools (*Mueller v. Allen*, 1983).

These cases notwithstanding, the Lemon Test has not always proved fatal when applied to legislation, and courts have not applied the Lemon Test to all cases. The Court has thus upheld Sunday closing or blue laws on the basis that they have a secular purpose and effect quite apart from any impact they may once be thought to have had in encouraging church attendance. Moreover, in *Marsh v. Chambers* (1983) the Supreme Court upheld the legitimacy of prayers by a chaplain at the beginning of state legislative sessions on the basis that such prayers are connected with a long history of past usage, including that of the first Congress, and that they do not pose the same threat of scorn to nonparticipants as do prayers in the more restrictive school environment. Similarly, in

Lynch v. Donnelly (1984), the Supreme Court upheld the display of a religious crèche on public property as part of a much larger Christmas display that included numerous secular symbols. By contrast, in *County of Allegheny v. American Civil Liberties Union, Greater Pittsburgh Chapter* (1989), the Court ruled that a religious crèche standing alone on the courthouse steps was unconstitutional, while simultaneously allowing a 13-foot Chanukah Menorah displayed next to a Christmas tree.

On other occasions, free exercise rights have prevailed over establishment concerns. Thus, in *Westside Community Board of Education v. Mergens* (1990), the Supreme Court upheld a congressional "equal access" law that provides that public schools open to noncurricular clubs must allow religious organizations to participate on the same basis as others.

The Free Exercise Clause and the Belief/Practice Dichotomy

While the second clause of the First Amendment guarantees the free exercise of religion, this guarantee is obviously not absolute. At least since the Supreme Court upheld the conviction of a Mormon for bigamy in *Reynolds v. United States* (1879), the distinction has often been made between religious belief and religious practice. While both have broad protection, the first obviously has the wider, because it is confined within an individual's mind. Religious practice will necessarily be more circumscribed because it so directly affects others.

Religious advocacy, or speech, occupies an intermediate category, to be regulated, as shall be apparent from subsequent discussions of freedom of speech, not so much according to content as according to time and place considerations. Thus, an individual has the right to believe in polygamy and, under most circumstances, to argue for legislation to repeal current antipolygamy laws. An individual who marries more than one spouse may, however, end up before the courts.

Application of the Free Exercise Clause

The Supreme Court has decided a number of free exercise cases. Two early cases that mixed religious and free speech issues involved saluting the American flag. In the first case, *Minersville School District v. Gobitis* (1940), the Court rejected pleas by Jehovah's

Witnesses—who consider the pledge to be a form of idolatry—that saluting the flag was an unconstitutional violation of their religious beliefs. It subsequently ruled, in *West Virginia State Board of Education v. Barnette* (1943), however, that its earlier decision was mistaken and that students could not be forced to affirm a belief against their principles. In a more recent free exercise case, *Wisconsin v. Yoder* (1972), the Court upheld the right of Amish parents to take their children out of public schools after the eighth grade rather than risk what they understand to be the threat of worldliness. In an earlier case, *Sherbert v. Verner* (1963), the Supreme Court prohibited a state from denying unemployment benefits to a Seventh-day Adventist who was fired from her job and would not accept other available employment because such jobs required that she work on Saturday, contrary to her convictions. Similarly, the case of *Lamb's Chapel v. Center Moriches Union Free School District* (1993) prohibited a school from specifically excluding religious groups from using school property after hours, and *Zobrest v. Catalina Foothills School District* (1993) ruled that a state could not deny a sign language interpreter to a student simply because that student was enrolled in a Roman Catholic high school.

In 1988 and 1990, many observers were alarmed by two decisions in which the Supreme Court appeared to be giving less scrutiny to laws affecting religious exercise than it had previously. In *Lyng v. Northwest Indian Cemetery Protective Association* (1988), the Court allowed the forest service to build a road through an area of national forests regarded by Native Americans as sacred. Similarly, in *Employment Division, Department of Human Resources of Oregon v. Smith* (1990), the Court accepted Oregon's denial of unemployment benefits to two Native Americans who had been fired from their jobs for ingesting peyote in connection with long-standing religious rituals.

Even before a new law, the Religious Freedom Restoration Act, went into effect urging the Court to give greater scrutiny to laws restricting religious freedom, however, the Court had already moved to strike down a Florida city ordinance restricting animal sacrifices as improperly motivated by a desire to restrict religious exercise (*Church of the Lukumi Babalu Aye v. City of Hialeah*, 1993). In *Rosenberger v. Rector and Visitors of the University of Virginia* (1995), the Court subsequently ruled that the University of Virginia—a state-supported institution—could not deny funding to a religious publication simply because it advanced religious views.

The latter decision rested largely on the doctrine that any restriction of freedom of speech must be content-neutral.

Amendment I. [Congress shall make no law] abridging the freedom of speech.

JUSTIFICATIONS FOR FREEDOM OF SPEECH

After delineating the rights relative to religion, the First Amendment proceeds to guarantee freedom of speech and press, rights almost inextricably linked both in legal theory and the popular mind. In *Palko v. Connecticut* (1937), Justice Cardozo listed freedom of speech as part of "the matrix, the indispensable condition, of nearly every other form of freedom," and so it is. Freedom of speech acknowledges individual worth. Moreover, in a democratic-republican government that depends upon the people to select their own rulers, it is critical that the people be permitted to discuss and write about these potential rulers without fear of recrimination.

The nineteenth century English philosopher, John Stuart Mill, argued in the essay *On Liberty* that speech was good not only as a means of ferreting out the truth, but also as a mechanism of helping individuals to understand their own beliefs. Unless beliefs are subject to challenge, he argued, people will not hold them with the same degree of understanding as they might otherwise have. It is not surprising that Americans often refer to the rights of freedom of speech and press in describing what it is that makes this society unique.

THE DEVELOPMENT OF FREE SPEECH TESTS

Granted that freedom of speech is critical, most would recognize that it, like almost all other rights, is not unlimited, as a reading of the First Amendment might first suggest. The most convincing argument for limits was made by Justice Oliver Wendell Holmes, Jr., in an early free speech case known as *Schenck v. United States* (1919). Confronted with a radical who had mailed pamphlets to potential draftees during World War I urging them to resist the draft, Holmes upheld Schenck's conviction under the Espionage Act of 1917 on the basis of what has come to be known as "the clear and present danger test." That is, he argued that, while Schenck would ordinarily be justified in communicating in the way he did, here the government had the right to suppress his speech because it created a clear and present danger that the government had the right to prevent, namely, interference with the war effort and national security.

Thus, observing that "the character of every act depends upon the circumstances in which it is done," Holmes went on to formulate what may be the most convincing example to demonstrate that freedom of speech is not absolute when he observed that "The most stringent protection of free speech would not protect a man in falsely shouting fire in a theater and causing a panic." Scholars still argue as to whether a clear and present danger was present in *Schenck* and whether it is an adequate test for all speech cases, but almost everyone agrees that Holmes formulated a convincing example of cases where governmental action is appropriate.

Not all judicial tests following in the wake of *Schenck* have been as liberal as Holmes's. Thus, in *Gitlow v. New York* (1925), a case involving prosecution under a New York criminal anarchy law of a socialist for distributing a little-noticed pamphlet advocating overthrow of the government, the Court reverted to what is often called the "bad tendency" test, or the "kill-the-serpent-in-the-egg approach," to suppress speech that did not present the wartime danger arguably present in *Schenck*. Noting that "A single revolutionary spark may kindle a fire that, smouldering for a time, may burst into a sweeping and destructive conflagration," the Court undermined protections for unpopular speech by focusing on the potential long-term negative effects of speech on public peace and safety.

Similarly, *Dennis v. United States* (1951) reformulated the clear and present danger test as a "gravity of the evil" test to convict leading American communists under the Smith Act—which made it a crime to advocate the forceful overthrow of the government or organize a party for this purpose—when confronted with what many believed to be a worldwide communist conspiracy to overthrow all capitalistic governments.

Over the course of time, however, the Supreme Court has reasserted the priority position of the right of free speech except in cases that threaten direct or imminent harm. Thus in *Brandenburg v. Ohio* (1969), the Court overturned Ohio's Criminal Syndicalism Act and its application to a member of the Ku Klux Klan who had uttered racial slurs at a Klan rally and spoken of "revengance" against representatives of the three branches of government. The opinion for the entire Court indicated that advocacy of ideas would only be illegal "where such advocacy is directed to inviting or producing imminent lawless action and is likely to incite or produce such action" (*Brandenburg v. Ohio*, 1969, p. 447). Moreover, in concurring opinions, Justices Black and Douglas announced the death of the more restrictive clear and present danger test, arguably leaving the nation with its strongest protection of free speech in the Court's history.

SUBSIDIARY PRINCIPLES

In addition to widening protections against alleged threats to state or national security, the courts have developed a number of rules designed to give special protection to free speech. Thus, under the "overbreath doctrine," the Supreme Court routinely strikes down laws that are so broad that they threaten to sweep in protected as well as unprotected speech. A law against obscenity, for example, must not define obscenity so broadly that it would also enjoin speech that is not obscene. Similarly, the Court often cites "the vice of vagueness" in voiding laws that do not clearly distinguish protected from unprotected speech, and it insists that the government use the "least means" necessary to regulate speech.

Apart from such special areas to be discussed later, the Court looks suspiciously upon any content-based restrictions of free speech, permitting certain time, place, and manner restrictions but insisting that they apply equally to all speeches and not be broader than necessary. A speaker could thus be prohibited from preaching in the middle of an interstate highway, or sound trucks might be barred from a public park in a residential neighborhood, but only if such regulations apply equally to all and are not administered in a discriminatory fashion. Moreover, although forbidding the distribution of all handbills might reduce littering, less embracive means could accomplish the same object without so broadly interfering with speech.

Speech has many purposes and comes in a variety of forms. Given the purposes of the Constitution and the aims of those who wrote it, there is good reason to believe that the document's primary concern is with what might be called "political" speech and, consistent with other guarantees within the First Amendment and elsewhere within the Constitution, speech of a religious or philosophic nature. One might further apply the First Amendment idea of speech to social, economic, personal, scientific, and aesthetic matters without thereby also recognizing an equal right to engage in libel, pander obscenity, or solicit individuals to criminal activities as in bribery or murder-for-hire cases (Van Alstyne, *Interpretations of the First Amendment*, pp. 40–42). Indeed, the Supreme Court has taken such an approach, carving out exceptions to what might be regarded as the generally broad protections given to political and related speech.

OBSCENITY

Thus, the Court has consistently ruled that obscenity is not a form of speech protected by the First Amendment. This formulation has not, of course, been conclusive because it has required that the Court get beyond Justice Potter Stewart's honest observation that "I know it when I see it" and devise a clearer test for what is obscene and what is not. For many years American courts applied what was known as the Hicklin Test. It provided that works would be judged according to "whether the tendency of the matter charged as obscene is to deprave and corrupt those whose minds are open to such immoral influence and into whose hands a publication of this sort may fall" (quoted in Abraham and Perry, *Freedom & the Court*, p. 206). In such cases as *Roth v. United States* (1957) and *Alberts v. California* (1957), the Court liberalized this standard, but, after experimenting with several tests, some justices, William Brennan being most prominent among them, decided that the attempt to define obscenity was impossible and should be abandoned.

Chief Justice Burger was determined to see that the Court did not abandon its supervision in this area. He successfully mustered his colleagues around a three-part test now known as the Miller Test because it was first formulated in *Miller v. California* (1973). In this case, the Court said that a work would be considered obscene: (1) if an average person, applying contemporary community standards, would find that the work taken as a whole appeals to a prurient (lustful) interest in sex; (2) if it depicts or describes in a patently offensive way sexual conduct specifically described by law; and (3) if the work lacks any serious literary, artistic, political, or scientific value. These standards have pushed much of the controversy over obscenity back to local communities, but the Supreme Court has still had to intervene on occasion to see that these standards were not applied arbitrarily or in a fashion that would threaten legitimate speech rights.

In recent years the Court has devoted increased attention to the regulation of pornography depicting children engaged in sexual activity, and it has allowed for some regulation of pornography through the use of zoning laws. Still, the Court recognizes that even performances of a sexual nature have some expressive value. In *Barnes v. Glen Theatre, Inc.*, (1991), it upheld a South Bend, Indiana statute that required dancers at the Kitty Kat Lounge and other establishments to wear at least pasties and G-strings during their performances.

Even before its *Miller* decision, the Court had indicated that it distinguished between that which was obscene and that which was merely offensive. In *Cohen v. California* (1971), a case that also has important implications for protection of symbolic speech, the Court ruled that a much used four-letter word with sexual connotations displayed on a jacket in reference to the military draft was not erotic and thus not obscene, even if worn in a public place. By contrast, the Court has ruled that the Federal Communications Commission can consider a station's use of sexual language (in this case the playing of George Carlin's discussion of "seven dirty words") when deciding whether to renew its license. In this case, the Court reasoned that the pervasiveness of the electronic media and their accessibility to children created special needs in this area (*Federal Communications Commission v. Pacifica Foundation*, 1978).

In part because of the maturity level of those involved, the Court has also permitted greater restrictions of both speech and press in school settings. In *Bethel School District No. 403 v. Fraser* (1986), the Court allowed a school to punish a student whose speech to a school assembly was judged to be lewd but not obscene. Similarly, in *Hazelwood School District v. Kuhlmeier* (1988), the Court allowed a school principal to censor articles about teenage pregnancy in a student newspaper that would obviously not be subject to such censorship if it were printed outside a school setting.

SYMBOLIC SPEECH

Symbolic speech is another issue inspiring a great deal of controversy. Is such speech protected by the First Amendment or is it to be regarded like other actions that have no constitutional protection? Judicial precedents suggest considerable willingness on the part of American courts to include such symbolism within the general ambit of freedom of speech. As indicated earlier, in overturning a decision rendered just a few years before, the Supreme Court in *West Virginia Board of Education v. Barnette* (1943) declared during World War II that freedom of speech meant that a child, who had religious beliefs against the practice—in this case a Jehovah's Witness who believed that saluting the flag was a form of idolatry—could not be required to salute the American flag. In more recent years, the Supreme Court has upheld the rights of high school students to wear black arm bands to school in protest over the Vietnam War (*Tinker v. Des Moines*, 1969).

In an even more controversial set of decisions (*Texas v. Johnson*, 1989, and *United States v. Eichman*, 1990), a closely divided Court upheld the right of protestors to burn the American flag, a decision that led to immediate, albeit initially unsuccessful, attempts backed by President Bush to reverse the decision via a constitutional amendment. While dissenters on the Supreme Court argued that the flag was a unique symbol deserving of special protection, the majority argued that, for freedom of speech to be meaningful, it had to be extended to cherished symbols as well as to others.

Sometimes, however, the line between permissible symbolic speech and illegal action becomes quite blurred. Thus, in an earlier case, the Court ruled that war protestors did not have the right to burn draft cards, which were considered government property and which were further considered a basic part of the selective service system and hence the nation's defense (*United States v. O'Brien*, 1968). In *R.A.V. v. St. Paul* (1992), however, the Supreme Court struck down the application of a city ordinance to a white teenager who burned a cross (a traditional symbol of white racism often associated with the Ku Klux Klan) on the lawn of a black neighbor. The five-member majority led by Justice Antonin Scalia and joined by Justices Rehnquist, Kennedy, Souter, and Thomas focused on the fact that the St. Paul Bias Motivated Crime Ordinance, which was directed specifically to speech acts likely to arouse "anger or alarm" on the basis of "race, color, creed, religion, or gender," was not content-neutral, but was directed to certain types of speech considered particularly offensive. The four other members of the Court agreed with the decision, but based their objection to the law on the fact that it was overbroad, potentially deterring speech protected by the First Amendment. While striking down this law, the Court left open the possibility of prosecution based on trespassing or similar statutes.

FIGHTING WORDS

As in the case of symbolic speech, the Court has carved out special standards in the case of so-called "fighting words." The theory is that certain derogatory words spoken directly in another person's face are not the kind of rational discussion intended to be protected by the First Amendment, but are rather like force itself. However compelling this logic may be, to date there is only one major Supreme Court decision, *Chaplinsky v. New Hampshire* (1942), directly in this area, and there is an obvious reluctance to expand this exception in a way that might undermine the high degree of protection generally conceded to support the First Amendment. There is, however, renewed interest in the fighting words doctrine, as some colleges have attempted to outlaw the use of certain derogatory terms directed against racial or other minorities. The aforementioned decision in *R.A.V. v. St. Paul* (1992) suggests that many such laws are likely to run afoul of judicially imposed standards that disallow regulations based on the specific content of speech.

LIBEL

Libel is another troublesome area in the realm of speech and press. Libel refers, of course, to the publication of false and damaging information about another. In the England familiar to the American framers, however, truth was no defense in a libel suit; indeed, such "libels" were regarded as even more dangerous than those that were false. Laws both in England and in the colonies attempting to restrict so-called seditious libel had demonstrated that libel laws that are too strict, especially in regard to public figures, risk interfering with legitimate criticism of public officials. Ever since *New York Times Co. v. Sullivan* (1964), a case vividly documented in Anthony Lewis's book, *Make No Law*, in which *The New York Times* and a number of black ministers were unsuccessfully sued by an Alabama police commissioner (whose name had not even been mentioned in the ad) for an advertisement that contained some factual inaccuracies, the Supreme Court has thus sought to establish relatively strict standards for such individuals to collect libel judgments in cases in which they believe they have been defamed.

To win such a case, these individuals must prove what is called "actual malice." That is, they must show that statements made about them were published with knowledge that they were false or with "reckless disregard" as to whether they were true or false. A number of years ago, comedian Carol Burnett was able to win a sizeable judgment against a publication under such a test, but it should be no surprise that, with such a burden of proof, many public figures simply leave scandalous stories about them unchallenged. The failure to challenge such stories is thus no guarantee of their veracity. Moreover, newspapers and other media may spend tens of thousands of dollars defending themselves against libel charges that eventually prove unfounded, thus chilling legitimate speech in the interim.

COMMERCIAL SPEECH

Believing that freedom of speech was developed primarily to protect political and related forms of speech, the Supreme Court did not until fairly recently recognize that the First Amendment might also protect commercial speech, or advertising. After striking down a law that prohibited advertisements for abortion in *Bigelow v. Virginia* (1975), however, the Court issued increasingly expansive decisions in this area. Thus, in *Rubin v. Coors Brewing Co.* (1995), it ruled against a federal law designed to prohibit advertisements from indicating how much alcohol was contained in its products, and in *44 Liquormart, Inc. v. Rhode Island* (1996) it struck down a state law which attempted to suppress information about alcohol prices. Lawyers have been permitted to advertise via the electronic media, and public utilities have been permitted to mail out promotional ads. Apart from laws designed to curb false or misleading advertising, it is thus often difficult to distinguish the levels of protection afforded this kind of speech from that afforded to others.

Amendment I. [Congress shall make no law . . . abridging the freedom of] the press

FREEDOM OF THE PRESS AND PRIOR RESTRAINT

Technically, oral speech defaming another is called slander, and written speech is called libel. So it is that freedom of speech is tied quite closely to freedom of the press. Historically, freedom of the press primarily meant freedom from "prior restraint." That is, whatever judgment to which a publisher might later be subject, there was a great reluctance, or strong presumption against, any attempts by the government to censure something before the public actually had a chance to see it and judge its contents. While the Supreme Court has not limited the meaning of the First Amendment to a presumption against prior restraint, the Court obviously considers this presumption an essential element of such a free press. The most obvious case of this presumption against prior restraint occurred in 1971 in the Pentagon Papers Case, *New York Times Company v. United States*. In this case, the U.S. attorney general went to court to restrain publication of a series of papers that critically analyzed American participation in the Vietnam War. Absent some showing that this publication would result in identifiable harms to specific individuals, the Supreme Court denied the government's request for a continuing injunction and gave the newspapers permission to publish them. The Court made it clear that, once published, the newspapers might still be prosecuted if the material they printed was libelous or if they had engaged in a crime to obtain it, but it held that such prosecutions would have to come later and it would give no sanction to prior restraint of publication.

Two recurring issues that involve freedom of the press concern whether the press should have special access to certain stories and what, if any, other privileges members of the press should have. In *Houchins v. KQED, Inc.*, (1978), a case involving press coverage of prisons, the Court indicated that it was generally reluctant to extend access to a prison to members of the press that it did not extend to others. Similarly, in a series of cases in 1972 (*Branzburg v. Hayes, In re Pappas*, and *United States v. Caldwell*), the Supreme Court ruled that members of the press were not exempt from grand jury inquiries about information they had gathered about criminal activity during the course of their investigations. Many states have subsequently adopted "shield laws" designed to protect reporters who gain such information in their regular course of business.

Moreover, the Court has generally struck down "gag orders" that would seriously limit reporters' ability to report information about an ongoing investigation or trial. In *Nebraska Press Association v. Stuart* (1976), a case involving reporting about the gruesome sexual assault and murder of family members in a small town, the Court noted that there were better means—for example, change of venue and jury sequestration—of protecting the integrity of a trial. It also observed that unchecked rumors might often prove more detrimental to the integrity of a trial than unvarnished reports by the media.

Because the rights of speech and press are so valued, and because the opportunities for such communication now involve a variety of media, the Supreme Court has rendered virtually scores of other cases on these topics. To date, at least, most such decisions have been extremely protective of such fundamental rights of expression.

Amendment I. [Congress shall make no law ... abridging] the right of the people peaceably to assemble and to petition the Government for a redress of grievances.

ASSEMBLY AND PETITION

Like the rights of freedom of speech and press, the rights of assembly and petition that round out the First Amendment are also closely related to the democratic-republican form of government. Without the right to assemble peaceably, political rallies could not be held. Without the right to appeal to those in power, there would be no effective way of influencing them. As Jefferson indicated in the Declaration of Independence, had George III responded positively to the petitions that the colonists had directed his way, the resort to arms might never have proven necessary.

The right of association is not specifically mentioned in the First Amendment, but the right of peaceable assembly certainly seems to imply such a right without which it would be impossible to form political organizations. It was on the basis of the right of association that the Supreme Court denied the right of the state of Alabama to get membership lists of the *National Association for the Advancement of Colored People* at a time when such lists could be used to persecute its members (*NAACP v. Alabama*, 1958).

Freedom of association and assembly does not, of course, apply to meetings for illegal purposes. Moreover, like other rights, such freedoms, if pushed to an extreme, may have an adverse effect on other rights. The Civil Rights Act of 1964 has thus allowed the government to impinge on the free association rights of those operating places of public accommodation who might otherwise choose to disassociate themselves from persons of other races. Similarly, in *Roberts v. U.S. Jaycees* (1984), the Court upheld the application of a Minnesota law prohibiting the exclusion of women from meetings of the United States Jaycees. The Court indicated, however, that it might have upheld such exclusion had the group been much smaller and more selective, so such a decision would be unlikely to apply to small private clubs.

Amendment II. A well regulated Militia, being necessary to the security of a free State, the right of the people to keep and bear Arms, shall not be infringed.

THE RIGHT TO BEAR ARMS

There are few areas of the Constitution that are more controversial than the Second Amendment. Here, perhaps more than anywhere else, popular understandings and scholarly commentary have tended to diverge. In the popular mind, gun ownership is often viewed as a fundamental right tied to basic needs for self-protection in what is viewed as an increasingly violent society. By contrast many scholars (undoubtedly influenced by their own concern over the increasing number of both intentional and accidental deaths from guns) have viewed the right to bear arms as an antiquated provision largely tied to the days when the nation was primarily defended by a citizen militia. Many constitutional law casebooks completely omit this amendment from discussion.

The very wording of the Second Amendment provides fuel for the controversy. Is the opening phrase of the amendment designed to limit the right to bear arms to members of the militia, or does it apply to everyone?

There is currently an explosion of scholarly commentary on the subject. Much of it is increasingly more supportive of popular understandings of the amendment. Scholars note that the concept of a militia was intended as a substitute for a standing army and as a safeguard against governmental oppression. Almost all writers agree, however, that like other rights listed in the Constitution, the right to bear arms is not unlimited.

To date, the Supreme Court has been almost completely silent on the subject, with its decision in *United States v. Miller* (1939) serving as a fairly ambiguous precedent allowing for some state and federal restrictions on gun ownership. These have included the five-day waiting period imposed by Congress in the so-called Brady Bill—named after Reagan's press secretary who was wounded in Hinckley's assassination attempt against the president—and the ban on certain types of semi-automatic weapons.

Given such inattention at the highest level of the judiciary, lower courts have sustained laws that have regulated and restricted gun possession. Given the increasing attention that scholars are devoting to this amendment and the diversity of existing lower court precedents, it would not be surprising to see greater judicial intervention, and attempted clarification, in this area in the near future.

Amendment III. No Soldier shall, in time of peace be quartered in any house, without the consent of the Owner, nor in time of war, but in a manner to be prescribed by Law.

THE PROHIBITION AGAINST
QUARTERING TROOPS

Constitutions are not written in a vacuum. In considering the rights that they hoped to protect, Americans had a particularly keen eye on abuses that they had encountered under British rule. One such abuse, especially prominent in cities like Boston, the scene of the so-called Boston Massacre, was the presence of English troops and their impositions upon private households. Indeed, in the Declaration of Independence, one of the charges against the English king and Parliament was that they were "quartering large bodies of armed troops among us." The Third Amendment thus provides that, in peacetime, such quartering of troops cannot take place without the owner's consent and in wartime, when exigencies may require such housing, that it be done by law. Fortunately, this has not been a subsequent problem in American history, perhaps less because of this amendment than because there is no further colonial attachment to another country.

REFERENCES AND SUGGESTIONS FOR
FURTHER STUDY

Cases

Abington School District v. Schempp, 374 U.S. 203 (1963).
Alberts v. California, 354 U.S. 476 (1957).
Barnes v. Glen Theatre, Inc., 501 U.S. 560 (1991).
Barron v. Baltimore, 32 U.S. 243 (1833).
Bethel School District No. 403 v. Fraser, 478 U.S. 675 (1986).
Bigelow v. Virginia, 421 U.S. 809 (1975).
Board of Education of the Westside Community Schools v. Mergens, 110 S. Ct. 2356 (1990).
Brandenburg v. Ohio, 395 U.S. 444 (1969).
Branzburg v. Hayes, In re Pappas, and United States v. Caldwell, 408 U.S. 665 (1972).
Chaplinsky v. New Hampshire, 315 U.S. 468 (1942).
Chicago, Burlington & Quincy Railroad Co. v. Chicago, 166 U.S. 226 (1897).
Church of the Lukumi Babalu Aye v. City of Hialeah, 113 S. Ct. 2217 (1993).
Cohen v. California, 403 U.S. 15 (1971).
County of Allegheny v. American Civil Liberties Union Greater Pittsburgh Chapter, 492 U.S. 573 (1989).
Dennis v. United States, 341 U.S. 494 (1951).
Employment Division, Department of Human Resources of Oregon v. Smith, 494 U.S. 872 (1990).
Engel v. Vitale, 370 U.S. 421 (1962).
Federal Communications Commission v. Pacifica Foundation, 438 U.S. 726 (1978).
44 Liquormart, Inc. v. Rhode Island, Docket No. 94-1140 (1996).

Gitlow v. New York, 268 U.S. 652 (1925).
Hazelwood School District v. Kuhlmeier, 482 U.S. 260 (1988).
Houchins v. KQED, Inc., 438 U.S. 1 (1978).
Hurtado v. California, 110 U.S. 516 (1884).
Lamb's Chapel v. Center Moriches Union Free School District, 113 S. Ct. 2141 (1993).
Lee v. Weisman, 112 S. Ct. 2649 (1992).
Lemon v. Kurtzman, 403 U.S. 602 (1971).
Lynch v. Donnelly, 465 U.S. 668 (1984).
Lyng v. Northwest Indian Cemetery Protective Association, 485 U.S. 439 (1988).
Marsh v. Chambers, 463 U.S. 783 (1983).
Miller v. California, 413 U.S. 15 (1973).
Minersville School District v. Gobitis, 310 U.S. 586 (1940).
Mueller v. Allen, 463 U.S. 388 (1983).
NAACP v. Alabama, 357 U.S. 449 (1958).
Nebraska Press Association v. Stuart, 427 U.S. 539 (1976).
New York Times Co. v. Sullivan, 376 U.S. 254 (1964).
New York Times Company v. United States, 403 U.S. 713 (1971).
Oregon v. Smith, 110 S. Ct. 1545 (1990).
Palko v. Connecticut, 302 U.S. 319 (1937).
R.A.V. v. St. Paul, 112 S. Ct. 2538 (1992).
Reynolds v. United States, 98 U.S. 145 (1879).
Roberts v. U.S. Jaycees, 468 U.S. 609 (1984).
Rosenberger v. Rector and Visitors of the University of Virginia, 115 S. Ct. 2510 (1995).
Roth v. United States, 354 U.S. 476 (1957).
Rubin v. Coors Brewing Co., 115 S. Ct. 1585 (1995).
Schenck v. United States, 249 U.S. 47 (1919).
Sherbert v. Verner, 374 U.S. 398 (1963).
Texas v. Johnson, 109 S. Ct. 2533 (1989).
Tinker v. Des Moines School District, 393 U.S. 503 (1969).
United States v. Eichman, 110 S. Ct. 2404 (1990).
United States v. Miller, 307 U.S. 174 (1939).
United States v. O'Brien, 391 U.S. 367 (1968).
Wallace v. Jaffree, 472 U.S. 38 (1985).
Walz v. Tax Commission, 397 U.S. 664 (1970).
West Virginia State Board of Education v. Barnette, 319 U.S. 624 (1943).
Westside Community Board of Education v. Mergens, 496 U.S. 226 (1990).
Wisconsin v. Mitchell, 113 S. Ct. 2194 (1993).
Wisconsin v. Yoder, 606 U.S. 205 (1972).
Zobrest v. Catalina Foothills School District, 113 S. Ct. 2462 (1993).

Books

Henry J. Abraham and Barbara A. Perry, *Freedom and the Court: Civil Rights and Liberties in the United States*, 6th ed. (New York: Oxford University Press, 1994).

Arlin M. Adams and Charles J. Emmerich, *A Nation Dedicated to Religious Liberty: The Constitutional Heritage of the Religion Clauses* (Philadelphia: University of Pennsylvania Press, 1990).

Ellen Alderman and Caroline Kennedy, *In Our Defense: The Bill of Rights in Action* (New York: William Morrow Co., 1991).

Raymond Arsenault, ed., *Crucible of Liberty: 200 Years of the Bill of Rights* (New York: The Free Press, 1991).

David J. Bodenhamer and James W. Ely, Jr., eds., *The Bill of Rights in Modern America After 200 Years* (Bloomington: Indiana University Press, 1993).

Andrea L. Bonnicksen, *Civil Rights and Liberties* (Palo Alto, CA: Mayfield, 1982).

John Brigham, *Civil Liberties and American Democracy* (Washington, DC: Congressional Quarterly Inc., 1984).

Irving Bryant, *The Bill of Rights: Its Origin and Meaning* (Indianapolis, IN: Bobbs-Merrill, 1965).

Stephen L. Carter, *The Culture of Disbelief* (New York: Basic Books, 1993).

Zechariah Chafee, Jr., *Free Speech in the United States* (Cambridge, MA: Harvard University Press, 1964).

Richard C. Cortner, *The Supreme Court and the Second Bill of Rights: The Fourteenth Amendment and the Nationalization of Civil Liberties* (Madison: The University of Wisconsin Press, 1981).

Clayton E. Cramer, *For the Defense of Themselves and the State: The Original Intent and Judicial Interpretation of the Right to Keep and Bear Arms* (Westport, CT: Praeger, 1994).

Maurice Cranston, *What Are Human Rights?* (New York: Taplinger Publishing Co., Inc., 1973).

Derek Davis, *Original Intent: Chief Justice Rehnquist and the Course of American Church/State Relations* (Buffalo, NY: Prometheus Books, 1991).

Mary Ann Glendon, *Rights Talk* (New York: The Free Press, 1991).

Mark A. Graber, *Transforming Free Speech* (Berkeley: University of California Press, 1991).

Kermit L. Hall, ed., *By and For the People: Constitutional Rights in American History* (Arlington Heights, IL: Harlan Davidson, Inc., 1991).

Alexander Hamilton, James Madison, and John Jay, *The Federalist Papers*, Clinton Rossiter, ed. (New York: New American Library, 1961).

James Davison Hunter, *Culture Wars: The Struggle to Define America* (New York: Basic Books, 1991).

Leonard W. Levy, *The Establishment Clause and the First Amendment* (New York: Macmillan, 1986).

Anthony Lewis, *Make No Law: The Sullivan Case and the First Amendment* (New York: Random House, 1991).

Donald S. Lutz, *A Preface to American Political Theory* (Lawrence: University Press of Kansas, 1992).

David Lyons, *Rights* (Belmont, CA: Wadsworth Publishing Company, Inc., 1979).

John Stuart Mill, *On Liberty* (Indianapolis, IN: The Bobbs-Merrill Company, Inc., 1956).

Stephen V. Monsma, *Positive Neutrality: Letting Religious Freedom Ring* (Westport, CT: Greenwood Press, 1993).

Mark A. Noll, ed., *Religion and American Politics: From the Colonial Period to the 1980s* (New York: Oxford University Press, 1990).

David M. O'Brien, *Constitutional Law and Politics*, Vol. 2, *Civil Rights and Liberties* (New York: W.W. Norton & Company, 1991).

Robert S. Peck, *The Bill of Rights and the Politics of Interpretation* (St. Paul, MN: West Publishing Company, 1992).

Lucas A. Powe, Jr., *The Fourth Estate and the Constitution: Freedom of the Press in America* (Berkeley: University of California Press, 1991).

C. Herman Pritchett, *Constitutional Civil Liberties* (Englewood Cliffs, NJ: Prentice-Hall, Inc., 1984).

A. James Reichley, *Religion in American Public Life* (Washington, DC: The Brookings Institution, 1985).

John Philip Reid, *Constitutional History of the American Revolution: The Authority of Rights* (Madison: University of Wisconsin Press, 1986).

Robert A. Rutland, *The Birth of the Bill of Rights, 1776–1791* (Chapel Hill: University of North Carolina Press, 1955).

Ellis Sandoz, *Conceived in Liberty: American Individual Rights Today* (North Scituate, MA: Duxberry Press, 1978).

Bernard Schwartz, *A History of the American Bill of Rights* (New York: Oxford University Press, 1977).

Bernard Schwartz, ed., *The Roots of the Bill of Rights*, 5 vols. (New York: Chelsea House, 1980).

Steven H. Shiffrin and Jesse H. Choper, *The First Amendment: Cases—Comments—Questions* (St. Paul, MN: West Publishing Company, 1991).

Rodney A. Smolla, *Jerry Falwell v. Larry Flint: The First Amendment on Trial* (New York: St. Martin's Press, 1988).

Rodney A. Smolla, *Suing the Press: Libel, the Media and Power* (New York: Oxford University Press, 1986).

Frank J. Sorauf, *The Wall of Separation: The Constitutional Politics of Church and State* (Princeton, NJ: Princeton University Press, 1976).

Robert J. Spitzer, *The Politics of Gun Control* (Chatham, NJ: Chatham House Publishers, Inc., 1995).

Herbert J. Storing, *What the Anti-Federalists Were For: The Political Thought of the Opponents of the Constitution* (Chicago: The University of Chicago Press, 1981).

Wayne R. Swanson, *The Christ Child Goes to Court* (Philadelphia, PA: Temple University Press, 1990).

Thomas L. Tedford, *Freedom of Speech in the United States* (New York: Random House, 1985).

Sanford J. Unger, *The Papers and the Papers* (New York: E.P. Dulton, 1972).

Melvin I. Urofsky, *The Continuity of Change: The Supreme Court and Individual Liberties, 1953–1986* (Belmont, CA: Wadsworth Publishing Company, 1991).

William W. Van Alstyne, *Interpretations of the First Amendment* (Durham, NC: Duke University Press, 1984).

Helen E. Veit, Kenneth R. Bowling, and Charles Bickford, *Creating the Bill of Rights* (Baltimore, MD: The Johns Hopkins University Press, 1991).

Chapter 8

The Bill of Rights and the Rights of the Accused—Amendments 4–7

Amendment IV. The right of the people to be secure in their persons, houses, papers, and effects, against unreasonable searches and seizures, shall not be violated, and no Warrants shall issue, but upon probable cause, supported by Oath or affirmation, and particularly describing the place to be searched, and the persons or things to be seized.

UNREASONABLE SEARCHES AND SEIZURES

The Fourth Amendment is related to the Third in that both rest implicitly on the notion prominent in English common law that one's home is one's castle. The term privacy is nowhere mentioned in the Constitution, but the Fourth Amendment certainly points in the direction of this concept by its high regard for the integrity of persons and their property. As in the case of the Third Amendment, the Fourth was written with specific British abuses in mind. In attempts to detect tax fraud and violations of various embargoed goods, British agents often swept down on suspects with general warrants that gave practically unlimited authority to search and that stimulated great resentment.

The Fourth Amendment thus seeks to protect the security of

persons, houses, papers, and effects, against unreasonable searches and seizures.

This language is necessarily ambiguous in that it fails specifically to define what "unreasonable" means. Some have linked this clause to the second half of the amendment that provides that

no Warrants shall issue, but upon probable cause, supported by Oath or affirmation, and particularly describing the place to be searched, and the persons or things to be seized.

This is not, however, a necessary connection. To take some obvious examples, it seems unreasonable for a police officer to get a warrant to see if a person just arrested is carrying a concealed weapon that might be turned on the officer. Thus in *Terry v. Ohio* (1968), the Supreme Court allowed for the brief "stop and frisk" of such suspects. Similarly, one would not expect a search warrant for contraband in plain view or in open fields or for vehicles that could be driven away before an officer could return with a warrant, or in cases where an officer is in hot pursuit of a suspect. With such exceptions in mind, the courts have ruled that circumstances exist in which a search warrant is not a necessary component of a reasonable search and seizure.

Such instances are necessarily exceptions, however, which should not disguise the Court's general regard for warrants. The extent of this commitment should be evident in the Court's decision to extend the search warrant requirements to electronic eavesdropping and wiretapping. In an early case, *Olmstead v. United States* (1928), the Court had decided that words over a phone line were not physical things such as appeared to be described in the Fourth Amendment that could be searched and seized, and that information gained from taps placed without force or physical penetration of a building was valid evidence. In subsequent cases like *Katz v. United States* (1967), however, the Supreme Court has decided that the Fourth Amendment language can be adopted to contemporary techniques and that warrants are required in such cases.

With a view to past English abuses, the Fourth Amendment does not permit the issuance of general warrants, or so-called "writs of assistance," giving broad and unspecified powers to officers to search wherever they please. Rather, warrants must particularly describe, "the place to be searched, and the persons or things to be seized." A police officer searching for an illegal bazooka has no authority to lift the lid of a cookie jar looking for weapons. By the same token, an officer who stumbles across a bazooka while looking for drugs could use this as the valid product of his search.

To get a warrant, an officer must appear before a neutral judge or magistrate—although, surprisingly, the Fourth Amendment does not precisely say so—and establish under "Oath or affirmation" what is called "probable cause." As this phrase suggests, probable cause requires more than mere suspicion, a requirement designed to assure that police do not simply go on "fishing expeditions" that invade personal privacy every time they suspect a violation of the law.

Administrative Searches

It is generally assumed that the Fourth Amendment was primarily intended to restrain police conduct, but, increasingly, searches are also conducted at offices and places of employment by supervisors and employers and at homes and places of business by administrative officials charged with maintaining public health and safety or accounting for governmental expenditures. In such cases, courts have attempted to balance private and public interests, requiring or not requiring warrants depending on the nature of the search or establishment and the reasonableness of an expectation of privacy in such locations (O'Brien, *Civil Rights & Liberties*, pp. 859-63). Thus, in *Wyman v. James* (1971), the Supreme Court decided that a social worker could conduct a warrantless search of a welfare recipient's home, and in *New Jersey v. T.L.O.* (1985), it ruled that a high school principal could search the purse of a student suspected of having drugs in her possession. A number of cases, most notably *National Treasury Employees v. Von Raab* (1989) and *Skinner v. Railway Labor Executives' Association* (1989), have also upheld mandatory drug testing programs, the first for employees of the U.S. Customs Service and the second for railway employees who have been involved in accidents.

THE EXCLUSIONARY RULE

If there is a defect in the Fourth Amendment, it is that it does not specify what will happen in cases in which officers of the law violate the amendment and make unreasonable searches and seizures, or proceed to make general searches without probable cause. It could be argued that nothing can in such circumstances be done to remedy the wrong that has been done, aside from the possibility that civil actions could be initiated against the officers involved in the illegal activity. Such cases may not be easy to win, however, and, even here, monetary compensation may provide little relief for persons emotionally traumatized by an illegal search.

Recognizing such problems, courts have come to enforce what is known as the exclusionary rule. That is, they exclude from trial evidence that has been seized illegally. This rule, of course, does nothing to remedy the violations of rights that have already occurred, but it arguably serves to deter future illegal conduct and helps keep judicial hands free of the taint of wrongdoing. More negatively, the exclusionary rule can result in the exclusion of some crucial evidence, causing some guilty individuals, as a consequence, to go free. Because of these consequences of the exclusionary rule—applied to the national government in *Weeks v. United States* (1914) and to the states in *Mapp v. Ohio* (1961)—it has always had its detractors.

Commentators have been particularly concerned about the impact that the exclusionary rule might have on successful law enforcement. To date, they have not succeeded in eliminating the rule, but its application has been limited in a number of cases. In *Nix v. Williams* (1984), for example, the Court established an "inevitable discovery" exception. Here the justices ruled that the introduction of the dead body of a ten-year old murder victim was permissible. Although her murderer had taken officers to the scene as part of what was later ruled to be an improperly obtained confession, search parties were in the vicinity, the victim's body was in plain view, and searchers would almost surely have discovered the body in pretty much the same state as the officers found it—it was almost Christmas, and the weather was freezing in Iowa where the girl's body was found. Similarly, in *United States v. Leon* (1984) and *Massachusetts v. Sheppard* (1984), the Court established a "good faith" exception to the exclusionary rule, believing that officers should not be held responsible for flaws in a warrant if they had acted in "good faith."

Amendment V. No person shall be held to answer for a capital, or otherwise infamous crime, unless on a presentment or indictment of a Grand Jury, except in cases arising in the land or naval forces, or in the Militia, when in actual service in time of War or public danger;

INDICTMENT BY GRAND JURY

The Fifth Amendment is usually described as protecting the rights of criminal defendants, but, since any of us can be accused of crimes, the amendment actually extends to all citizens. Although the Constitution does not specifically say so, it establishes an accusatorial rather than an inquisitorial system. Thus, the Fifth Amendment, like the one that follows, is based on the presumption that an individual is legally innocent until proven guilty, and that it is better for many guilty individuals to go free than for any innocent person to be falsely convicted. Perhaps even more broadly, these amendments rest on an understanding that individuals do not cease to be persons deserving of humane treatment even when judged guilty. In such cases, of course, it is sometimes easiest to lose sight of the notion of rights that undergirds the Constitution and other important founding documents.

The first part of the Fifth Amendment provides for indictment by a grand jury in capital cases (cases involving a possible death penalty); in trials for other "infamous crimes," other than those arising in the military (which fall under congressional regulatory powers under Article I, Section 8); or in cases of war or public danger. The grand jury needs to be clearly distinguished from the petit jury. Whereas the latter decides a defendant's guilt and, in some cases, on an appropriate penalty, a grand jury has the function of deciding whether there is sufficient evidence to prosecute an individual. Such a jury is intended to shield individuals from venal or overzealous prosecutors. Some states still use a system of "information" for indictment, believing that grand juries are not always the effective shield against abuse that they seem to be—how many members of a grand jury will feel confident challenging a professional prosecutor's judgment that he has enough evidence to proceed with a trial? This is one of the few provisions of the Bill of Rights that has not been applied to the states through the due process clause of the Fourteenth Amendment.

Amendment V. nor shall any person be subject for the same offence to be twice put in jeopardy of life or limb;

THE DOUBLE JEOPARDY PROVISION

Another protection for criminal defendants is found in the next provision of the Fifth Amendment, which prohibits an individual from being "twice put in jeopardy of life or limb" for the same crime. Without this provision against double jeopardy, a prosecutor could wear down a defendant with legal costs and court appearances even after such defendant had been declared not guilty of a given crime. This provision has not been interpreted as an absolute bar against separate state and federal prosecutions in cases where a crime is an offense against both, however, nor is it considered double jeopardy to retry an individual in the case of a hung (or divided) jury, or in cases where an initial trial is voided because of the introduction of illegally seized evidence or some other prosecutorial indiscretion. Thus, in the famous case of *Gideon v. Wainwright* (1963), after Mr. Gideon's conviction was thrown out because he had been denied state-funded assignment of counsel, he was tried again, albeit not convicted on retrial for his original crime. More recently, Byron de Le Beckwith was reindicted, and eventually convicted, on the basis of new evidence in the murder of civil rights leader Medgar Evers. Two earlier juries had failed to reach a verdict.

Amendment V. nor shall be compelled in any criminal case to be a witness against himself

PROTECTION AGAINST SELF-INCRIMINATION

Many citizens have heard of "taking the Fifth." This expression is a description for the next part of the Fifth Amendment, which provides that individuals will not in criminal cases be compelled to testify against themselves. This guarantee applies only in criminal cases. Thus, although O.J. Simpson did not take the stand in his criminal trial for murder, he was subsequently forced to testify in the civil action brought by the victims' families. The unstated premise here is that it is the government's duty to provide evidence against defendants and not the responsibility of the defendants themselves; this is the essence of an accusatorial, rather than an inquisitorial, system. Moreover, current laws prevent adverse comments on individuals' decisions to exercise their rights. Certainly, there are cases in which innocent persons fear they will not present a believable appearance in court, and the Fifth Amendment is designed to ensure that their rights are protected. Under current law, individuals on trial cannot exercise their Fifth Amendment rights on a selective basis. That is, they may choose to testify or not, but once on the stand, they cannot individually select which questions they would decline to answer for fear of incriminating themselves. The decision whether to allow a defendant to testify can obviously be critical to the outcome of many cases.

Fifth Amendment protections have been extended to congressional hearings where individuals are under oath. Thus, in the congressional hearing involving Oliver North, who was accused of illegally arranging for an arms-for-hostages deal, diverting money from Latin America to the Middle East, North demanded immunity for any incriminating testimony he would give to Congress. Indeed, his conviction was later thrown out—recall the exclusionary rule—on the basis that the Special Prosecutor's case had been tainted by material gleaned from the hearings.

Amendment V. nor [shall any person] be deprived of life, liberty, or property, without due process of law;

THE DUE PROCESS CLAUSE

The next provision of the Fifth Amendment is arguably one of the most far-reaching in the entire Constitution. It prohibits governmental deprivations of "life, liberty, or property, without due process of law." If one agrees with the legal theorist Ronald Dworkin that the Constitution contains both very specific provisions, or conceptions, and more generalizable concepts, or principles (*Law's Empire*, pp. 70–72), the due process clause would clearly fall in the latter category. That is, the nature of due process is arguably broader than any other provision within the Fifth Amendment. Whereas it is a relatively simple matter to ascertain whether an individual has been indicted by a grand jury or subject to double jeopardy, it is far more problematical to decide whether, all things considered before and after a trial, that individual has been accorded due process of law. Perhaps this was the founders' way of letting subsequent generations know that they were aiming not simply for a specific set of procedures, however important these may be, but for more general fairness in the trial of defendants.

When future framers of the Fourteenth Amendment would look for a way to defend the rights of the newly freed slaves, it is perhaps significant that they utilized a similar strategy. In an ironic development, the Court in turn would subsequently read an equal protection component into the due process clause, permitting the Court in *Bolling v. Sharpe* (1954) to apply to the national government (here the District of Columbia) the same requirements for racial desegregation as it applied in a companion case to the states.

Amendment V. nor shall private property be taken for public use, without just compensation.

THE TAKINGS CLAUSE

The last provision of the Fifth Amendment switches focus away from criminal defendants to those who have property that the state needs for a public purpose. Those who know the story in Hebrew Scriptures of King Ahab and Queen Jezebel and their desire for Naboth's vineyard know that great abuses can occur when those in power desire that which belongs to those who are not in power. Most countries recognize a right of eminent domain in cases where land is needed to build roads, form a public park, or the like; in some communist countries, land has simply been expropriated from its owners, often branded enemies of the people for their wealth and/or class status. The last provision of the Fifth Amendment is designed to assure that, when the government of the United States makes such an appropriation, it must provide just compensation.

The Supreme Court has generally given relatively free range to compensated governmental takings, interpreting the "public use" provision relatively broadly. Thus, confronted with oligopolistic land ownership in the state, in *Hawaii Housing Authority v. Midkiff* (1984), the Court allowed the Hawaii legislature to condemn land owned by lessors and sell it to families who had been leasing such property. There is, then, little recourse available to those who would contest governmental takings except to make the best case possible for what they believe the value of their land to be.

As governmental regulations over environmental impacts and land usages have become more pervasive, property owners have looked increasingly to the takings clause to provide some limits. In *Nollan v. California Coastal Commission* (1987), California home-owners thus successfully fought a state attempt to force them to grant uncompensated public access to their beachfront property as a condition for building a new house on the property. Similarly, in *Lucas v. South Carolina Council* (1992), the Supreme Court ruled that a South Carolina regulation prohibiting a property owner from building on a beachfront lot (thus making the land practically worthless for its intended purpose) constituted a regulatory taking for which the government had to provide compensation.

The takings clause was the first in the Bill of Rights to be applied by the federal courts to both state and national governments. Given the renewed attention by some conservative legal theorists—who believe that the current Court has not paid enough attention to property rights in this provision—it might be a good clause to watch for further legal developments.

Amendment VI. In all criminal prosecutions, the accused shall enjoy the right to a speedy and public trial, by an impartial jury of the State and district wherein the crime shall have been committed; which district shall have been previously ascertained by law

RIGHT TO A PETIT JURY

The Sixth Amendment continues the delineation of the rights of those accused of crimes, focusing again on the rights of such defendants at trial. By this amendment, such trials are to be both "speedy and public." The former requirement is a matter of degree left open for future decisions, and the latter is designed to assure adequate publicity to deter untoward procedures and protect both the rights of those on trial and the integrity of the judicial process.

Perhaps most importantly, individuals are guaranteed the right to an impartial jury, that is, a jury free from preconceived bias, a jury that is further drawn from the district where the crime was committed—a provision that does not prohibit a defendant's plea for a change of venue in cases where the defendant thinks a fair trial is impossible in his or her own district.

The jury referred to here is a petit jury, which determines guilt or innocence and, in some cases, advises as to the appropriate penalty. As an institution, the jury has its roots deep in English common law and was considered both as a good fact-finding body—partly on the principle that twelve heads are better than one—and as a way to deter abuse on behalf of governmental officials. It can also be argued, as did Alexis de Tocqueville, the astute French observer of nineteenth-century America, that such juries have an important educative function, allowing citizens to become familiar with the laws and to have at least indirect input into their application (*Democracy in America*, pp. 270–76).

While a twelve-member jury was standard under English law, the Constitution neither explicitly requires that a jury have this precise number of individuals, nor does it specifically require that juries render unanimous verdicts. Over some rather loud protests, the Supreme Court has permitted states to innovate in both areas in recent years. Thus, in *Williams v. Florida* (1970), the Court upheld the use of six-person juries in non-capital cases—later rejecting juries of five in *Ballew v. Georgia* (1978) and verdicts of 5 to 1 in *Burch v. Louisiana* (1979). In earlier decisions, the Court had already allowed for jury verdicts by margins of 9–3, 10–2, and 11–1 (*Johnson v. Louisiana*, 1972, and *Apodaca v. Oregon*, 1972). It should be added that, while a defendant has the right to a petit jury, this is not a right that must be exercised, even if that individual chooses a trial over a plea bargain—a deal with the prosecutor whereby a defendant pleads guilty in hopes of receiving a lesser penalty than would otherwise be given. In criminal cases, juries are instructed that a conviction requires a showing of evidence beyond a reasonable doubt; but, however fundamental and firmly fixed this notion is in American jurisprudence, this rule is not specifically stated in the Constitution.

It is so important that a jury be free from bias that various mechanisms have been devised to assure this. Typically, during the so-called *voir dire* examination of potential jurors, lawyers for either side can dismiss an unlimited number of jurors for cause, that is for reasons such as relationship to or obvious bias against the defendant. Lawyers are usually also given a number of so-called peremptory challenges, that is, challenges that can be exercised without a stated cause. As the number of such challenges granted increases, so too does the possibility that one or the other side of a case will try to stack the jury with individuals believed for demographic or other reasons to be in sympathy with, or antagonistic to, the defendant. Recent Supreme Court decisions—most notably *Batson v. Kentucky* (1986) and *Edmonson v. Leesville Concrete Co.* (1991)—have limited the use of peremptory challenges to exclude individuals from juries on the basis of race and gender. In a related matter, the Supreme Court has reversed course and permitted the use of so-called "death qualified" juries, in which those who say they could not vote for the death penalty are excluded (*A.L. Lockett v. McCree*, 1986).

Amendment VI. [the accused shall enjoy the right] to be informed of the nature and cause of the accusation; to be confronted with the witnesses against him; to have compulsory process for obtaining witnesses in his favor

THE RIGHTS OF NOTIFICATION, CONFRONTATION, AND COMPULSORY PROCESS

The next provision of the Sixth Amendment stipulates that individuals must be informed of the charges and confronted with witnesses against them. Without such a provision, there would be no way for defendants and their attorneys to contest the charges for which they are on trial, and to examine hostile witnesses to see if they are telling the truth. By the same token, the possibility of such confrontation might sometimes deter witnesses from coming forward or pressing charges, especially in cases where the age of the victims might make them particularly sensitive or the nature of the crimes against them (rape or sexual harassment, for example) could prove to be an embarrassment. In at least one highly controversial case, the Supreme Court has limited the right of an alleged child molester to confront his alleged victim, who was permitted to testify out of court on a one-way, closed circuit television (*Maryland v. Craig*, 1990). Just as defendants are entitled to cross-examine hostile witnesses, so too they have the Sixth Amendment right to use "compulsory process" to obtain witnesses who might be able to exonerate them.

Amendment VI. [the accused shall] have assistance of counsel for his defence.

THE RIGHT TO COUNSEL

Perhaps most importantly, all defendants are guaranteed the right to counsel. This latter right has been significantly extended in this century from a guarantee that merely allowed a person to hire an attorney if he or she could afford one, to a judicially enforceable rule that defendants must be told of their right to an attorney and provided with an attorney by the state if they cannot hire one on their own. Indeed, many states now have elected or appointed public defenders for this very purpose.

Earlier in this century, the Supreme Court ruled that states must provide attorneys only to those who, by reason of the seriousness of the crimes with which they were charged or other special circumstances surrounding their case, had special need for one. It was on this basis that the judgment against the Scottsboro Boys was voided in *Powell v. Alabama* (1932) after the state had failed to provide adequate counsel despite the fact that the crime alleged against the black boys (rape) was a serious one and that they were uneducated, away from home, and in a hostile environment.

Over time, however, the Court began to recognize that even in noncapital felony cases where defendants were not especially ignorant or disadvantaged, few could defend themselves adequately. Thus, in *Gideon v. Wainwright* (1963), a case appealed to the Supreme

Court on a handwritten *in forma pauperis*, or in the form of a pau-
per or poor person petition, and engagingly documented in
Anthony Lewis's book *Gideon's Trumpet*, this right was extended
to all felony cases. Subsequently, this right was extended in all
criminal cases involving possible imprisonment (*Argersinger v.
Hamlin*, 1972).

The right to an attorney at trial might not, of course, be particularly efficacious in cases where defendants have already incrimi-
nated themselves. Thus, the Supreme Court began to realize that an
attorney might be needed even before a trial began. In *Escobedo v.
Illinois* (1964), the Court accordingly overturned a conviction
obtained when police refused to honor the request of a suspect in
custody at the police station for a lawyer.

By the time of *Miranda v. Arizona* (1966), the Supreme Court had
been confronted with a large number of cases in which various kinds
of pretrial police misconduct had been alleged. Perhaps as a way of
terminating such cases, or at least severely restricting them, the
Court issued a most far-reaching decision in this case. It decided that
once the police had actually gotten to the stage of focusing on a specific suspect, they needed to inform such suspects of their rights. Few
can watch a modern television detective show without being aware
of these rights, which include the right to an attorney, appointed by
the state in the case of indigence; the right to remain silent; information that all statements can be used against a suspect; and the
information that a suspect is under no compulsion to speak.

Miranda was, and continues to be, a highly controversial ruling
(Rothwax, *Guilty*, 1996). Not only had the Court extended a mandate that reached far beyond the confines of the case, but its meticulous rules seemed more in the nature of a piece of legislation than
of case-by-case decision-making. Many predicted that no criminals
would ever confess to anything after being subjected to so many
warnings. There are still disputes about the impact of *Miranda*, but
general agreement is that it did not stop confessions. Moreover, in
the course of time, some police officers have even come to prefer the
specificity of the decision in that it leaves few areas for subsequent
judicial decision-making. So too, some variations from the precise
wording of the *Miranda* warning might be such as to constitute
"harmless error" (*Duckworth v. Eagen*, 1989).

Like the Fourth, the Fifth and Sixth Amendments have been
enforced by judicially created exclusion of evidence obtained short
of the *Miranda* ruling. Again, too, certain limited exceptions have

been recognized. A police officer fearful that a loaded gun might be picked up by an unsuspecting child might not have time, for example, to warn a criminal of the incriminating consequences of giving an answer before inquiring as to where such a weapon was located. By and large, however, such cases are still exceptions, and the *Miranda* rules remain remarkably undisturbed.

Amendment VII. In Suits at common law, where the value in controversy shall exceed twenty dollars, the right of trial by jury shall be preserved, and no fact tried by a jury shall be otherwise reexamined in any Court of the United States, than according to the rules of the common law.

PETIT JURIES IN COMMON LAW CASES

Whereas the amendments immediately preceding deal with federal criminal trials, the Seventh Amendment deals with federal civil trials, such as diversity of citizenship cases and the like. The Seventh Amendment provides the right to a jury trial in all civil cases exceeding 20 dollars, today such a petty sum that one wonders why it was included in the constitutional text at all. The amendment, whose guarantees have been extended to cover cases falling under federal statutes (of which there are now obviously many more than in 1787), further provides that the fact-finding function of a jury shall not be re-examined other than "according to the rules of the common law." Knowing that jurors would not always be experts in the law, the framers continued to believe that the collective judgment of juries would be superior to the individual judgment of magistrates in ascertaining the facts of a case.

REFERENCES AND SUGGESTIONS FOR FURTHER STUDY

Cases

A.L. Lockett v. McCree, 476 U.S. 836 (1986).
Apodoca v. Oregon, 406 U.S. 404 (1972).
Argersinger v. Hamlin, 407 U.S. 25 (1972).
Ballew v. Georgia, 435 U.S. 223 (1978).
Batson v. Kentucky, 476 U.S. 79 (1986).
Bolling v. Sharpe, 347 U.S. 497 (1954).
Burch v. Louisiana, 441 U.S. 130 (1979).
Duckworth v. Eagen, 492 U.S. 195 (1989).
Edmonson v. Leesville Concrete Co., 111 S. Ct. 2077 (1991).

Escobedo v. Illinois, 386 U.S. 478 (1964).
Gideon v. Wainwright, 372 U.S. 335 (1963).
Hawaii Housing Authority v. Midkiff, 467 U.S. 229 (1984).
Johnson v. Louisiana, 406 U.S. 356 (1972).
Katz v. United States, 389 U.S. 347 (1967).
Lucas v. South Carolina Council, 112 S. Ct. 2886 (1992).
Mapp v. Ohio, 367 U.S. 643 (1961).
Maryland v. Craig, 497 U.S. 836 (1990).
Massachusetts v. Sheppard, 468 U.S. 981 (1984).
Miranda v. Arizona, 384 U.S. 436 (1966).
National Treasury Employees v. Von Raab, 489 U.S. 656 (1989).
New Jersey v. T.L.O., 469 U.S. 325 (1985).
Nix v. Williams, 467 U.S. 431 (1984).
Nollan v. California Coastal Commission, 483 U.S. 825 (1987).
Olmstead v. United States, 277 U.S. 438 (1928).
Powell v. Alabama, 287 U.S. 45 (1932).
Skinner v. Railway Labor Executives' Association, 489 U.S. 609 (1989).
Terry v. Ohio, 392 U.S. 1 (1968).
United States v. Leon, 468 U.S. 902 (1984).
Weeks v. United States, 232 U.S. 383 (1914).
Williams v. Florida, 399 U.S. 78 (1970).
Wyman v. James, 400 U.S. 309 (1971).

Books

Henry J. Abraham and Barbara A. Perry, *Freedom and The Court: Civil Rights and Liberties in the United States*, 6th ed. (New York: Oxford University Press, 1994).

Liva Baker, *Miranda: Crime, Law and Politics* (New York: Atheneum, 1983).

David J. Bodenhamer, *Fair Trial: Rights of the Accused in American History* (New York: Oxford University Press, 1991).

Dan T. Carter, *Scottsboro: A Tragedy of the American South* (New York: Oxford University Press, 1969).

Ronald Dworkin, *Law's Empire* (Cambridge, MA: The Belknap Press of Harvard University Press, 1986).

James W. Ely, Jr., *The Guardian of Every Other Right: A Constitutional History of Property Rights* (New York: Oxford University Press, 1992).

Malcolm M. Feeley, *The Process is the Punishment: Handling Cases in a Lower Criminal Court* (New York: Russell Sage Foundation, 1979).

David Fellman, *The Defendant's Rights Today* (Madison: University of Wisconsin Press, 1976).

Marvin F. Frankel, *Criminal Sentences: Law Without Order* (New York: Hill and Want, 1973).

Alfredo Garcia, *The Sixth Amendment in Modern American Jurisprudence: A Critical Perspective*, (New York: Greenwood Press, 1992).

Kermit L. Hall, *The Magic Mirror: Law in American History* (New York: Oxford University Press, 1989).

James P. Levine, *Juries and Politics* (Pacific Grove, CA: Brooks/Cole Publishing Company, 1992).

Leonard W. Levy, *A License to Steal: The Forfeiture of Property* (Chapel Hill: The University of North Carolina Press, 1996).

Leonard W. Levy, *Origins of the Fifth Amendment* (New York: Oxford University Press, 1968).

Anthony Lewis, *Gideon's Trumpet* (New York: Vintage Books, 1964).

Peter W. Lewis and Kenneth D. Peoples, *Constitutional Rights of the Accused—Cases and Comments* (Philadelphia, PA: W.B. Saunders Company, 1979).

Stuart S. Nagel, *The Rights of the Accused in Law and Action* (Beverly Hills, CA: Sage Publications, 1972).

David O'Brien, *Civil Rights and Liberties*, Vol. II of *Constitutional Law and Politics*, 2nd ed. (New York: W.W. Norton & Company, 1995).

Harold J. Rothwax, *Guilty: The Collapse of Criminal Justice* (New York: Random House, 1996).

Alexis de Tocqueville, *Democracy in America*, J.P. Mayer, ed. (Garden City, NY: Anchor Books, 1969).

Jon M. Van Dyke, *Jury Selection Procedures: Our Uncertain Commitment to Representative Panels* (Cambridge, MA: Ballinger Publishing Company, 1977).

Alan F. Westin, *Privacy and Freedom* (New York: Atheneum, 1967).

Bruce Yandle, ed., *Land Rights: The 1990s' Property Tax Rebellion* (Lanham, MD: Rowman & Littlefield Publishers, Inc., 1995).

Chapter 9

The Bill of Rights and Contemporary Amendments—Amendments 8–12

Amendment VIII. Excessive bail shall not be required, nor excessive fines imposed, nor cruel and unusual punishments inflicted.

THE EIGHTH AMENDMENT

Elsewhere in this book, we have noted that while some constitutional provisions have a high degree of specificity, others leave matters of degree to future generations to decide. The provisions in the Eighth Amendment seem to fit squarely within the latter category. The amendment respectively prohibits "excessive bail," "excessive fines," and "cruel and unusual punishments." Terms like "excessive" almost beg for some guidance, and both courts and legislatures have tried to provide it. It is difficult to set precise rules here, since the nature of both bail and fines is necessarily set by the crime of which a defendant is accused and judgments about his or her character. It would arguably be excessive to require a jaywalker to post any bail at all; on the other hand, courts might decide that a million dollars would not be enough to guarantee that a billionaire madman or wealthy drug dealer would appear at trial.

The concept of cruel and unusual punishment may be even more elusive. The notion of cruelty obviously varies from one age to another. Americans would certainly be shocked to see criminals being drawn and quartered, as in colonial England, and most would probably react adversely even to the public whippings in use at the time the Constitution was written. This notion led some to hope for the eventual judicial invalidation of the death penalty. Clearly, the penalty had been in force at the time of the Constitution and long after, as indicated by the due process clauses (with provisions for deprivation of life) of both the Fifth and Fourteenth Amendments, and the reference in the Fifth Amendment to "capital" crimes. Still, perhaps the courts would rule that society has now advanced to the point where such punishments could be considered excessively cruel and/or unusual.

It appeared that the Supreme Court might be adopting such a stance when, in *Furman v. Georgia* (1972), it invalidated existing state death penalty laws on the basis that they were excessively arbitrary. Subsequently, however, a large number of states adopted new laws dividing the trial and sentencing stages of a trial, and giving clearer directions to juries about aggravating and mitigating factors they should consider when deciding whether to impose the death penalty.

In *Gregg v. Georgia* (1976) and cases that followed, the Supreme Court subsequently accepted such laws in the face of intense arguments by Justices Brennan and Marshall, both since retired from the Court, that any imposition of the death penalty was a cruel and unusual violation of basic human dignity. The Court rejected arguments, however, that would permit states to impose an automatic death penalty in the case of certain crimes. Similarly, it would reject death penalty legislation, as in the case of other penalties, that seemed disproportionate to the crime. Currently, the only crimes for which the courts would accept the death penalty are those involving murder; one could not be legally executed for shoplifting or even for a crime as heinous as rape, as long as these crimes were not tied to the deaths of other individuals.

As in other areas of law, recent years have witnessed the emergence of new issues relative to the death penalty. In *Penry v. Lynaugh* (1989), for example, the Supreme Court held that it was not unconstitutional to execute someone who was mildly retarded. In *McCleskey v. Kemp* (1987), the Supreme Court rejected statistical evidence that seemed to show that the death penalty was administered in a racially discriminatory fashion. In that case, the Court found that there was no evidence indicating discrimination against this specific defendant, a black man who had been convicted of two counts of armed robbery and the murder of a white man. Similarly, after deciding in *Thompson v. Oklahoma* (1988) that the Eighth Amendment prohibited the execution of individuals who had committed murder at the age of 15, it ruled a year later in *Stanford v. Kentucky* that individuals who were 16 years old when they murdered could be executed.

Amendment IX. The enumeration in the Constitution of certain rights shall not be construed to deny or disparage others retained by the people.

THE NINTH AMENDMENT AND THE RIGHT TO PRIVACY

In the arguments between Federalists and Antifederalists about the necessity for a bill of rights, the Federalist supporters of the new Constitution initially argued that a bill of rights would be unnecessary because, as a government of enumerated powers, the national government would have no authority other than that which was specifically designated. Moreover, adoption of a bill of rights could even prove dangerous, some Federalists argued, if this list of rights came to be viewed as exclusive and someone were to find a right inadvertently excluded from the listing and conclude that the government therefore had a right to restrict it. Could a person be sentenced to prison for not tipping a hat to a government official simply because the right not to tip one's hat was not listed in the Bill of Rights? This was a central problem the Ninth Amendment was designed to address.

It provides that the enumeration of certain constitutional rights, "shall not be construed to deny or disparage others retained by the people." This amendment leads to two immediate questions, perhaps neither of which has yet been answered satisfactorily. First, specifically which unenumerated rights are covered? Second, which branch of government is specifically entrusted with their protection? Neither question can be adequately answered from the text of the Ninth Amendment alone; consequently, this amendment, while much discussed, has had little practical application. Judge Robert Bork, an unsuccessful nominee for a Supreme Court appointment, has compared the Ninth Amendment to an inkblot. While not all would agree, the use of the Ninth Amendment is sometimes suspect precisely because it is most likely to be invoked by parties who turn to it simply because they can find no other constitutional leg upon which to stand.

The most notable exception to the general disuse into which this amendment has fallen centers around the developing law of the right to privacy. Quite early in this century, Justice Louis Brandeis argued that the right to privacy, or the right to be let alone, as he called it, was one of the most fundamental personal rights. Most privacy litigation, however, then revolved around interpretations of the Fourth and Fifth Amendments. Initially, the Court had a great deal of difficulty in applying the words of these amendments to innovations like wiretapping. While this hurdle was eventually overcome, some areas of governmental intrusions still seemed clearly beyond its scope and yet were not specifically forbidden elsewhere in the Constitution.

Matters of family life and sexuality, neither mentioned specifically in the U.S. Constitution, were among the most discussed of these areas. After a number of delaying actions, the Supreme Court was finally faced with this issue in *Griswold v. Connecticut* (1965). During the so-called Comstock Era, the Connecticut legislature had passed a law prohibiting individuals from using any means of artificial birth control. Even more obtrusively, the act had prohibited doctors from prescribing birth control devices, even in cases where the health of a woman might be jeopardized by a pregnancy. Many regarded such a law as clearly beyond the realm of governmental authority, state or national; and because of the incorporation doctrine, most rights now applied to protect individuals against the national government also applied against the states. But which specific guarantees prohibited a law like Connecticut's?

The Supreme Court's answer was ambiguous. Writing on behalf of that body, Justice William O. Douglas indicated that, while not specifically mentioned in the Constitution, that document clearly contemplated a right of privacy. Such intentions could be found in the First Amendment's protection of assembly and hence of association, in the Third Amendment's protection for the home, in the Fourth Amendment's provisions for search warrants, and in the Fifth Amendment's provision against self-incrimination. Moreover, Justice Douglas continued, the Ninth Amendment further indicated penumbral rights connected with those that were enumerated but not specifically stated. Thus, Connecticut's birth control law was struck down. In a concurring opinion, Justice Arthur Goldberg relied even more firmly on this argument from the Ninth Amendment. While few Americans could deny the ensuing favorable result, constitutional scholars have debated to this day whether Douglas's and Goldberg's reasoning, and particularly their reliance on the Ninth Amendment, was justified.

Disputes over *Griswold* would, however, pale beside the firestorm that greeted the Supreme Court's decision in *Roe v. Wade* in 1973. At issue was a Texas anti-abortion law now challenged as an undue infringement on the very kinds of privacy rights—those related to sexuality and family matters—alleged in *Griswold v. Connecticut* to be protected by the Ninth Amendment and other penumbras of the Bill of Rights. The rights of a woman were now in more obvious conflict with the rights of the unborn, believed by many to be "persons" who fell under the Fifth and Fourteenth Amendment protections against deprivation of "life" without due process of law.

The Court, in an opinion written by Justice Harry Blackmun, said it was no more able than philosophers to decide when human life, or personhood, began, although it did note that references to all persons "born or naturalized" in the first section of the Fourteenth Amendment seemed limited to postnatal as opposed to prenatal life. Thus deciding that the question of personhood would essentially have to be bypassed, the Court went on to fashion a decision that built upon earlier privacy analysis in *Griswold*. In examining the origin of American abortion laws in the latter half of the nineteenth century, Blackmun argued that their primary purpose was to protect the health of the woman. Whereas all abortions could be dangerous prior to the discovery of antiseptics to prevent infections, abortions at certain stages of pregnancy could today actually be less risky for a woman than carrying a child to term. Blackmun thus ruled that in the first trimester (three months) of pregnancy, when modern risks of abortion for a woman were so minimal, the state had no right to legislate against abortion at all.

In the second trimester, he ruled that state interests were limited to health concerns such as the licensing of doctors and facilities where abortions could safely take place. Only in the third trimester, the typical point of "viability" where most fetuses could now survive outside their mothers' wombs, would a state have the right to restrict abortion on behalf of fetal life; and, even here, exceptions would have to be made in cases where the life or health of mothers was severely threatened. Blackmun thus attempted to steer between those who considered abortion an absolute right tied to the unlimited right of a woman to control her own body and those who, on behalf of fetal rights and other state interests, would permit complete state control over abortions.

Roe v. Wade hardly settled controversies over the myriad of related issues, including the rights of fathers, the obligation of states to fund abortions, the notification of parents in cases where juveniles under their guardianship sought abortion, and whether states could require a waiting period before an abortion, or mandate that women be given information on fetal development. The more such cases have arisen, the more clear it has become how difficult such issues are to resolve under an amendment as ambiguous as the Ninth.

In a recent decision, *Planned Parenthood v. Casey* (1992), five justices reaffirmed a "liberty interest" in a woman's decision to choose abortion and sought to exempt such a choice from only "undue burden"; at the same time, the Court majority (led by three moderate conservatives, Justices O'Connor, Kennedy, and Souter) weakened *Roe*'s rigid trimester analysis and upheld state requirements for parental consent for minors (with the possibility of a judicial bypass), a twenty-four hour waiting period, and counseling on the risks of, and alternatives to, abortion. This same decision rejected requirements that a married woman get spousal consent. Moreover, in *Bowers v. Hardwick* (1986), the Court, by a razor-thin five-to-four vote, refused to extend privacy protection to acts of consensual sodomy that were contrary to state law. Perhaps with a view toward the difficulty of its abortion decisions, the Court decided that it might be unwise to push interpretations of the Ninth Amendment much further.

Still, while not explicitly evoking the Ninth Amendment, the Court has in a number of other decisions endorsed the importance of rights that, not being stated elsewhere in the Constitution, it might arguably have sought to ground in the Ninth Amendment. To cite but two examples, the Supreme Court has gone so far as to say, in *Shapiro v. Thompson* (1969), that the right to travel—nowhere explicitly mentioned in the Constitution—is a fundamental right deserving of constitutional protection. So too, in *Pierce v. Society of Sisters of the Holy Name* (1925), the Court affirmed the right of parents to send their students to a parochial school. *Pierce* might be justified under the free exercise clause of the First Amendment, but the free exercise clause probably would not fully explain the Court's decision in *Meyer v. Nebraska* (1923) prohibiting the state from outlawing the teaching of a modern foreign language in school. The right to teach a foreign language, the right to privacy, and the right to travel appear to be unenumerated rights, power over which the people never intended to give to either the state or the national government.

Amendment X. The powers not delegated to the United States by the Constitution, nor prohibited by it to the States, are reserved to the States respectively, or to the people.

THE TENTH AMENDMENT AND STATES' RIGHTS

Like the Ninth Amendment, the Tenth Amendment is phrased in such general language that it can be taken to mean almost anything or almost nothing. Whereas the Ninth Amendment has been the favorite of contemporary liberals, historically the Tenth Amendment has been a favorite among conservatives. More than any other amendment in the Bill of Rights, the Tenth Amendment was designed to address the Antifederalists' fears that the new national government would simply swallow the rights of the states. In protecting the states, this amendment further indicated that the national government would be a government of enumerated powers. As the last amendment in the Bill of Rights, it seems especially fitting that the Tenth Amendment, like the preamble to the Constitution, ends with a reference to "the people."

It is relatively easy to look to Article I, Section 10 for most of the powers specifically denied to the states. It is much more difficult to ascertain which powers have been delegated to the national government, however, because such powers include not only those specifically listed in Article I, Section 8 and elsewhere, but also those that can be reasonably implied from the necessary and proper clause and from other grants of powers. In the same case in which Chief Justice Marshall upheld the constitutionality of the national bank (*McCulloch v. Maryland*, 1819), he was faced with the argument that, because it was not mentioned in the Constitution, the power to create a bank was a power reserved to the states. In response, Marshall correctly noted that the Tenth Amendment did not refer to "the powers not *specifically* delegated," but simply to "the powers not delegated" to the United States, thus leaving open the possibility of implied powers. Thus, the powers "reserved to the States respectively, or to the people," are not all that easily identified. Justice Stone was hence prompted in *United States v. Darby* (1941) to remark that the Tenth Amendment "states but a truism that all is retained which has not been surrendered."

The obstacle of generality notwithstanding, the Tenth Amendment has had an important place in American history, especially during the first one hundred and fifty years or so. From the Tenth Amendment came the ideas of reserved powers, sometimes called state police powers. The idea behind both notions is that in regard to certain functions like the health, welfare, education, land management, and policing of its own citizens, state powers should be paramount. It was on this basis that the scope of the Sherman Anti-Trust Act was limited in *United States v. E.C. Knight* (1895) when the Supreme Court somewhat unrealistically declared that the regulation of monopolies was a matter for state governments to handle.

Similarly, many other national economic regulations involving child labor, the hours of labor, minimum wages, and the like were once voided on the basis that such matters were left to the states under the Tenth Amendment. Eventually, national powers under the taxing power, interstate commerce clause, and war-powers provisions have eroded any notion that certain areas of the economy are left completely free of national control. By and large, the Supreme Court has expected states to protect their own interests through their legislators in Congress, most notably those in the Senate where each state has two delegates. As discussed earlier in this book, however, in *United States v. Lopez* (1995), the Supreme Court indicated that it would scrutinize congressional legislation to see if it was a justified exercise of federal power. Similarly, in *New York v. United States* (1992), the Court majority struck down a provision of the Low-Level Radioactive Waste Policy Amendments Act of 1985 that the majority believed attempted to commandeer states into a federal regulatory scheme. Such cases may signal an increasing willingness on the Court's part to enforce some limits on federal power. The Tenth Amendment, with its continuing testimony to the framers' desire to preserve the degree of state autonomy necessary to perpetuate a distinctly federal, as opposed to unitary, form of government, might well receive increased attention from the Court in coming years.

Amendment XI. [1798] The Judicial power of the United States shall not be construed to extend to any suit in law or equity, commenced or prosecuted against one of the United States by Citizens of another State, or by Citizens or Subjects of any Foreign State.

THE ELEVENTH AMENDMENT AND SUITS AGAINST THE STATE

The Eleventh Amendment is probably one of the least known amendments in the entire Constitution. The fact that it was proposed by Congress in 1794 and ratified by the necessary number of states in 1798 suggests, however, that it can properly be understood, like the Bill of Rights, almost as a product of the Founding Period. The amendment is perhaps most important because it is the first to overturn a Supreme Court decision. The decision at issue, *Chisholm v. Georgia* (1793), had declared that a state could be sued by a citizen of another state, in this case a citizen claiming that he had never been paid for debts owed him from the Revolutionary War era. Some states were naturally sensitive about such suits, which might subject them to payments they hoped to avoid. Moreover, such suits, however consistent they appeared to be with the language of Article III, contradicted assurances given by some Federalists at state ratifying conventions where they had indicated that states, as sovereign entities, could not be sued under the new Constitution without their consent (the doctrine of sovereign immunity). Despite adoption of the Eleventh Amendment, Chief Justice John Marshall ruled in *Osborn v. Bank of the United States* (1824) that the amendment did not bar suits against state officials and in *Cohens v. Virginia* (1821) that it did not bar appeals to federal courts when states instituted suits.

The Eleventh Amendment received its biggest boost in the years following the Civil War and Reconstruction when the Court expanded interpretation of the amendment—most notably in *Hans v. Louisiana* (1890)—to bar suits brought against state governments by their own citizens as well as by citizens of other states. Subsequent cases involving the exercise of federal powers under the commerce clause and the enforcement of Fourteenth Amendment rights have somewhat narrowed state immunity. However, in a recent case—*Seminole Tribe v. Florida* (1996)—the Court seemingly reaffirmed the broad ruling in *Hans* by deciding that the Eleventh Amendment barred Indian tribes from suing a state over what they alleged to be a failure of the state to negotiate in good faith over establishing casinos on Indian lands.

Amendment XII. [1804] The Electors shall meet in their respective states, and vote by ballot for President and Vice President, one of whom, at least, shall not be an inhabitant of the same state with themselves; they shall name in their ballots the person voted for as President, and in distinct ballots the person voted for as Vice-President, and they shall make

distinct lists of all persons voted for as President, and of all persons voted
for as Vice-President, and of the number of votes for each, which lists
they shall sign and certify, and transmit sealed to the seat of the government of the United States, directed to the President of the Senate;—The
President of the Senate shall, in the presence of the Senate and House of
Representatives, open all the certificates and the votes shall then be
counted;—The person having the greatest number of votes for President,
shall be the President, if such number be a majority of the whole number
of Electors appointed; and if no person have such majority, then from the
persons having the highest numbers not exceeding three on the list of
those voted for as President, the House of Representatives shall choose
immediately, by ballot, the President, But in choosing the President, the
votes shall be taken by states, the representation from each state having
one vote; a quorum for this purpose shall consist of a member or members from two-thirds of the states, and a majority of all the states shall be
necessary to a choice. *And if the House of Representatives shall not choose
a President whenever the right of choice shall devolve upon them, before
the fourth day of March next following, then the Vice-President shall act as
President, as in the case of the death or other constitutional disability of the
President.*—The person having the greatest number of votes as Vice-
President, shall be the Vice-President, if such number be a majority of
the whole number of Electors appointed, and if no person have a majority, then from the two highest numbers on the list, the Senate shall
choose the Vice-President; a quorum for the purpose shall consist of
two-thirds of the whole number of Senators, and a majority of the whole
number shall be necessary to a choice. But no person constitutionally
ineligible to the office of President shall be eligible to that of Vice-
President of the United States.

THE TWELFTH AMENDMENT AND
THE ELECTORAL COLLEGE

Like the Eleventh Amendment, the Twelfth was designed to remedy a problem that developed under the new Constitution. The cause
of this problem was the development of political parties that were
not anticipated, at least not in their modern form (recall, however,
Madison's discussion of "factions" in *Federalist* No. 10), by the
Founding Fathers. Because of this development, candidates for president and vice president began running together on a ticket. When, in
the election of 1800, all electoral delegates who voted for Jefferson as
president also cast their votes for fellow Republican Aaron Burr, the
result was a tie in the election, which threw the selection to the
House of Representatives. If Burr had not been so mistrusted (by

among others, Alexander Hamilton, a Federalist whom Burr would later kill in a duel), the popular will could very well have been frustrated by representatives who were not from Jefferson's own party.

To prevent this possibility, the Twelfth Amendment provided that when casting their two votes, each elector was to designate that one was the choice for president and the second the choice for vice president. If no one received a majority, the amendment now further provided that the top three candidates—rather than, as Article II, Section 1 had specified, the top five—would be sent to the House of Representatives for a choice. In such a case, each state delegation has a single vote, whether it be a populous state like California or a thinly populated state like Wyoming. Moreover, in cases where results diverged, members of the House would have to decide whether to cast their votes according to the popular majority in their district, state, or the nation; or according to the party affiliation of the candidate. When the election of 1824, which featured four presidential candidates, went to the House, John Quincy Adams was selected as president over Andrew Jackson, who had received more popular votes. Similarly, in the elections of 1876 and 1888, the winners of the popular vote were not the winners of the electoral vote. These elections, as well as scenarios possible in cases with three or more presidential candidates—for example, the election of 1968, which featured George Wallace as a third party candidate and the election of 1992, which featured Ross Perot in this capacity—show that the electoral college has been the source of continuing controversy.

The most frequently proposed alternative to the electoral college is popular election (many such plans requiring a run-off if no candidate receives 40 percent or more of the vote), but other plans would award electoral votes by districts or by an electoral proportion of each state, rather than by the winner-take-all formula currently used by most states. There are also plans to eliminate so-called "faithless electors," who vote for a candidate other than the one to whom they are pledged. Another proposal would allow for a run-off between the top two candidates, rather than allowing the members of the House of Representatives to make this choice, in cases where no candidate wins a majority of the electoral college. The existing electoral college still has its defenders, however, particularly among those who see this system as a continuing support for federalism, as well as those who believe that the electoral college performs an important function in magnifying the electoral margins by which most presidents now come into office.

REFERENCES AND SUGGESTIONS FOR FURTHER STUDY

Cases

Bowers v. Hardwick, 478 U.S. 186 (1986).
Chisholm v. Georgia, 2 U.S. 419 (1793).
Cohens v. Virginia, 19 U.S. 264 (1821).
Furman v. Georgia, 408 U.S. 238 (1972).
Garcia v. San Antonio Metropolitan Transit Authority, 469 U.S. 528 (1985).
Gregg v. Georgia, 428 U.S. 153 (1976).
Griswold v. Connecticut, 381 U.S. 479 (1965).
Hans v. Louisiana, 134 U.S. 1 (1890).
McCleskey v. Kemp, 481 U.S. 279 (1987).
McCulloch v. Maryland, 17 U.S. 316 (1819).
Meyer v. Nebraska, 262 U.S. 390 (1923).
New York v. United States, 112 S. Ct. 2408 (1992).
Osborn v. Bank of the United States, 9 Wheat (22 U.S.) 738 (1824).
Penry v. Lynaugh, 492 U.S. 302 (1989).
Pierce v. Society of Sisters of the Holy Name, 268 U.S. 510 (1925).
Planned Parenthood v. Casey, 60 LW 4795 (1992).
Roe v. Wade, 410 U.S. 113 (1973).
Seminole Tribe v. Florida, 116 S. Ct. 1114 (1996).
Shapiro v. Thompson, 394 U.S. 618 (1969).
Stanford v. Kentucky, 429 U.S. 361 (1989).
Thompson v. Oklahoma, 487 U.S. 815 (1988).
United States v. Darby Lumber Company, 312 U.S. 100 (1941).
United States v. E.C. Knight Company, 156 U.S. 1 (1895).
United States v. Lopez, 115 S. Ct. 1624 (1995).

Books

Randy Barnette, ed., *The Rights Retained by the People: The History and Meaning of the Ninth Amendment* (Fairfax, VA: George Mason University Press, 1989).

Walter Berns, ed., *After the People Vote: A Guide to the Electoral College*, rev. ed. (Washington, DC: American Enterprise Institute, 1992).

Judith Best, *The Case Against Direct Election of the President: A Defense of the Electoral College* (Ithaca, NY: Cornell University Press, 1975).

Judith A. Best, *The Choice of the People: Debating the Electoral College* (Lanham, MD: Rowman & Littlefield, 1996).

Barbara H. Craig and David M. O'Brien, *Abortion and American Politics* (Chatham, NJ: Chatham House Publishers, Inc., 1993).

Lee Epstein & Joseph F. Kobylka, *The Supreme Court & Legal Change: Abortion & the Death Penalty* (Chapel Hill: The University of North Carolina Press, 1992).

David J. Garrow, *Liberty & Sexuality: The Right to Privacy and the Making of Roe v. Wade* (New York: Macmillan Publishing Company, 1994).

Alexander Hamilton, James Madison, and John Jay, *The Federalist Papers*, Clinton Rossiter, ed. (New York: New American Library, 1961).

Clyde E. Jacobs, *The Eleventh Amendment and Sovereign Immunity* (Westport, CT: Greenwood Press, Inc., 1972).

Tadahisa Kuroda, *The Origins of the Twelfth Amendment: The Electoral College in the Early Republic, 1787–1804* (Westport, CT: Greenwood Press, 1994).

Leonard W. Levy, *Original Intent and the Framers' Constitution* (New York: Macmillan Publishing Company, 1988).

Michael Meltsner, *Cruel and Unusual: The Supreme Court and Capital Punishment* (New York: William Morrow & Company, Inc., 1974).

James C. Mohr, *Abortion in America: The Origins and Evolution of National Policy, 1800–1900* (New York: Oxford University Press, 1978).

John V. Orth, *The Judicial Power of the United States: The Eleventh Amendment in American History* (New York: Oxford University Press, 1987).

Bennett B. Patterson, *The Forgotten Ninth Amendment* (Indianapolis, IN: Bobbs-Merrill, 1955).

Neal R. Pierce, *The People's President: The Electoral College in American History and the Direct-Vote Alternative* (New York: Simon and Schuster, 1968).

Laurence H. Tribe, *Abortion: The Clash of Absolutes* (New York: W.W. Norton & Company, 1990).

Chapter 10

The Post–Civil War Amendments— Amendments 13–15

BACKGROUND

Of all the changes made in the U.S. Constitution, few are as profound as those adopted at the end of the Civil War, the nation's bloodiest conflict. While the causes of this war were complex, differences between the North and South and their varying views of the institution of slavery were certainly fundamental. Initially waged as a war primarily to preserve the Union, it became increasingly clear to Abraham Lincoln that a war that had resulted in such carnage would require a higher justification. Gradually, he came to see this goal as the emancipation and protection of the former slaves.

During the war itself, Lincoln issued his famous Emancipation Proclamation; but, important as this declaration was, it was limited both in scope and legal foundation. Essentially a war measure taken under the president's authority as commander-in-chief, the Emancipation Proclamation applied only behind enemy lines where the North's ability to enforce it was necessarily initially limited. Moreover, as a presidential directive, the Proclamation lacked the constitutional permanency that one might hope for such an important innovation. It should not be surprising that many including Lincoln himself thought such guarantees should have wider reach and firmer constitutional foundations.

Between 1865 and 1870, three constitutional amendments were proposed and ratified, the result of intense political debate and acrid controversy. Each amendment had a different objective. The first, the Thirteenth, was adopted to ensure that slavery would end, such "involuntary servitude" now permitted only as punishment for crimes. The Fourteenth Amendment, whose ratification was required by Congress as a condition of renewed recognition of southern state delegations there, was designed to overturn the notorious *Dred Scott* decision of 1857 and allow blacks to become citizens with rights now protected under the Constitution. This amendment was further designed to reverse the restrictive black codes enacted by a number of southern states in the wake of Emancipation as a way of regulating the movements and other freedoms of those formerly held as slaves. The Fifteenth Amendment focused more explicitly on voting rights.

Amendment XIII. [1865] Section 1. Neither slavery nor involuntary servitude, except as a punishment for crime whereof the party shall have been duly convicted, shall exist within the United States, or any places subject to their jurisdiction.
   Section 2. Congress shall have power to enforce this article by appropriate legislation.

THE THIRTEENTH AMENDMENT AND THE END OF SLAVERY

Of these three amendments, the Thirteenth proved the easiest to enforce. While it did not necessarily eliminate the economic dependency that would soon be manifest in the system of sharecropping that developed in the South after the Civil War, the amendment did do away once and for all with the earlier system of chattel slavery.

Slavery involved much more than physical bondage, of course, and there has accordingly been controversy as to how far the enforcement provision of the Thirteenth Amendment might extend in eliminating what Justice John Marshall Harlan I referred to in the *Civil Rights Cases* of 1883 as "the badges of slavery and servitude." While broad interpretations of the scope of the Thirteenth Amendment have sometimes been accepted by the courts, the adoption of the Fourteenth Amendment has provided far firmer footing for most civil rights claims made by black Americans.

Amendment XIV. [1868] Section 1. All persons born or naturalized in the United States and subject to the jurisdiction thereof, are citizens of the United States and of the State wherein they reside.

CITIZENSHIP PROVISIONS OF THE FOURTEENTH AMENDMENT

Many realized that eliminating the institution of slavery was but a first step toward assuring the rights of those once held in bondage. The most ambitious attempt to assure such rights came with the ratification of the Fourteenth Amendment, which was divided into five sections. The first section of this amendment extended citizenship rights to

All persons born or naturalized in the United States and subject to the jurisdiction thereof.

This was the specific clause that overturned the *Dred Scott* decision, which had ruled in 1857 that blacks were not and could not be considered citizens of the United States under the Constitution of 1787. The only ambiguity in the opening phrase of the Fourteenth Amendment—namely, the elusive "subject to the jurisdiction thereof"—was intended to exempt those like children of foreign ambassadors who are born in the nation but not, because of principles connected with diplomatic immunity, subject to its laws. For a time, the Court interpreted this phrase so as to exclude Native Americans from citizenship, but in 1924 Congress overturned this narrow reading. Congress has passed legislation clarifying the provision applied to persons born in the United States to include not only those actually born on U.S. soil (legally called *jus soli*, law of the soil), but also those born to an American citizen or citizens abroad (*jus sanguinis*, law of the blood). In the latter case, if a person born of only one American parent wants to claim U.S. citizenship, that person's parent must meet a residency requirement and the person must live for ten years in the United States, including five continuous years from age 14 to 28.

Amendment XIV. Section 1. No State shall make or enforce any law which shall abridge the privileges or immunities of citizens of the United States; nor shall any State deprive any person of life, liberty, or property, without due process of law; nor deny to any person within its jurisdiction the equal protection of the laws.

THREE IMPORTANT GUARANTEES

The meat of the Fourteenth Amendment is found in the next sentence, which can be divided into three primary guarantees—the privileges and immunities clause, the due process clause, and the equal protection clause. Whereas the Bill of Rights was designed to protect citizens against arbitrary actions by the national government, the Fourteenth was adopted to protect citizens' rights against the states. This is a significant change. Eventually, the Fourteenth Amendment (and, specifically, the due process clause) would be the vehicle by which the judicial branch extended to the states as well the rights once protected in the Bill of Rights only against federal action.

If the Fourteenth Amendment would eventually have such far-reaching impact, its initial influence would be much more limited. The central problem was that while there was a great deal of concern for the newly freed slaves, there was also a continuing desire to preserve the federal system with its emphasis on state decision-making, and these two goals were not always compatible. Moreover, as Reconstruction ended and federal troops were withdrawn from the South in 1877, a desire to return to some kind of normalcy translated to less support nationally for black rights. The result, evident in a series of Supreme Court decisions, nearly proved disastrous for American blacks.

SUPREME COURT DECISIONS LIMITING THE IMPACT OF THE FOURTEENTH AMENDMENT

Under the Fourteenth Amendment, blacks, like other persons— and the language of the Fourteenth Amendment, while prompted by concern for the rights of blacks, was phrased in general terms—were to be guaranteed

the privileges and immunities of citizens of the United States,

a phrase that also appears in Article IV of the Constitution. Potentially, such privileges and immunities could have been considered quite wide indeed, but the wider such interpretations had been, the greater the potential threat posed to traditional notions of the respective rights of states in regard to their own citizens. The width of such rights would necessarily await judicial construction.

The first cases that came before the Court were called *The Slaughterhouse Cases* (1873), and they effectively reduced the privileges and immunities clause to an empty shell. At issue was a law passed by the Louisiana legislature that had required that all butcherings take place in specific abattoirs, a measure at once motivated by legitimate health and sanitation concerns and by the taint of political corruption. When challenged by butchers whose livelihood was threatened, the Supreme Court had to decide whether the right to employment was a privilege and immunity of U.S. citizenship, or whether the protection of such rights rested where they had always been, namely at the state level. While the dissenters argued that the Fourteenth Amendment had been designed to end state control over fundamental liberties, the majority argued that such an interpretation would stand the Constitution on its head, and that such a revolutionary interpretation could not be accepted without more conclusive constitutional language. Accordingly, the majority defined privileges and immunities about as narrowly as possible (referring, for example, to the right to use seaports and to come to the seat of government), leaving to this day little of substance for the privileges and immunities clause to defend. If the rights of newly freed blacks were to be protected, they would have to depend on the due process or equal protection clauses.

As discussed in an earlier chapter, the due process clause would eventually be the vehicle by which the chief guarantees of the Bill of Rights would be applied to the states through a process usually referred to as "absorption" or "incorporation." Throughout the nineteenth and early twentieth centuries, however, the due process clause served as more of a protection for American businesses interested in staving off governmental regulations than for those it had been primarily designed to serve. Advocates of such businesses were able to persuade the courts that corporations were "persons" under the law, and that laws that interfered with what were considered to be natural economic laws of supply and demand were unconstitutional.

This development still left defenders of black rights with the potentially powerful weapon of the equal protection clause, a clause that had finally incorporated Jefferson's noble assertion of equality in the Declaration of Independence into the fundamental law of the land. Initially, however, this clause too would be practically decimated by two Supreme Court rulings. The first setback occurred in the *Civil Rights Cases* of 1883. At issue was the Civil Rights Act of 1875, a far-ranging law that had prohibited discrimination in places of public accommodation. Receiving a challenge to this law after federal troops had been withdrawn from the South, the Court focused on the words "no State shall." Distinguishing such illegal state action from permissible private discriminatory action, the Court majority argued that the Constitution prohibited the former alone. Thus, while a state could not deny an individual the equal protection of the laws, individuals could continue to do as they pleased. In short, not every private wrong had a corresponding governmental remedy.

That such an interpretation was not completely unreasonable is perhaps shown by the fact that today's far more liberal court still requires illegal state action before it will bring the equal protection clause into play. In one modern case, for example, it held that discriminatory membership policies of a Moose Lodge were not state action simply because the Lodge had received a liquor license from the state (*Moose Lodge No. 107 v. Irvis*, 1972). Because of this state action requirement, the Civil Rights Act of 1964 that now prohibits discrimination in places of public accommodation has thus been upheld on the basis of congressional powers under the commerce clause, rather than by the equal protection clause.

However it might have been justified by an appeal to the state action language of the Fourteenth Amendment, the decision in 1883 was a real setback, and it would be compounded still further in 1896. By the 1890s, a whole system of segregation or so-called Jim Crow laws had developed. Now states were not only allowing individuals to discriminate, but they were actually mandating segregation. These laws were at issue in the case of *Plessy v. Ferguson* (1896) involving a Louisiana law euphemistically designated as "a law to promote the comfort of passengers" as applied to an individual who was one-eighth black. The Court, over the vigorous dissent of John Marshall Harlan I—himself a former Kentucky slaveholder—ruled that there was nothing discriminatory about separate facilities for whites and blacks as long as such facilities were equal. Harlan thundered that:

in view of the Constitution, in the eye of the law, there is in this country no superior dominant ruling class of citizens. There is no caste here. Our Constitution is color-blind, and neither knows nor tolerates classes among citizens. In respect of civil rights, all citizens are equal before the law.

The Court majority, however, ruled that blacks neither had need for special protection from the courts, nor did they have reason to assume that such separate facilities were intended to designate their inferiority. Despite Harlan's argument that it was no more reasonable to require racial segregation than the separation of natural born and naturalized citizens or Catholics and Protestants, the majority ruled that segregation laws were reasonable adaptations to local circumstances that would promote peace, and that states were free to mandate them under their police powers. Such was the construction put on the equal protection clause until 1954.

BROWN AND THE REBIRTH OF THE FOURTEENTH AMENDMENT

By 1954, it had become clear, however, that the American treatment of blacks was far more separate than equal. In a number of prior cases, most relating to the field of higher education, the Supreme Court began signaling that it would now give increased emphasis to the requirement for equality, but legitimate questions remained as to whether a separate system could indeed be equal. This was the question the Supreme Court confronted in the historic *Brown v. Board of Education* decision of 1954, which was argued on behalf of the National Association for the Advancement of Colored People by Thurgood Marshall, later to become the first black Supreme Court justice and, for the segregating schools, by John Davis, prominent attorney and onetime Democratic presidential candidate.

After examining the psychological damage that segregation had wrought and the important role of education in modern life, the Court decided in a unanimous decision guided by newly appointed Chief Justice Earl Warren, that "separate educational facilities are inherently unequal." This decision, applied by a companion case, *Bolling v. Sharpe* (1954), to the District of Columbia via the due process clause of the Fifth Amendment, was soon extended to other areas of segregation as well. The next 30 years would show, however, that mandating change and actually effecting it could be quite different things.

Among the questions the Court had to decide was the reach of permissible remedies to bring about racial desegregation. School busing has been a particularly emotional issue. In *Swann v. Charlotte-Mecklenburg Board of Education* (1971), the Court, without mandating rigid quotas, did sanction the use of busing to achieve racial balance and to remedy the effects of past *de jure* segregation, or segregation by law. In *Milliken v. Bradley* (1974), however, the Court subsequently ruled that remedies would have to be confined to counteracting prior violations of the law. It thus voided an ambitious interdistrict busing plan in Detroit that had been formulated by a lower court to remedy prior *de facto* segregation.

Long after the adoption of the Fourteenth Amendment, racial classifications were used invidiously to discriminate against African Americans and members of other racial groups whose members constituted racial minorities in the United States. More recently, advocates of minority rights have supported using racial classifications to extend privileges designed to make up for past discrimination, provide for role models in minority communities, assure the delivery of certain services to minority members (by, for example, minority graduates of law and medical schools), and promote greater diversity. Opponents of such "affirmative action" programs have criticized such racial preferences as a form of "reverse discrimination."

To this point in time, the Supreme Court has tolerated some use of racial preferences, while simultaneously limiting their scope. The best known case in this area is still the *Bakke* case of 1978. At issue was a program instituted by the medical school at the University of California at Davis that had no prior history of *de jure*, or legally mandated, segregation. Under this program, 16 of 100 entry-level slots were allocated to racial minorities. The result was that Bakke, a white, was denied entry while others less qualified than he were accepted under the quota program. Few cases have been more complex. Four justices, generally considered to be liberals, saw Davis's program as justified. They saw quotas as a legitimate means of overcoming the effects of past racial discrimination and assuring that minorities would achieve specified goals. Four justices, usually branded as conservatives, opposed not only Davis's quota system, but all considerations of race. In the middle was Justice Lewis Powell of Virginia, who rejected Davis's quota program as too rigid and thus believed Bakke should be admitted to the medical school at Davis, but who also thought that race could be considered a plus when the university sought the most diverse student body it could achieve. This decision thus upheld some use of race but struck down strict quotas like that at Davis.

Subsequent cases have not clarified the picture significantly. In *Fullilove v. Klutznich* (1980), for example, the Supreme Court upheld a congressional law setting aside ten percent of its public-work contracts to minority-owned businesses, but in *City of*

Richmond v. J.A. Croson (1989), it struck down a program created by the Richmond city council with a 30 percent set-aside. Just a year later, however, in *Metro Broadcasting v. Federal Communications Commission*, the Court permitted the Federal Communications Commission to consider race positively in deciding to whom to award station licenses.

Recently, focus has shifted back, as in *Bakke*, to the university setting. In 1995, a U.S. circuit court voided race-based scholarship awards at the University of Maryland. In 1996, another circuit court ruled that race-based admission preferences in Texas were in violation of the Fourteenth Amendment. Future review of such cases by the Supreme Court might further clarify the situation, but for now, the Court appears to be deciding cases on something of an *ad hoc* basis.

EQUAL PROTECTION AND GENDER CLASSIFICATIONS

Although the Fourteenth Amendment was motivated chiefly by concerns about disparate treatment based on race, the equal protection clause does not specifically mention racial discrimination, and, in recent years, the Supreme Court has used the clause to extend heightened scrutiny to classifications based on gender. Recognizing that, like race, gender is a noticeable characteristic with which a person is born and that has been used for many years to discriminate against individuals, at least four justices of the U.S. Supreme Court have argued that classifications based on gender should also be regarded as suspect. As discussed in the chapter on the judiciary, a Court majority has yet to go this far, but it has extended "heightened scrutiny" to gender classifications.

This approach reversed decades during which the Court refused to apply the equal protection clause to gender classifications. In *Bradwell v. Illinois* (1873), for example, the Court upheld a law banning women from the practice of law as reasonable and consistent with natural law. While the majority decision was based, like *The Slaughterhouse Cases*, on a restrictive reading of the privileges and immunities clause, a concurring opinion written by Justice Joseph Bradley and joined by two other justices said that, "The paramount destiny and mission of woman are to fulfill the noble and benign offices of wife and mother. This is the law of the Creator."

In more recent years, however, a Court majority, while refusing to regard gender as a suspect category, has nonetheless formulated an intermediate test by which to see that gender classifications are based on and substantially related to important governmental interests, rather than simply being based on sexual stereotypes. Thus, in *Reed v. Reed* (1971) the Court struck down a law that automatically regarded a male, rather than a female, as better qualified to be an executor of an estate. In *Frontiero v. Richardson* (1973), it voided a federal statute that assumed that spouses of male servicemen were dependent upon their husbands, but made spouses of females prove such dependency before receiving extra allowances. In *Craig v. Borden* (1976), the Court also struck down an Oklahoma law (designed to reduce highway fatalities) allowing 18-year-old females to purchase beer that contained 3.2 percent alcohol but preventing the sale of such beverages to males. In June, 1996, the Supreme Court announced in a seven to one ruling that the historic all-male Virginia Military Academy (VMI) would have to admit women applicants or become a private, rather than a state-supported, institution. As VMI contemplated its course before deciding to admit women, the Citadel in South Carolina, the only other state-supported all-male institution of its kind, announced that it would open its doors to women; it had previously accepted one woman under court order, but she had left during her first week.

The Court has also ruled both that direct sexual harassment and the creation of a hostile environment in the workplace may be prohibited by federal laws passed under authority of the Fourteenth Amendment. While striking down many sexual classifications as unreasonable, in *Rostker v. Goldberg* (1981) the Supreme Court upheld the decision by Congress to require that men, but not women, upon turning 18 years old register for the Selective Service System. Arguably, this would have changed had the proposed Equal Rights Amendment been adopted, but it fell three states short of the necessary number needed for ratification. Some believe that the Court's own liberal stance toward gender rights might have undercut some arguments for the urgency and necessity of the Equal Rights Amendment.

EQUAL PROTECTION AND OTHER CLASSIFICATIONS

Increasingly, the concept of equal protection has been applied to classifications based on such characteristics as age, wealth, alienage, legitimacy, mental or physical disability, and homosexuality. In some of these areas, the Supreme Court has taken at least halting steps, but, to date, none has received as intensive scrutiny as have racial and gender classifications.

In a number of cases, for example, the Court has struck down laws that appear to discriminate arbitrarily against those born out of wedlock. However, in *Michael H. v. Gerald D.* (1989), the Court upheld the presumption that a child born to a married couple resulted from that union, thus making it difficult for a third party to establish paternity.

Recognizing that classifications based on mental or physical disabilities are sometimes needed so as to extend care to such individuals, the Court has basically allowed law-makers to formulate protections in this area. Even applying its lowest level of scrutiny (the "rational basis" test), however, the Court did in *City of Cleburne, Texas v. Cleburne Living Center* (1985), strike down a city ordinance designed to prevent mentally retarded persons from living in group homes.

In a number of cases, the Court has struck down laws that deny benefits to poor persons, albeit not always on equal protection grounds. As discussed in an earlier chapter, in *Gideon v. Wainwright* (1963), the Court extended the right to appointed counsel to indigents; similarly, in *Griffin v. Illinois* (1956), the Court ruled that a state could not deny transcripts to indigents who needed them to file appeals. Relying chiefly on what it perceived to be interference with the right to travel, rather than on wealth per se, in *Shapiro v. Thompson* (1969), the Court invalidated a state's one year residency requirement for recipients of Aid to Families with Dependent Children, and in *Plyler v. Doe* (1982), the Court ruled that schools could not visit punishment on the children of illegal aliens by denying them education in the public schools. Ironically, almost a decade earlier, the Court had ruled in *San Antonio v. Rodriguez* (1973) that the equal protection clause did not mandate equal state funding of public schools. Although that decision had left in place a Texas system that relied heavily on local property taxes, the state courts later invalidated this system on the basis of its state constitution.

Most prohibitions against age discrimination have come from Congress rather than from the courts. Thus, in *Massachusetts Board of Retirement v. Murgia* (1976), the Court upheld a state law requiring uniformed police officers to retire at 50, and, in *Gregory v. Ashcroft* (1991), it upheld a Missouri law setting a retirement age of 70 for public employees.

More recently, in *Romer v. Evans* (1996), the Supreme Court invalidated a Colorado referendum that had adopted an amendment to the state's constitution (Amendment 2) striking down all local civil rights laws specifically designed to protect or promote the interests of homosexuals. Writing for a 6-3 majority of the Court, Justice Anthony Kennedy said that the law raised "the inevitable inference that the disadvantage imposed is born of animosity toward the class of persons affected." Citing the Court's earlier decision in *Bowers v. Hardwick* (1986) upholding laws against homosexual sodomy—treated in this book under discussions of the Ninth Amendment—Justice Antonin Scalia argued in dissent that, if states could adopt such laws, they could also prohibit special benefits on behalf of those engaged in such activities. He also denied that homosexuals suffered as a class from the same lack of influence as did other groups to whom the Court had extended special scrutiny. This debate could well continue in future cases.

EQUAL PROTECTION AND LEGISLATIVE APPORTIONMENT

In the twentieth century, the equal protection clause has taken a whole new meaning that might have surprised many of its early advocates. This clause has become the vehicle by which the federal courts have supervised both congressional and state legislative apportionment, eventually settling on the principle of "one person, one vote," a development that was slow in coming. As late as the 1940s, the Supreme Court declared that issues involving state legislative apportionment were political questions best left to the other branches of government. At the state level, of course, this proved something of a cruel dilemma, the branch alleged to be malapportioned, thus being the branch that would have to reform itself. Eventually, in *Baker v. Carr* (1962), the Supreme Court reversed its stance and declared apportionment a justiciable issue. In *Gray v. Sanders* (1963), the Supreme Court articulated the "one person, one vote" standard in invalidating Georgia's county unit system of deciding primary elections. The Court later applied this standard to congressional districts in *Wesberry v. Sanders* (1964) and to both houses of the state legislature in *Reynolds v. Sims* (1964) and subsequent cases. The Court has, however, recognized that some population variances are permissible. Generally, it has allowed greater deviations among state legislative districts, where it is often advisable to follow county lines and other historic divisions, than it has in drawing congressional district lines.

Some dissenters on the Court, as well as some historians of the Fourteenth Amendment who thought its interpretation should be limited to the original intent of its framers, cried foul at the "one person, one vote" standard. The Court majority had, however, found a way to remedy an evil that otherwise seemed insoluble, and despite attempts to reverse its decisions, they still stand. Indeed, some legal commentators, John Hart Ely among them, have argued that such decisions on behalf of representational responsiveness demonstrate the operation of the courts at their best (Ely, *Democracy and Distrust*).

Recent cases have underscored the manner in which even simple constitutional guidelines like "one person, one vote" can become complicated in their application. It is thus possible to continue the process of gerrymandering, or drawing districts so as to favor one party or group, even while assigning relatively equal populations to districts. Moreover, the Court has given increased attention to cases in which such gerrymandering, once used to discriminate against African Americans and other minorities, is now employed with the hope of creating districts in which such minorities can be elected. In 1995 and 1996, the Supreme Court voided oddly shaped districts in Georgia, North Carolina, and Texas that were configured so as to maximize representation for racial minorities. The Court appeared to stop short, however, of saying that race could never be used in drawing districts, and it will probably take a number of other decisions to clarify policy in this area.

Such controversies continue to show the potential of the brief words of Section 1 of the Fourteenth Amendment. Over time, at least, these words have literally brought about a revolution in American constitutional law.

Amendment XIV. Section 2. Representatives shall be apportioned among the several States according to their respective numbers, counting the whole number of persons in each State, excluding Indians not taxed. But when the right to vote at any election for the choice of electors for President and Vice President of the United States, Representatives in Congress, the Executive and Judicial officers of a State, or the members of the Legislature thereof, is denied to any of the male inhabitants of such State, being *twenty-one* years of age, and citizens of the United States, or in any way abridged, except for participation in rebellion, or other crime, the basis of representation therein shall be reduced in the proportion which the number of such *male* citizens shall bear to the whole number of male citizens 21 years of age in such State.

REVERSING THE THREE-FIFTHS CLAUSE

Section 2 of the Fourteenth Amendment reverses the three-fifths clause by providing that a state's votes will now be determined by counting "the whole number of persons in each State, excluding Indians not taxed." In short, no longer would blacks count for less than a whole person. This raised an immediate political problem. If states that formerly held slaves were now given increased votes, the consequences might be a gain in their own political power, a gain that might not only have weakened Republican congressional advantages, but that might well work against the goals the Civil War had been fought to win. It was even possible that their gain would come at the same time that they disenfranchised blacks. Section 2 of the Fourteenth Amendment was designed to assure that if such disenfranchisement occurred, at least in regard "to any of the male inhabitants of such State, being 21 years of age, and citizens of the United States," it would be at the cost of representation. Moreover, Section 2 of the Fourteenth Amendment proved to be a special disappointment for leaders of the movement for women's suffrage in that it provided the first recognition within the text of the Constitution that voting was regarded as a male prerogative. It is little wonder that in *Minor v. Happersett* (1875), the Court ruled that the Fourteenth Amendment did not prohibit discrimination against women at the polls—a decision not effectively overturned until adoption of the Nineteenth Amendment in 1920. The provision in Section 2 providing for reduced state representation proved difficult to enforce, and was soon followed by the Fifteenth Amendment.

Article XIV. Section 3. No person shall be a Senator or Representative in Congress, or elector of President and Vice President, or hold any office, civil or military, under the United States, or under any State, who, having previously taken an oath as a member of Congress, or as an officer of the United States, or as a member of any State legislature, or as an executive or judicial officer of any State, to support the Constitution of the United States, shall have engaged in insurrection or rebellion against the same, or given aid or comfort to the enemies thereof. But Congress may by a vote of two-thirds of each House, remove such disability.

RESTRICTIONS ON FORMER REBELS

While Section 2 addressed the voting power of the former confederate states, Section 3 addressed the eligibility of former congressmen and other civil and military personnel who had joined the Confederacy in insurrection against the United States. By the terms of this section, such persons, guilty of treason under the Constitution, were now barred from office absent a two-thirds vote of each house. In 1872, Congress voted by the required two-thirds majority to remove the restrictions on most southerners (Grimes, *Democracy and the Amendments to the Constitution*, p. 55).

Amendment XIV. Section 4. The validity of the public debt of the United States, authorized by law, including debts incurred for payment of pensions and bounties for services in suppressing insurrection or rebellion, shall not be questioned. But neither the United States nor any State shall assume or pay any debt or obligation incurred in aid of insurrection or rebellion against the United States, or any claim for the loss or emancipation of any slave; but all such debts, obligations and claims shall be held illegal and void.

VALID AND INVALID PUBLIC DEBTS

Section 4 addressed yet another issue, making it clear that the United States would be responsible for debts it had incurred during the war, but not for debts entered into by the Confederacy. This section further exempted the government from paying compensation for "the loss or emancipation of any slave," a reminder that such a remedy, like thoughts of transporting blacks back to Africa, had at one time been seriously contemplated as a way of ending this institution. Indeed, when Congress abolished slavery in the District of Columbia in 1862, prior to the ratification of the Thirteenth Amendment, it provided compensation for owners who were loyal to the Union (Urofsky, *A March of Liberty*, p. 419).

Amendment XIV. Section 5. The Congress shall have power to enforce, by appropriate legislation, the provisions of this article.

ENFORCEMENT OF THE FOURTEENTH AMENDMENT

Finally, the Fourteenth Amendment ends with a fifth section that gives Congress power—"by appropriate legislation"—to enforce its provisions. This section has been rediscovered in recent years. On occasion, the courts have recognized that Congress has wide latitude of action under this provision, a latitude that might even be broader than that of the Court acting alone. Thus, for example, in *Katzenbach v. Morgan* (1966) the Supreme Court accepted the congressional assertion of authority in the Voting Rights Act of 1965 to prohibit state-mandated literacy tests, even though their constitutionality had previously been upheld against equal protection challenges. In this case, Justice William Brennan likened the powers of Congress under Section 5 of the Fourteenth Amendment to its broad powers under the necessary and proper clause. Congressional powers under Section 5 may also help explain why the Supreme Court sometimes is more tolerant of federal affirmative action programs than it has been of programs enacted at the state or local level.

Amendment XV. [1870] Section 1. The right of citizens of the United States to vote shall not be denied or abridged by the United States or by any State on account of race, color, or previous condition of servitude.
    Section 2. The Congress shall have power to enforce this article by appropriate legislation.

THE FIFTEENTH AMENDMENT

The Thirteenth Amendment, then, provided the legal basis for the freedom of the slaves. The Fourteenth Amendment was designed to extend to these former slaves various legal and civil rights. In a democracy, however, the best form of help may well be self-help, for those who can vote will by this very fact have significant political power. This is the right embodied in the Fifteenth Amendment, which prohibits voting discrimination on the basis of race and again gives Congress appropriate remedial authority so to provide.

Even more than the provisions of the Fourteenth Amendment, the guarantees of the Fifteenth Amendment would lie dormant for nearly a century, victim of grandfather clauses, literacy tests (often applied quite unevenly to whites and blacks), poll taxes, all-white primaries, and even physical intimidation on the part of the Ku Klux Klan and other such organizations. Eventually, however, the words of the amendment would be used to strike down a number of these mechanisms (as in *Smith v. Allright*, 1944, voiding the all-white primary), and would be given renewed vigor by the Voting

Rights Act of 1965 and its various extensions. Today, at least, the amendment is no longer a hollow set of words, but a living guarantee that has brought dignity and power to those who were for so long held in bondage.

THE LESSON OF THE POST–WAR AMENDMENTS

Surveying the Civil War Amendments as a whole, they stand witness to the tremendous power inherent in the constitutional amending process. Court decisions can be overturned, rights extended, and whole new classes of persons brought within constitutional protection. In this respect, the Civil War Amendments have nearly been as important as the Bill of Rights. By the same token, it took many years for many of the guarantees in the post–Civil War Amendments to be realized; these amendments do much to demonstrate that interpretations of constitutional language can sometimes take strange twists and turns, as affected by the temper of the times as by the original language employed.

REFERENCES AND SUGGESTIONS FOR FURTHER STUDY

Cases

Baker v. Carr, 369 U.S. 186 (1962).
Bakke v. Regents of the University of California, 438 U.S. 265 (1976).
Bolling v. Sharpe, 347 U.S. 497 (1954).
Bowers v. Hardwick, 478 U.S. 186 (1986).
Bradwell v. Illinois, 83 U.S. 130 (1873).
Brown v. Board of Education, 347 U.S. 483 (1954).
City of Cleburne, Texas v. Cleburne Living Center, 473 U.S. 432 (1985).
City of Richmond v. J.A. Croson, 488 U.S. 469 (1989).
The Civil Rights Cases, 109 U.S. 3 (1883).
Craig v. Borden, 429 U.S. 190 (1976).
Dred Scott v. Sandford, 60 U.S. 393 (1857).
Frontiero v. Richardson, 411 U.S. 677 (1973).
Fullilove v. Klutznick, 448 U.S. 448 (1980).
Gideon v. Wainwright, 372 U.S. 335 (1963).
Gray v. Sanders, 372 U.S. 368 (1963).
Gregory v. Ashcroft, 111 S. Ct. 2395 (1991).
Griffin v. Illinois, 351 U.S. 12 (1956).
Katzenbach v. Morgan, 384 U.S. 641 (1966).

Massachusetts Board of Retirement v. Murgia, 427 U.S. 307 (1976).
Metro Broadcasting v. Federal Communications Commission, 497 U.S. 547 (1990).
Michael H. v. Gerald D., 491 U.S. 116 (1989).
Milliken v. Bradley, 418 U.S. 717 (1974).
Minor v. Happersett, 88 U.S. 161 (1875).
Moose Lodge No. 107 v. Irvis, 407 U.S. 163 (1972).
Plessy v. Ferguson, 163 U.S. 537 (1896).
Plyler v. Doe, 474 U.S. 202 (1982).
Reed v. Reed, 404 U.S. 71 (1971).
Reynolds v. Sims, 377 U.S. 533 (1964).
Romer v. Evans, 116 S. Ct. 1620 (1996).
Rostker v. Goldberg, 453 U.S. 57 (1981).
San Antonio v. Rodriguez, 411 U.S. 1 (1973).
Shapiro v. Thompson, 394 U.S. 618 (1969).
The Slaughterhouse Cases, 83 U.S. 36 (1873).
Smith v. Allright, 321 U.S. 649 (1944).
Swann v. Charlotte-Mecklenburg Board of Education, 402 U.S. 1 (1971).
Wesberry v. Sanders, 376 U.S. 1 (1964).

Books

Henry J. Abraham and Barbara A. Perry, *Freedom and the Court: Civil Rights and Liberties in the United States*, 6th ed. (New York: Oxford University Press, 1994).

Raoul Berger, *Government by Judiciary: The Transformation of the Fourteenth Amendment* (Cambridge, MA: Harvard University Press, 1977).

Daniel M. Berman, *It Is So Ordered: The Supreme Court Rules on School Segregation* (New York: W.W. Norton & Company, Inc., 1966).

Margorie A. Bingham, *Women and the Constitution: Student Textbook* (Atlanta, GA: The Carter Center of Emory University, 1990).

Taylor Branch, *Parting the Waters: America in the King Years, 1954–63* (New York: Simon and Schuster, 1988).

Richard C. Cortner, *The Supreme Court and the Second Bill of Rights: The Fourteenth Amendment and the Nationalization of Civil Liberties* (Madison: University of Wisconsin Press, 1981).

Ward E. Y. Elliott, *The Rise of Guardian Democracy: The Supreme Court's Role in Voting Rights Disputes, 1845–1969* (Cambridge, MA: Harvard University Press, 1974).

John Hart Ely, *Democracy and Distrust: A Theory of Judicial Review* (Cambridge, MA: Harvard University Press, 1980).

Don E. Fehrenbacher, *The Dred Scott Case: Its Significance in American Law and Politics* (New York: Oxford University Press, 1978).

Eric Foner, *Reconstruction: America's Unfinished Revolution, 1863–1877* (New York: Harper & Row, 1988).

John Hope Franklin and Alfred A. Moss, Jr., *From Slavery to Freedom*, 6th ed. (New York: A.A. Knopf, 1988).

Alan P. Grimes, *Democracy and the Amendments to the Constitution* (Lexington, MA: Lexington Books, 1978).

Robert J. Harris, *The Quest for Equality* (Baton Rouge: Louisiana University Press, 1960).

Harold M. Hyman, *A More Perfect Union: The Impact of the Civil War and Reconstruction on the Constitution* (Boston: Houghton Mifflin Company, 1975).

Donald W. Jackson, *Even the Children of Strangers: Equality Under the U.S. Constitution* (Lawrence: University Press of Kansas, 1992).

Harry V. Jaffa, *Crisis of the House Divided: An Interpretation of the Issues in the Lincoln–Douglas Debates* (Chicago: University of Chicago Press, 1982).

Joseph B. James, *The Ratification of the Fourteenth Amendment* (Macon, GA: Mercer University Press, 1984).

Richard Kluger, *Simple Justice*, 2 vols. (New York: Alfred A. Knopf, 1975).

Earl M. Malz, *Civil Rights, The Constitution, and Congress, 1863–1869* (Lawrence: University Press of Kansas, 1990).

James M. McPherson, *Abraham Lincoln and the Second American Revolution* (New York: Oxford University Press, 1991).

William E. Nelson, *The Fourteenth Amendment: From Political Principle to Judicial Doctrine* (Cambridge, MA: Harvard University Press, 1988).

David A.J. Richards, *Conscience and the Constitution: History, Theory, and Law of the Reconstruction Amendments* (Princeton, NJ: Princeton University Press, 1993).

Allan P. Sindler, *Bakke, DeFunis, and Minority Admissions: The Quest for Equal Opportunity* (New York: Longman, 1978).

Dorothy M. Stetson, *Women's Rights in the U.S.A.: Policy Debates and Gender Roles* (Pacific Grove, CA: Brooks/Cole Publishing Company, 1991).

Bernard Taper, *Gomillion v. Lightfoot* (New York: McGraw-Hill Book Company, Inc., 1962).

Melvin I. Urofsky, *A March of Liberty: A Constitutional History of the United States* (New York: Alfred A. Knopf, 1988).

J. Harvie Wilkinson III, *From Brown to Bakke* (New York: Oxford University Press, 1979).

Juan Williams, *Eyes on the Prize: America's Civil Rights Years, 1954–1965* (New York: Viking, 1967).

Garry Wills, *Lincoln at Gettysburg: The Words That Remade America* (New York: Simon & Schuster, 1992).

C. Vann Woodward, *The Strange Career of Jim Crow*, 3rd rev. ed. (New York: Oxford University Press, 1974).

John R. Wunder, *"Retained by the People:" A History of American Indians and the Bill of Rights* (New York: Oxford University Press, 1994).

Tinsley E. Yarbrough, *A Passion for Justice* (New York: Oxford University Press, 1987).

Chapter 11

The Progressive Era Amendments—
Amendments 16–19

The ratification of the Bill of Rights in a single year and of three amendments from 1865 through 1870 should be enough to indicate that amendments tend to be ratified in clusters, the majority necessary to propose and ratify one amendment often reflecting sentiment strong enough to initiate other such changes. It should not therefore be surprising to see that, after a 43 year hiatus during which some scholars began to despair about the possibility that any new amendments could be adopted (Vile, *The Constitutional Amending Process in American Political Thought*, chapter 8), amendments 16 through 19 were all adopted within the seven-year span from 1913 to 1920. This period roughly corresponds to the Progressive Era in American politics, an era dominated by reformers who sought to root out corruption, refine American politics, and make it more democratic. All four amendments reflect such sentiments, albeit not always in ways that would be familiar today.

Amendment XVI. [1913] The Congress shall have power to lay and collect taxes on incomes, from whatever source derived, without apportionment among the several States, and without regard to any census or enumeration.

THE SIXTEENTH AMENDMENT AND THE
NATIONAL INCOME TAX

The Sixteenth Amendment was designed to give constitutional authority for a national income tax. The original Constitution had provided in Article I, Section 9, that

No Capitation, or other direct, Tax shall be laid, unless in Proportion to the Census or Enumeration herein before directed to be taken.

On the basis of this elusive language that did not specifically define a "direct tax," the Supreme Court had, in *Pollock v. Farmer's Loan and Trust Company* (1895), declared that a tax on income was a direct tax and that, as a tax on such income rather than on a state's population, it was therefore void. The Sixteenth Amendment reversed this judgment, the third such amendment to overturn a Supreme Court decision.

There are at least two ties between this amendment and the Progressive Era. In the first place, it is practically impossible to use government as a positive force for change if that government has no stable and adequate source of revenue. Especially in times of war, when foreign commerce can be severely disrupted, an income tax provides such a steady source of income, allowing government to engage in activities of social improvement that it might not otherwise be able to carry out. Second, however, the income tax is, at least in theory, a fairer tax in that it can be adapted to income. One of the reasons the Supreme Court apparently struck down the income tax in 1895 was its fear that the tax would be used in socialistic fashion to redistribute income, taxing the rich at higher rates and funneling such money back to the poor in terms of governmental expenditures on social programs. While such a measure is not necessarily considered socialistic today, the progressive income tax—that is, a tax levied at a higher percentage for those with higher incomes—is often praised for its fairness and because it does not, like more regressive taxes often employed by state and local governments (sales and property taxes, for example) fall disproportionately on those who are sometimes least able to pay.

Amendment XVII. [1913] The Senate of the United States shall be composed of two Senators from each State, elected by the people thereof, for six years; and each Senator shall have one vote. The electors in each State shall have the qualifications requisite for electors of the most numerous branch of the State legislatures.

When vacancies happen in the representation of any State in the Senate, the executive authority of such State shall issue writs of election to fill such vacancies: *Provided,* That the legislature of any State may empower the executive thereof to make temporary appointments until the people fill the vacancies by election as the legislature may direct.

This amendment shall not be so construed as to affect the election or term of any Senator chosen before it becomes valid as part of the Constitution.

THE SEVENTEENTH AMENDMENT AND THE ELECTION OF U.S. SENATORS

Of all the institutions established in the U.S. Constitution, perhaps none was more designed to reflect the federal nature of the Union than the Senate. Each state was guaranteed equal representation (two senators) in that body and, under provisions of Article I, Section 2, senators were to be selected by the state legislatures, making it clear that they were in Washington to protect such state interests. However much this might have accorded with the idea of federalism, it also led to charges that the Senate had become a "millionaires' club" composed of wealthy people with inordinate influence in the states. Moreover, the system of indirect election was obviously not as democratic as direct election. A scholar has noted that the system of selecting senators was subject to such problems as deadlocks, bribery and corruption, stampeded elections, unfilled vacancies which denied states their equal representation, misrepresentation of the popular will, interference with regular state legislative business and the corruption of state politics (Haynes, *The Senate of the United States*, pp. 86–95).

The provision for congressional proposal of amendments shows its weaknesses in few places more than in cases of amendments designed to reform the Congress itself. How can two-thirds of the senators who have come to power under one electoral scheme be expected to propose a scheme under which they would now be required to be elected by popular vote? This was the dilemma facing those who thought the existing system was undemocratic and in need of reform. Many began to pursue the alternate route under Article V, whereby Congress would be obligated to call a convention if it received proposals from two-thirds of the states to this end. The pressure generated by such calls was largely responsible for propelling Congress to action, and the amendment was quickly ratified, applying, however, only to future elections. Whereas Article I, Section 2 had allowed the state executive to make temporary appointments that would then be filled by the legislature in cases of senatorial vacancies, the Seventeenth Amendment now provided that the state executive could make temporary appointments, if so empowered by the state legislature, until the legislature could provide for elections to fill such vacancies.

Few amendments have done more to democratize the Constitution and tie the legislative branch closer to the people. While thus furthering democracy, the amendment has also arguably made the Senate a less deliberative body (Hoebeke, *The Road to Mass Democracy*). The amendment is also occasionally criticized for undermining the link between the Senate and the federal system. It is certainly probable that senators now see themselves less as representatives of their states as institutions than as representatives of the people of their states. Such perceptions can obviously have both positive and negative consequences.

Amendment XVIII. [1919] Section 1. *After one year from the ratification of this article the manufacture, sale, or transportation of intoxicating liquors within, the importation thereof into, or the exportation thereof from the United States and all territory subject to the jurisdiction thereof for beverage purposes is hereby prohibited.*

Section 2. *The Congress and the several States shall have concurrent power to enforce this article by appropriate legislation.*

Section 3. *This article shall be inoperative unless it shall have been ratified as an amendment to the Constitution by the legislatures of the several States, as provided in the Constitution, within seven years from the date of the submission hereof to the States by the Congress.*

THE EIGHTEENTH AMENDMENT AND THE NATIONAL PROHIBITION OF ALCOHOL

If ever an amendment might seem less progressive to most modern ears, it is the Eighteenth Amendment, which provided for the prohibition of "the manufacture, sale or transportation . . . importation . . . or the exportation" of alcohol "for beverage purposes" throughout the United States. This provision was to be concurrently, that is, jointly, enforced by Congress and the states, with no provisions made for those who already owned or operated businesses devoted to such sales. Surely, few restrictions could be less libertarian and more intrusive upon personal liberty than this.

Many reformers in the Progressive Era obviously did not see things in this light. Encouraged by sacrifices already made during World War I on behalf of the war effort, many began to imagine the tremendous benefits that might be reaped if alcohol and the saloons that dispensed it could be eliminated once and for all. Their notion was not altogether different from modern opponents of illegal drugs who can justly point to the high social costs involved in such consumption. There may well have been more than a tinge of class bias among prohibitionists as well. Drawn disproportionately from white Anglo-Saxon Protestants with a moralistic heritage much less sympathetic to drinking than were other cultures, many progressives probably associated drinking with newly arrived Catholic immigrants from Ireland and southern European nations with whose cultures reformers had little sympathy or understanding.

Whatever the mix of moralistic and class-based motives, the dream of national reform through national prohibition proved illusory. The Eighteenth Amendment encountered increasing circumvention prior to its eventual abolition by the Twenty-First Amendment at the outset of Franklin Roosevelt's first administration in 1933 (the only amendment to have been ratified at congressional specification by special state conventions rather than by existing state legislatures, at the time more likely to be controlled by rural dry forces than conventions would be). An amendment designed as a reform actually stimulated organized crime, with many gangsters illegally gaining their fortunes by providing the alcohol that the Eighteenth Amendment had banned. A bit of the legacy of the Eighteenth Amendment remained even after its repeal, in that Section 2 of the Twenty-First Amendment still explicitly permitted individual states to regulate alcohol within their own jurisdictions, regulations that often lead to local option.

In the chapter on Article V, it was noted that the Constitution does not specify the length of time during which an amendment may be ratified. The Eighteenth Amendment was the first of several amendments designed to remedy this arguable defect, providing within its own text a provision that, to be valid, the amendment would have to be ratified within seven years of its submission to the states. As a provision within the text of the amendment itself, such a limit is presumably self-executing although, over time, they also appear unnecessarily to load down the Constitution with provisions lacking continuing relevance.

Amendment XIX. [1920] The right of citizens of the United States to vote shall not be denied or abridged by the United States or by any State on account of sex.

Congress shall have power to enforce this article by appropriate legislation.

THE NINETEENTH AMENDMENT AND WOMEN'S SUFFRAGE

The association between the Progressive Era and direct democracy is seldom more evident than in the Nineteenth Amendment—sometimes called the Susan B. Anthony Amendment after one of its earliest and most dedicated supporters. From the time of the Seneca Falls Convention in New York in 1848, women had petitioned for the right to vote, but it took almost 75 years before the Nineteenth Amendment was finally ratified. Prior to this time, of course, the U.S. Constitution did not specifically prohibit women from voting in national elections, but since such qualifications had been left to the states, many had chosen to limit such suffrage to males. A number of western states (Wyoming being the first) had chosen to extend this right to citizens regardless of gender, but such half-steps were obviously not enough for those who believed that voting was a necessary concomitant to effective citizenship and representation.

The proposal of voting rights for women was met by both derision and fear. In the face of arguments that voting was a privilege of citizenship, it was argued that women were already represented by their husbands and fathers, and that they were clearly designed by their Creator for domestic concerns, not for the rough and tumble of the political arena. Perhaps partly as a way of meeting such arguments, many progressive reformers accepted the assumption that women might vote differently from men. They attempted to argue that women would in fact help to refine the political process, freeing it from much of its corruption and bringing ethical issues to the fore. However influential this argument might have proven to be, and however much political scientists have since looked for a so-called "gender gap," women do not in practice appear to vote much differently than men. Certainly, however, the nation can be proud that the rights of women to participate in politics have been recognized in the Constitution, and that no individuals can now be disenfranchised simply on the basis of their gender.

REFERENCES AND SUGGESTIONS FOR FURTHER STUDY

Case

Pollock v. Farmers' Loan & Trust Company, 157 U.S. 429 (1895).

Books

Alan P. Grimes, *Democracy and the Amendments to the Constitution* (Lexington, MA: Lexington Books, 1978).

Richard H. Hamm, *Shaping the 18th Amendment: Temperance Reform, Legal Culture, and the Polity, 1880–1920* (Chapel Hill: The University of North Carolina Press, 1995).

George H. Haynes, *The Senate of the United States: Its History and Practice* (New York: Russell and Russell, 1960).

C.H. Hoebeke, *The Road to Mass Democracy: Original Intent and the Seventeenth Amendment* (New Brunswick: Transaction Publishers, 1995).

Richard Hofstader, *The Age of Reform: From Bryan to F.D.R.* (New York: Vintage Books, 1955).

Aileen S. Kraditor, *The Ideas of the Women's Suffrage Movement, 1890–1920* (New York: Columbia University Press, 1965).

David E. Kyvig, *Alcohol and Order: Perspectives on National Prohibition* (Westport, CT: Greenwood Press, 1985).

Charles Leedham, *Our Changing Constitution* (New York: Dodd, Mead & Company, 1964).

Arthur S. Link and Richard L. McCormick, *Progressivism* (Arlington Heights, IL: Harlan Davidson, Inc., 1983).

John R. Vile, *The Constitutional Amending Process in American Political Thought* (New York: Praeger, 1992).

Majorie S. Wheeler, ed., *One Woman, One Vote: Rediscovering the Woman Suffrage Movement* (Troutdale, OR: New Sage Press, 1995).

Majorie S. Wheeler, ed., *Votes for Women: The Woman Suffrage Movement in Tennessee, the South, and the Nation* (Knoxville: The University of Tennessee Press, 1995).

Robert Wiebe, *The Search for Order, 1877–1920* (New York: Hill and Wang, 1967).

Chapter 12

The Other Amendments— Amendments 20–27

Amendment XX. [1933] Section 1. The terms of the President and Vice President shall end at noon on the 20th day of January, and the terms of Senators and Representatives at noon on the 3d day of January, of the years in which such terms would have ended if this article had not been ratified; and the terms of their successors shall then begin.

Section 2. The Congress shall assemble at least once in every year, and such meeting shall begin at noon on the 3d day of January, unless they shall by law appoint a different day.

THE LAME-DUCK AMENDMENT

The Twentieth Amendment is often designated the lame-duck amendment because its central purpose was to shorten the time that so-called lame-duck presidents, vice presidents, and legislators would remain in office. A lame-duck representative is one who is still in office but has been defeated for re-election, and who could thus propose or pass legislation with no threat to his or her own electoral future. It was such lame-duck representatives, it will be recalled, who created the judicial seats that came to be contested in the case of *Marbury v. Madison* (1803), which established the principle of judicial review of national legislation.

Under a law enacted by the Articles of Confederation, the first Congress met on March fourth; prior to the adoption of the

Seventeenth Amendment, this enabled state legislatures, many of which met in January, to choose their senators. Because Article I, Section 4 of the Constitution specified that the annual meeting of Congress should begin on the first Monday in December, a new Congress did not come into session until 13 months after the November election.

Such extensive service after electoral defeat certainly undermines the entire notion of representation. Under the provisions of the Twentieth Amendment, new members of Congress now take office at noon on the third day of January, rather than in March. The president is now inaugurated on the twentieth day of January. The convening day for Congress in January replaces the date in December originally set under Article I.

Amendment XX. Section 3. If, at the time fixed for the beginning of the term of the President, the President elect shall have died, the Vice President elect shall become President. If a President shall not have been chosen before the time fixed for the beginning of his term, or if the President elect shall have failed to qualify, then the Vice President elect shall act as President until a President shall have qualified; and the Congress may by law provide for the case wherein neither a President elect nor a Vice President elect shall have qualified, declaring who shall then act as President, or the manner in which one who is to act shall be selected, and such person shall act accordingly until a President or Vice President shall have qualified.

Section 4. The Congress may by law provide for the case of the death of any of the persons from whom the House of Representatives may choose a President whenever the right of choice shall have devolved upon them, and for the case of the death of any of the persons from whom the Senate may choose a Vice President whenever the right of choice shall have devolved upon them.

Section 5. Sections 1 and 2 shall take effect on the 15th day of October following the ratification of this article.

Section 6. This article shall be inoperative unless it shall have been ratified as an amendment to the Constitution by the legislatures of three-fourths of the several States within seven years from the date of its submission.

PRESIDENTIAL VACANCIES

Section 3 of the Twentieth Amendment is designed to deal with cases in which a president-elect dies before inauguration or those in which a new president is not chosen before the newly set inauguration date. In both cases, the vice president-elect serves. Section 4 goes on to authorize congressional legislation to deal with cases where one of the presidential or vice presidential nominees dies before Congress breaks an electoral deadlock. Given that the last such deadlock Congress faced resulted from the election of 1824, it should not be surprising to find that it has not exercised its legislative powers under this provision.

Amendment XXI. [1933] Section 1. The eighteenth article of amendment to the Constitution of the United States is hereby repealed.

Section 2. The transportation or importation into any State, Territory, or possession of the United States for delivery or use therein of intoxicating liquors, in violation of the laws thereof, is hereby prohibited.

Section 3. This article shall be inoperative unless it shall have been ratified as an amendment to the Constitution by conventions in the several States, as provided in the Constitution, within seven years from the date of the submission hereof to the States by the Congress.

THE REPEAL OF NATIONAL ALCOHOLIC PROHIBITION

Little needs to be said here about the Twenty-First Amendment since it repealed national alcoholic prohibition as established in the Eighteenth Amendment. It should perhaps be noted that, while repealing the earlier amendment, the Twenty-First explicitly recognizes previously exercised state police powers to prohibit the "transportation or importation . . . or possession" of alcohol within its borders. Many states have, in turn, made the regulation of alcohol a local option permitting significant variations.

Amendment XXII. [1951] Section 1. No person shall be elected to the office of the President more than twice, and no person who has held the office of President, or acted as President, for more than two years of a term to which some other person was elected President shall be elected to the office of the President more than once. But this Article shall not apply to any person holding the office of President when this Article was proposed by the Congress, and shall not prevent any person who may be holding the office of President, or acting as President, during the term within which this Article becomes operative from holding the office of President or acting as President during the remainder of such term.

Section 2. This Article shall be inoperative unless it shall have been ratified as an amendment to the Constitution by the legislatures of three-fourths of the several States within seven years from the date of its submission to the States by the Congress.

A LIMIT ON PRESIDENTIAL TERMS OF OFFICE

Of all the amendments that have been adopted, few are more controversial than the Twenty-Second, which limits a president to serving two full terms, or, in the case of a vice president who comes to office during another's term, to no more than ten years. Ratified in 1951, this amendment was stimulated both by genuine fears of increased presidential powers and by partisan Republican frustrations over the repeated election of the Democrat Franklin D. Roosevelt. Prior to Roosevelt, presidents had followed the example of Washington, who had left office after two terms; this rule had been so well established that, by the 1920s, it could be rightly cited as an example of America's unwritten constitution. Roosevelt's terms called the continuing validity of such a custom into question.

It can certainly be argued that the two-term limit would have been better left as an unwritten practice, subject to change in cases of national emergency like World War II, than embodied into the written Constitution. It can indeed be further argued that the two-term limit is undemocratic, serving to limit the people's will. The most effective criticism raised, however, is that the Twenty-Second Amendment works in a fashion probably never intended; that is, to undercut a president's powers in his second term, where he is something of a lame duck whose influence is likely to decline as the end of his final term draws near.

Still, this is hardly the kind of issue likely to generate a groundswell of opinion, and, given the perception that the modern presidency is already something of an "imperial" power, the amendment still has many supporters. Certainly, short-term prospects for repeal of the Twenty-Second Amendment would not appear strong. The amendment does with the Eighteenth, however, show that constitutional changes can sometimes result in quite unintended consequences and is therefore something of a warning against precipitous constitutional change.

Amendment XXIII. [1961] Section 1. The District constituting the seat of Government of the United States shall appoint in such manner as the Congress may direct:

A number of electors of President and Vice President equal to the whole number of Senators and Representatives in Congress to which the District would be entitled if it were a State, but in no event more than the least populous State; they shall be in addition to those appointed by the States, but they shall be considered, for the purposes of the election of President and Vice President, to be electors appointed by a State; and they shall meet in the District and perform such duties as provided by the twelfth article of amendment.

Section 2. The Congress shall have power to enforce this article by appropriate legislation.

ELECTORAL VOTES FOR THE DISTRICT OF COLUMBIA

Few constitutional mechanisms are more complex than the electoral college by which the president and vice president are selected. The mechanism was, it may be recalled, amended by the Twelfth Amendment in the aftermath of an unexpected tie between the presidential and vice presidential nominees in the election of 1800. The Twenty-Third Amendment provides for an additional, albeit not nearly as far-reaching, change.

Prior to 1961, residents of the nation's capital, the District of Columbia, lacked any voice in the electoral college, which apportioned votes only to states, determining each state's vote by adding the number of their representatives and senators. As a district with neither, the nation's capital received no votes, a situation that seemed unfair for a nation where the president was intended to represent everyone. The Twenty-Third Amendment remedies this defect by giving the District a number of electoral votes to be no greater than that of the smallest state. Such states are already somewhat overrepresented in the electoral college, since every state is entitled to a minimum of one representative and two senators. Effectively, then, the District of Columbia has three electoral votes, these votes now counting the same as others. Currently, there are 538 electoral votes, resulting from the 435 representatives in the House of Representatives, 100 senators, and the District of Columbia's three votes. To win the presidency without going to the House of Representatives, a candidate needs a majority of votes, that is, 270 or more.

As discussed in the section of this book that deals with congressional powers under Article I, Section 8, to oversee the District of Columbia, the District still does not have voting representation in Congress. An amendment proposed by Congress in 1978 to grant the District representation equivalent to what it would have if it were a state was defeated.

Amendment XXIV. [1964] Section 1. The right of citizens of the United States to vote in any primary or other election for President or Vice President, for electors for President or Vice President, or for Senator or Representative in Congress, shall not be denied or abridged by the United States or by any State by reason of failure to pay any poll tax or other tax.

Section 2. The Congress shall have power to enforce this article by appropriate legislation.

THE PROHIBITION OF POLL TAXES

No topic has been a more frequent subject of amendment than the right to vote, a right expanded by the Seventeenth, Nineteenth, Twenty-Third, Twenty-Fourth, and Twenty-Sixth Amendments. The Twenty-Fourth Amendment is unique in that it is the only amendment specifically to extend both to primary and general elections for national offices—although the Supreme Court had already declared in *United States v. Classic* (1941) that primaries were so integral to the electoral process that they were limited by constitutional restrictions. The subject of the Twenty-Fourth Amendment is the poll tax, one of the mechanisms used in the past to keep the poor, among whom numbered a higher proportion of blacks, from voting. The Twenty-Fourth Amendment voids the use of such a tax in national elections; in *Harper v. Virginia Board of Elections* (1966), the Supreme Court subsequently voided the use of such poll taxes in state elections on the authority of the equal protection clause of the Fourteenth Amendment. The right to vote can now be exercised regardless of one's ability to pay for this privilege.

Amendment XXV. [1967] Section 1. In case of the removal of the President from office or of his death or resignation, the Vice President shall become President.

Section 2. Whenever there is a vacancy in the office of the Vice President, the President shall nominate a Vice President who shall take office upon confirmation by a majority vote of both Houses of Congress.

Section 3. Whenever the President transmits to the President pro tempore of the Senate and the Speaker of the House of Representatives his written declaration that he is unable to discharge the powers and duties of his office, and until he transmits to them a written declaration to the contrary, such powers and duties shall be discharged by the Vice President as Acting President.

Section 4. Whenever the Vice President and a majority of either the principal officers of the executive departments or of such other body as Congress may by law provide, transmit to the President pro tempore of the Senate and the Speaker of the House of Representatives their written declaration that the President is unable to discharge the powers and duties of his office, the Vice President shall immediately assume the powers and duties of the office as Acting President.

Thereafter, when the President transmits to the President pro tempore of the Senate and the Speaker of the House of Representatives his written declaration that no inability exists, he shall resume the powers and duties of his office unless the Vice President and a majority of either the principal officers of the executive department or of such other body as Congress may by law provide, transmit within four days to the President pro tempore of the Senate and the Speaker of the House of Representatives their written declaration that the President is unable to discharge the powers and duties of his office. Thereupon Congress shall decide the issue, assembling within forty-eight hours for that purpose if not in session. If the Congress, within twenty-one days after receipt of the latter written declaration, or, if Congress is not in session, within twenty-one days after Congress is required to assemble, determines by two-thirds vote of both Houses that the President is unable to discharge the powers and duties of his office, the Vice President shall continue to discharge the same as Acting President; otherwise, the President shall resume the powers and duties of his office.

VACANCIES AND DISABILITIES

The Twenty-Fifth Amendment, like the Twentieth, deals with the presidency and vice presidency, and the possibility of a death or disability in these offices. This problem has become more acute given America's important role in the modern world and its possession of nuclear weapons. In such circumstances, it is especially important to know who is in control and to be assured that such person is capable of adequately performing his duties. Several events in this country have brought the problem to attention. President Woodrow Wilson suffered a paralyzing stroke while in office, Franklin D. Roosevelt died, several presidents have survived unsuccessful attempts on their lives, Eisenhower had a heart attack while in office and Johnson had had one previously, and Kennedy was assassinated. When a vice president assumed the office of president, the vice president's office became vacant; had he died, the office would have gone to the Speaker of the House, who was not always fitted for such a responsibility.

Vacancies in the Vice Presidency

Section 2 of the Twenty-Fifth Amendment attempts a remedy by providing that vacancies in the vice presidency will be filled by the president supported by a majority vote of both Houses of Congress, a process somewhat different from the confirmation process for most other presidential appointments, which requires a majority vote of the Senate. Under provisions of the Twenty-Fifth Amendment, Gerald Ford was selected to replace Vice President Spiro Agnew, who resigned in the wake of charges that he had, as a state official, accepted bribes. When Nixon later resigned, Ford thus became the nation's first unelected president. President Ford in turn nominated Nelson Rockefeller to be his vice president, a choice again confirmed by Congress.

Cases of Presidential Disability

While such vacancies have proven relatively easy to fill, continuing questions exist about handling cases of presidential disability. Section 3 deals with the easiest scenario by providing that when the president submits a written statement to the president pro tempore of the Senate and the speaker of the House of Representatives informing them that "he is unable to discharge the powers and duties of his office," the vice president shall serve, until informed otherwise by the president, as "Acting President." It is not altogether clear, however, that this section gives the vice president much more power than he already had without it.

The really difficult issue is what to do about a disabled president who refuses to acknowledge his condition. This is the problem addressed in Section 4. This section provides that a vice president shall assume presidential duties when, acting in conjunction with a majority of the president's cabinet or "of such other body as Congress may by law provide," he and this designated body shall transmit to the congressional leaders

their written declaration that the President is unable to discharge the powers and duties of his office.

However, what happens if the president contests this finding? Here the Twenty-Fifth Amendment has probably done about as well as human words can do in providing for the unpredictable, but the mechanism established is hardly fail-safe. It provides that the president is to resume his powers when he informs congressional officers that he is no longer disabled. If the vice president and a majority of cabinet or other officers contest this assertion in writing within four days, however, the Congress is left with the decision, assembling within 48 hours for this purpose and voting within 21 days. Absent a two-thirds vote by both houses that the president is unable to discharge his duties, he resumes his powers. It is not altogether clear who would be president in the interim.

Amendment XXVI. [1971] Section 1. The right of citizens of the United States, who are eighteen years of age or older, to vote shall not be denied or abridged by the United States or by any State on account of age.

Section 2. The Congress shall have power to enforce this article by appropriate legislation.

EIGHTEEN-YEAR-OLDS AND THE RIGHT TO VOTE

This amendment was added to the Constitution more than 20 years ago. Like many others before it, this amendment widened the right to vote, this time extending the franchise to all who were eighteen years or older. As in the case of women and the vote, the Constitution had not actually prohibited those between eighteen and twenty-one from voting (see, however, the language of Section 2 of the Fourteenth Amendment), but had left the matter to state discretion where most states had so stipulated. An attempt to extend the franchise to eighteen-year-olds by legislation was struck down by the Supreme Court in *Oregon v. Mitchell* (1970), congressional power being recognized in the case of federal but not state elections. The Twenty-Sixth Amendment was quickly ratified to eliminate this disparity.

A number of factors motivated the extension of the franchise to eighteen-year-olds. Most prominent was the view that such persons were better educated than ever before and thus better able to participate in the political process. Moreover, at the time the amendment was ratified, many young people were risking their lives in Vietnam—as they had done in previous wars—on behalf of their country. It seemed ironic to argue that eighteen-year-olds were old enough to die for their country and yet not old enough to participate in its political processes.

If there is any irony in the amendment, it is that, as a group, eighteen- to twenty-one-year-olds are among the least likely to vote. The fact that so many choose not to do so does not, of course, mean that none should have been given this right, but it does again suggest that the results of amendments are not always predictable beforehand. At least as long as eighteen remains the age at which most people graduate from high school, the voting age is unlikely to be raised or lowered by further amendments.

Amendment XXVII [1992]. No law, varying the compensation for the services of the Senators and Representatives, shall take effect, until an election of Representatives shall have intervened.

A TWENTY-SEVENTH AMENDMENT?

One of the more bizarre developments in American constitutional history occurred in 1992 with the putative ratification of an amendment designed to prevent a sitting Congress from raising its salaries, thus addressing a problem that has surfaced periodically throughout American history. What made the ratification so problematic, however, was the fact that the amendment ratified was identical to that listed in 1789 by James Madison as one of twelve proposals, ten of which became the Bill of Rights. Originally ratified by six of the eleven states required, the amendment was ratified by a seventh state in 1873 and an eighth in 1978. Gregory Watson, a student majoring in economics and taking a political science class at the University of Texas at Austin, rediscovered the amendment when writing a term paper and, as an aide to a Texas legislator, subsequently led a movement, largely financed out of his own pocket, to get the requisite state ratifications.

Watson's timing was nearly perfect. Not only had there been opposition to recent congressional pay raises, but Congress's reputation was suffering from a number of other scandals, which led many to believe that its members were no longer adequately representing the wishes of their constituents. The result was that on May 8, 1992, the last state necessary for a three-fourths majority ratified the amendment, which was subsequently certified by the National Archivist.

Is the amendment valid? At this point, it is difficult to say with certainty. On the negative side, ratifications spread out over a two-hundred-year period stretch the idea, articulated in *Dillon v. Gloss* (1921), that an amendment should reflect a contemporary consensus to its limit. On the positive side, the question of assessing such contemporaneousness has been left in *Coleman v. Miller* (1939) to Congress, and it accepted the amendment by an overwhelming vote on May 20, 1992. If the amendment remains in the Constitution without being successfully challenged in the courts in the near future, it may well be accepted, whatever perceived irregularities are present in its ratification. Whether it remains so or not, the amendment has probably sent an unmistakable message to Congress, which is unlikely to try again to vote a raise for itself (albeit not necessarily for future congresses) whether the amendment remains on the books or not.

POSTSCRIPT ON THE AMERICAN FUTURE

The author indicated in the Preface to this book that he considers the U.S. Constitution much as he does a close companion. It is indeed difficult to study the Constitution and its subsequent amendments without developing great admiration and empathy for those who have written and interpreted it. Reminders that the Constitution and the government it created are not perfect should perhaps always be balanced both by the acknowledgement that no governments involving the rule of human beings by other human beings can ever be so, and by the recognition that the U.S. government has come reasonably close to providing protection for the rights mentioned in the Declaration of Independence and for securing many of the goals stated in the Constitution's preamble.

The great beauty of a government that depends upon the people and of a Constitution that provides mechanisms for participation and even for its own amendment is the challenge to detractors not to tear down, but to join in bettering the polity or even the fundamental law itself. Viewed thusly, the Founding Fathers initiated a colloquy about the purposes and structures of government that has continued for the last two hundred years. Given a continuing dedication to civil responsibilities and respect for the rule of law, the American system of government may well last for two hundred more.

REFERENCES AND SUGGESTIONS FOR FURTHER STUDY

Cases

Coleman v. Miller, 307 U.S. 433 (1939).
Dillon v. Gloss, 256 U.S. 368 (1921).
Harper v. Virginia State Board of Elections, 383 U.S. 663 (1966).
Marbury v. Madison, 5 U.S. 137 (1803).
Oregon v. Mitchell, 400 U.S. 112 (1970).
United States v. Classic, 313 U.S. 299 (1941).

Books

Herbert Abrams, *The President Has Been Shot: Confusion, Disability and the 25th Amendment in the Aftermath of the Attempted Assassination of Ronald Reagan* (New York: W.W. Norton, 1992).

John D. Feerick, *The Twenty-Fifth Amendment: Its Complete History and Earliest Applications* (New York: Fordham University Press, 1976).

Alan P. Grimes, *Democracy and the Amendments to the Constitution* (Lexington, MA: Lexington Books, 1978).

David E. Kyvig, *Repealing National Prohibition* (Chicago: University of Chicago Press, 1979).

Steven F. Lawson, *Black Ballots: Voting Rights in the South, 1944–1969* (New York: Columbia University Press, 1976).

Frederic Ogden, *The Poll Tax in the South* (Tuscaloosa: University of Alabama Press, 1958).

Ratification of the Twenty-First Amendment to the Constitution of the United States: State Convention Records and Laws, compiled by Everett Somerville Brown (Ann Arbor: University of Michigan Press, 1938).

Ronald Reagan, et al., *Restoring the Presidency: Reconsidering the Twenty-Second Amendment* (Washington, DC: National Legal Center for the Public Interest, 1990).

Earl Spangler, *Presidential Tenure and Constitutional Limitation* (Washington, DC: University Press of America, Inc., 1979).

The Twenty-Fifth Amendment: Preparing for Presidential Disability. Special issue of the Wake Forest Law Review, Fall 1995.

Fifty Leading Cases

One difficulty in studying the Constitution is that most disputed issues are ultimately resolved by the Supreme Court. As a consequence, even a book like this, which tries to keep a general reader in mind, can cite literally hundreds of case names that can overwhelm a reader. Below the author has listed and described the verdicts in fifty cases—all cited in this text—that he thinks are the most important for students to learn.

Abington v. Schempp (1963): Followed up on *Engel v. Vitale* (1962) by deciding that the establishment clause of the First Amendment outlawed public readings from the Bible and recitations of the Lord's Prayer in public school classrooms.

Baker v. Carr (1962): Established that the issue of legislative apportionment would no longer be considered a "political question" but could be adjudicated in courts.

Barron v. Baltimore (1833): Ruled that the Bill of Rights applied only to the national government and not to the states. This decision has been subsequently modified by decisions that have been rendered after the adoption of the Fourteenth Amendment.

Bowers v. Hardwick (1954): Ruled that a state could adopt and enforce laws prohibiting homosexual sodomy.

Brown v. Board of Education (1954): Overturned the doctrine of "separate but equal" that had been established in *Plessy v. Ferguson*

(1896) and decided that such racial discrimination would now be considered inherently unequal.

Chisholm v. Georgia (1793): Decided that a state could be sued by citizens of other states. This case was subsequently overturned by the Eleventh Amendment.

Civil Rights Cases (1883): In overturning the Civil Rights Act of 1875, the Court ruled that the Fourteenth Amendment outlawed only discriminatory state action and not discriminatory private action.

Cooley v. Board of Wardens (1851): Established the doctrine of "selective exclusiveness" according to which it was recognized that some areas of commerce require a single uniform national rule and others permit state and local variations.

Dred Scott v. Sandford (1857): Declared that African Americans were not, and could not be, American citizens. This case, which also invalidated the Missouri Compromise of 1820, helped serve as a catalyst to the Civil War and was overturned by the Fourteenth Amendment.

Engel v. Vitale (1962): On the basis of the establishment clause of the First Amendment, this decision outlawed the public recitation of a nonsectarian prayer composed by the New York State Board of Regents for public schools.

Frontiero v. Richardson (1973): Struck down a military regulation whereby families of male members of the military were assumed to be dependent upon them (thus making the serviceman eligible for an extra allowance) whereas females were required to prove dependency by their family members.

Furman v. Georgia (1972): Struck down state capital punishment laws on the basis that, as then administered, such laws were in violation of the cruel and unusual punishment provision of the Fourteenth Amendment.

Gibbons v. Ogden (1824): Overturned a monopoly granted to steamboats by the state of New York on the basis that this monopoly interfered with piloting licenses granted to pilots of other ships by the national government.

Gideon v. Wainwright (1963): Extended the Sixth Amendment's right to appointed counsel to indigents in all felony cases.

Gitlow v. New York (1925): In upholding a conviction of a Socialist who had distributed incendiary literature, the Supreme Court used the "dangerous tendency" test rather than Holmes's "clear and present danger" standard. However, Justice Edward

Sanford did acknowledge that First Amendment protections of speech and press were protected by the Fourteenth Amendment, thus helping to launch the movement for incorporation of other such guarantees in the Bill of Rights into the Fourteenth Amendment where they would restrain the states.

Gregg v. Georgia (1976): Upheld, as constitutional, new state capital punishment laws. Such laws provided for separate trials to determine guilt or innocence and settle on a penalty as well as for the consideration of aggravating and mitigating circumstances.

Griswold v. Connecticut (1965): In striking down a Connecticut law prohibiting the use or prescription of birth control devices, the Court formulated a broad right to privacy that subsequently served as a basis for the rulings on abortion in *Roe v. Wade* (1973) and subsequent cases.

Home Building and Loan Association v. Blaisdell (1934): In upholding the Minnesota Mortgage Moratorium Law, the Court indicated that it would give a much more liberal reading to the contract clause than the Court had given in the nineteenth century.

Katz v. United States (1967): Effectively overturned *Olmstead v. United States* (1928) by declaring that police would be required to get search warrants before engaging in electronic surveillance.

Korematsu v. United States (1944): Sanctioned the exclusion of Japanese Americans from areas in California where they were thought to pose a military threat. In this case, however, Justice Hugo Black said that any classifications based on race were "immediately suspect" and would be subject to increased scrutiny.

Lemon v. Kurtzman (1971): Established a three-part test, known as the Lemon Test, by which courts can ascertain whether laws infringe on the establishment clause of the First Amendment. The test requires that legislation have a secular legislative purpose, that its primary effect neither advances nor inhibits religion, and that it avoids excessive entanglement with religion.

Lochner v. New York (1905): A case, often cited as the epitome of the kind of laissez-faire jurisprudence typical of the Court before 1937, in which the Court struck down a New York law designed to regulate the working hours of bakers.

Marbury v. Madison (1803): In turning away a request by an individual who had been appointed as a justice of the peace but had never received his commission, the Court ruled that a section of the Judiciary Act of 1789 that seemed to grant the Court original jurisdiction was unconstitutional and therefore void, therefore asserting the Court's power of judicial review.

McCulloch v. Maryland (1819): Ruled that Congress had the implied power to establish a national bank and that the state of Maryland had no authority to tax it.

Miller v. California (1973): Established a three-part test for identifying obscenity that, with minor modifications, is still in effect today. The standard is based on local community standards.

Miranda v. Arizona (1966): In invalidating the conviction of Ernesto Miranda for kidnapping and rape, the Court established a set of guidelines that police officers must follow and a set of warnings they should give when interrogating criminal suspects.

Myers v. United States (1926): Established the president's sole right to fire executive officers that he had appointed with the advice and consent of the Senate.

New York Times Co. v. Sullivan (1964): Established "actual malice" as the standard that the Court would apply in adjudicating cases in which public figures allege that they are victims of libel.

New York Times Company v. United States (1971): The so-called "Pentagon Papers" Case in which the Court reaffirmed the strong presumption against prior restraint and permitted publication of papers relative to the history of United States involvement in Vietnam.

Palko v. Connecticut (1937): In deciding that the double jeopardy provision did not apply to the states—a decision later overturned in *Benton v. Maryland* (1969)—Justice Benjamin Cardozo forcefully articulated the doctrine of selective incorporation whereby only those rights considered to be fundamental were applied to the states via the due process clause of the Fourteenth Amendment.

Plessy v. Ferguson (1896): Upheld state Jim Crow laws by establishing the doctrine of "separate but equal," a doctrine not overturned until the decision in *Brown v. Board of Education* (1954).

Pollock v. Farmers' Loan & Trust Co. (1895): Invalidated the income tax as unconstitutional; the decision was overturned by ratification of the Sixteenth Amendment.

Reed v. Reed (1971): Used the equal protection clause of the Fourteenth Amendment to overturn a state law that automatically preferred males to females as administrators of an estate.

Reynolds v. Sims (1964): Applied the principle of "one person, one vote" to both houses of state legislatures.

Roe v. Wade (1973): Held that the right to privacy encompassed a woman's right to procure an abortion in the first and second trimester of pregnancy and in cases in the third trimester where her life or health was at stake.

Romer v. Evans (1996): Overturned a Colorado amendment, which had been adopted by popular referendum, that outlawed all local laws designed to extend special benefits or protections to homosexuals. The relation of this case to *Bowers v. Hardwick* (1986) has yet to be established.

Schenck v. United States (1919): In upholding the conviction of a Socialist who had mailed pamphlets to potential draftees encouraging them to avoid the draft, Justice Holmes articulated the "clear and present danger" test designed to give broad protection to speech while indicating that it was not unlimited.

The Slaughterhouse Cases (1873): In rejecting the pleas of New Orleans' butchers who were required under state law to pursue their calling in specified abattoirs, the Court gave a very narrow reading to the privileges and immunities clause of the Fourteenth Amendment.

Swann v. Charlotte-Mecklenburg Board of Education (1970): Upheld the limited use of mandatory school busing as a means of dealing with prior *de jure* segregation.

Texas v. Johnson (1989): In a decision later reaffirmed in *United States v. Eichman* (1990), the Court ruled that a Texas law prohibiting flag desecration was an unconstitutional infringement of the First Amendment freedom of speech.

Tinker v. Des Moines Independent County School District (1969): Established the right of public school students to engage in nonviolent symbolic speech, in this case, the wearing of black arm bands in protest of the war in Vietnam.

United States v. Carolene Products Company (1939): The occasion for Justice Harlan Fiske Stone's famous footnote number four where he suggested that certain subjects within the Constitution—most notably the first ten amendments, provisions providing for keeping the democratic processes open, and those involving the rights of minorities—would be subject to more exacting judicial scrutiny than others.

United States v. Curtiss-Wright Export Corp. (1936): In upholding a presidentially declared boycott of goods to a warring area of South America, the Supreme Court said that the president has especially broad powers in the area of foreign affairs.

United States v. Lopez (1995): Overturned a federal law prohibiting guns near school grounds on the basis that such power was not directly related to congressional powers under the commerce clause.

United States v. Nixon (1974): Established that a president's executive privilege was limited and that President Nixon would have to turn over select Washington tapes to the Watergate Special Prosecutor.

U.S. Term Limits v. Thornton (1995): Decided that the qualifications listed for members in the Constitution were exclusive and that states could not add to this requirement by imposing their own term limits.

Wesberry v. Sanders (1964): Formulated the "one person, one vote" standard in invalidating Georgia's apportionment of its congressional districts.

West Coast Hotel v. Parrish (1937): In upholding a Washington State minimum wage law, the Court overturned an earlier decision in *Adkins v. Childrens' Hospital* (1923) and instituted the "switch in time that saved nine," by deflecting criticism that had led to Franklin D. Roosevelt's court-packing plan. From this case forward, the Court has generally given less attention to governmental regulations of economic matters than to other issues.

West Virginia State Board of Education v. Barnette (1943): Overturned the earlier decision in *Minersville School District v. Gobitis* (1940) and said that public school students with religious objections could not be disciplined for refusing to salute the American flag.

Youngstown Sheet & Tube Co. v. Sawyer (1952): A case, often simply called the Steel Seizure Case, in which the court ruled that President Truman did not have inherent authority as commander in chief to seize the American steel industry in order to avert a strike that threatened supplies needed to pursue the conflict then being waged in Korea.

Glossary

Actual Malice: A standard applied by courts in cases where public officials are suing for libel. This standard specifies that they must show either that such statements were published with knowledge that they were false or with reckless disregard of their truth or falsity.

Actual Representation: The position advocated by the American colonists in their dispute with Britain whereby they argued that they could not be taxed by the British Parliament unless they actually had representatives sitting in that body.

Advice and Consent: The power of the Senate to approve or disapprove treaties signed by the president and/or nominees that he has nominated for office.

Advisory Opinions: Nonbinding court decisions which, by long-standing practice, U.S. courts will not issue.

Affirmative Action Programs: The name given to a variety of programs designed to increase minority representation that may or may not include racial preferences or quotas.

Alien and Sedition Acts: Laws adopted by the Federalist Congress in 1798. The former made it more difficult for aliens to establish citizenship, and the latter made it a criminal offense to criticize the government or its officials. The laws were directed toward, and strongly opposed by, the Democratic-Republicans.

Amicus Curiae Briefs: "Friend of the court" briefs filed by groups or individuals who are not party to a suit but who want to call their legal views to the court's attention.

Annapolis Convention: The meeting attended by representatives of five states that preceded the Constitutional Convention of 1787. Called originally to discuss the problems of commerce and navigation under the Articles, the Annapolis Convention served as a springboard for the Constitutional Convention that followed.

Antifederalists: Opponents of the Constitution of 1787. Antifederalist opposition to the document is generally credited with exerting pressure on Federalist supporters of the Constitution to agree to the adoption of a bill of rights.

Appellate Jurisdiction: Refers to cases heard "on appeal," usually over issues of law rather than fact.

Articles of Confederation: The loose confederation of states, or league of friendship, in effect from 1781 to 1789. Under the Articles, the primary powers of government rested with individual states.

Bad Tendency Test: A test for freedom of speech, utilized both before and after development of the clear and present danger test, that allows governments to suppress speech judged to present a dangerous tendency.

Bail: Money that defendants in a criminal trial put up as a condition for release from custody while awaiting a trial. The Eighth Amendment prohibits such bail from being "excessive."

Bicameralism: Provides for the division of the legislative branch into two houses or chambers.

Bill of Rights: The first ten amendments to the U.S. Constitution that provide for the protection of basic civil rights and liberties.

Bills of Attainder: Legislative punishments inflicted without the benefit of a trial. Such bills are outlawed by Article I, Section 9 of the Constitution.

Blue Laws: Laws requiring the closure of certain businesses or forbidding the sale of certain items on Sundays.

Cabinet: The heads of the executive agencies and other individuals the president may choose to consult about governmental policies.

Checks and Balances: A governmental system like that created by the U.S. Constitution in which differing individuals and institutions exercise different powers, thus serving to prevent any single individual or institution from abusing its powers.

Chief Justice: The head of the U.S. Supreme Court. Regarded as *primus inter pares*, or first among equals, the chief is designated by the Constitution to preside over trials of impeachment of the president in the Senate.

Circuit Courts of Appeal: Thirteen courts in the federal system that are midway between the District Courts and the U.S. Supreme Court. Such circuit courts deal mostly with cases on appeal.

Citizenship: An acknowledgment of membership in a nation. The Fourteenth Amendment provides that persons born in the United States or naturalized are citizens. Congress is granted the power of naturalization in Article I, Section 8.

Clear and Present Danger Test: A test applied to laws regulating freedom of speech devised by Justice Oliver Wendell Holmes, Jr. in *Schenck v. United States* (1919) and designed to indicate that speech is highly protected but not absolute. Under this test governments can legitimately suppress speech that poses a "clear and present danger" that such governments have a right to prevent.

Commander-in-Chief: The title designating the president's power over the U.S. armed forces. Vesting this power in the presidency assures civilian control over the military.

Commerce Clause: The provision in Article I, Section 8 granting Congress power to regulate commerce "with foreign Nations, and among the several States, and with the Indian tribes." This has proved to be one of Congress' most expansive powers. The Congress under the Articles of Confederation did not have this authority.

Common Sense: A work published in January 1776, in which Thomas Paine argued against monarchy and hereditary succession and argued that the time had come for the colonists to declare their independence.

Concurrent Jurisdiction: Authority over an area or subject that is shared by more than one court or law enforcement agency.

Concurrent Powers: Powers, like taxation and spending, that are jointly exercised by both the state and national governments.

Concurring Opinion: A judicial decision in which one or more justices agree with the decision but write separately to give their own explanations and/or express their reservations.

Confederal Government: A government, like that under the Articles of Confederation or the Confederate States of America, under which the constituent state governments hold primary power.

Connecticut Compromise: The Compromise adopted at the Constitutional Convention of 1787 whereby Congress would be a bicameral body in which states were represented according to population in the House of Representatives and equally in the Senate.

Constitutional Convention of 1787: The meeting held in Philadelphia from May through September. Ostensibly called to revise the Articles of Confederation, the Convention decided instead to redraw the government.

Constitutional Conventions: Article V of the Constitution specifies that Congress is obligated to call a convention to propose amendments when requested to do so by two-thirds of the states. To date, no such Article V conventions have been called, and questions remain as to how they would operate.

Constitutional Courts: American courts created under the authority of Article III and subject to various protections specified therein.

Continental Congresses: Meetings of American colonial representatives that were called to discuss grievances and formulate strategy against the British. The First Continental Congress met in 1774. The Second Continental Congress, which began meeting in 1775, approved the Declaration of Independence.

Contract Clause: The provision in Article I, Section 10 that prohibits states from passing laws "impairing the obligations of Contracts."

Council of Revision: A prominent provision of the Virginia Plan that would have allowed the executive and members of the judiciary to veto acts of state and national legislation.

Court-Packing Plan: After the Supreme Court voided many of his New Deal programs, Franklin Roosevelt proposed adding one justice (up to 15) for every justice over age 70. Congress rejected this plan which, while not illegal, appeared to threaten the independence of the judiciary.

Cruel and Unusual Punishments: Unspecified penalties prohibited by the Eighth Amendment.

Death-Qualified Jury: A jury from which opponents to the death penalty have been dismissed.

Declaration of Independence: The document, written largely by Thomas Jefferson and adopted by the Second Continental Congress in 1776, declaring the reasons for the colonists' decision to declare their independence from Great Britain.

de Facto: Caused by forces other than the law.

de Jure: Mandated by law.

Dickinson, John: The Pennsylvania delegate who drew up the initial Articles of Confederation, a document subsequently modified to vest greater power in the states.

Direct Taxes: Unidentified taxes, prohibited from being laid by Article I, Section 9 except according to a state's population. The prohibition against direct taxes has been superseded by the legalization of the income tax in the Sixteenth Amendment.

Dissenting Opinion: An opinion written by a justice who does not agree with the majority opinion of the court.

District Courts: The lowest rung of the U.S. federal court system, of which there are currently 94. Such courts are largely courts of original jurisdiction, hearing cases in the first instance.

District of Columbia: The area called Washington, DC, which is designated as the nation's capital. Under the Constitution, Congress legislates for this area which has been given votes in the electoral college but whose citizens still have no voting members in the Congress.

Double Jeopardy: Trying an individual for a crime of which that individual has already been declared not guilty. Such double jeopardy is disallowed by the Fifth Amendment.

Dual Federalism: A view of governmental relations, prevalent prior to the New Deal, in which both state and federal authorities were thought to have distinct spheres of authority.

Due Process Clauses: Provisions found in the Fifth and Fourteenth Amendments prohibiting the government from taking a person's life, liberty, or property without due process of law. The later provision has been the primary vehicle by which the guarantees in the Bill of Rights have been applied by judicial decisions to the states.

During Good Behavior: A constitutional phrase indicating that federal judges serve until they die or resign, or until they are impeached, convicted, and removed from office.

Elastic Clause: The last sentence of Article I, Section 8, granting Congress all powers "necessary and proper" for carrying out its delegated powers. The clause has since been the primary basis for the doctrine of implied powers.

Electoral College: The indirect system used in the United States to select the president and vice president. This system has been modified by the Twelfth Amendment.

Emancipation Proclamation: A presidential order issued by Abraham Lincoln on January 1, 1863 declaring freedom for slaves held behind Confederate lines. Adopted as a war measure, the proclamation was later expanded with the Thirteenth Amendment's complete abolition of slavery.

Eminent Domain: The power of governments to demand the sale of private property needed for public use. The Fifth Amendment requires that the government provide just compensation in the case of such takings.

Emoluments: A constitutional term used to refer to salaries or other monetary rewards.

Enumerated Powers: Powers listed in the Constitution. The powers of Congress are chiefly granted, or enumerated, in Article I, Section 8.

Entrenchment Clauses: Two provisions listed in Article V of the Constitution limit the scope of amendments. One such provision, dealing with slave importation, has expired; the other provides that no state may be deprived of its equal representation in the Senate without its consent. Questions have been raised as to whether there are any additional implicit limits on the amending process.

Equal Protection Clause: A provision found within the Fourteenth Amendment requiring that state governments extend equal treatment to all persons.

Equal Rights Amendment: An amendment proposed by Congress to eliminate discrimination based on sex; the amendment fell three states shy of ratification.

Establishment Clause: The provision in the First Amendment prohibiting government from making laws "respecting an establishment of religion."

Exclusionary Rule: A judge-made rule, applied first to the national government and subsequently to the states, prohibiting the introduction in court of illegally obtained evidence. The rule has been defended both as a means of deterring illegal police conduct and as a mechanism to keep governmental hands clean of wrongdoing; it has been criticized for allowing some criminals to go free.

Executive Agreements: Agreements made between the president and foreign governments that are not, like treaties, submitted to the Senate for approval. Most such agreements cover relatively minor matters.

Executive Branch: The branch of government headed by the president and responsible for executing, that is, enforcing, the laws. The American president is a single individual who serves as both head of government and head of state.

Executive Privilege: The asserted right of a president to withhold documents relating to or to refuse to testify about matters considered to be confidential. In *United States v. Nixon* (1974), the Supreme Court recognized that such a claim was subject to limits.

Ex Post Facto Laws: Retroactive criminal laws, which are forbidden in Article I, Section 9 of the Constitution.

Extradition: The process by which states return a fugitive back to the state from which such a fugitive fled in order that such an individual may be tried for crimes committed or alleged to have been committed there. The provision for extradition is found in Article IV, Section 2 of the Constitution.

Federal Government: A governmental system in which power is divided between state and national authorities. In such systems, powers are almost always delineated by a written constitution, and both state and national governments have powers—as, for example, through taxation—to operate directly upon individual citizens.

Federalist Papers: A series of 85 articles published in New York newspapers in defense of the Constitution. Written under the pen name of Publius, its authors were Alexander Hamilton, James Madison, and John Jay. The most famous of the *Federalist Papers* is No. 10 in which James Madison praised republican government as a cure for the mischief of factions.

Federalists: The name of those who supported ratification of the U.S. Constitution. This name was also later used to designate the political party founded by Alexander Hamilton that favored strong national powers.

Fighting Words: Highly emotional and inflammatory words expressed in a face-to-face setting that may be prohibited as having the effect of force. In *Chaplinsky v. New Hampshire* (1942), the Supreme Court said that such words were not protected by the First Amendment.

Franchise: The right to vote.

Free Exercise Clause: The provision in the First Amendment barring the government from "prohibiting the free exercise of" religion.

Fugitive Slave Clause: A provision found in Article IV, Section 2 of the Constitution requiring that states shall deliver persons "held to Service or labor in one State, under the Laws thereof, escaping into another." Friction over this clause was particularly intense in the period leading up to the Civil War.

Full Faith and Credit Clause: The provision in Article IV, Section 1 of the Constitution according to which states are obligated to recognize civil acts of other states.

Gag Orders: Orders, now severely limited by the courts, intended to squelch reports of ongoing hearings or trials in order to guarantee the fairness of trials.

Gerrymandering: The process of configuring districts so as to give an advantage to a particular group.

Good Faith: A recognized exception to the exclusionary rule designed to apply where police officers acted in good faith and without knowledge that a warrant was flawed.

Grand Jury: A body of citizens convened to determine whether there is sufficient evidence to bring an individual to trial.

Grandfather Clauses: Provisions, directed against racial minorities and eventually overturned by the courts, which restricted voting to those who could prove that their grandfathers had voted prior to 1867, that is, prior to the time that African Americans were given this right.

Granted Powers: See enumerated powers.

Gravity of the Evil Test: A reformulation of the clear and present danger test that was applied by the Court in *Dennis v. United States* (1951).

Guarantee Clause: The provision in Article IV, Section 4 of the Constitution providing that the United States shall guarantee each state a republican, or representative, form of government.

Head of Government: The nation's chief elected official—in parliamentary systems, usually the prime minister, in the United States, the president.

Head of State: The individual—in the United States, the president—who meets with diplomats and serves as the nation's overarching symbol.

Heightened Scrutiny: The intermediate level of review generally applied by the Supreme Court to classifications based on gender.

Hereditary Succession: The principle by which monarchy is passed from one generation to another on the basis of noble birth.

Hicklin Test: A standard, since abandoned, according to which a work was judged to be obscene if its tendency was such as to deprave and corrupt those whose minds were open to such influence and into whose hands such a work might fall.

High Crimes and Misdemeanors: The grounds listed in the Constitution, along with bribery and treason, as grounds for impeachment. While the parameters of high crimes and misdemeanors are vague, most scholars agree that this phrase is designed to prohibit impeachment and conviction of officers simply because of disagreements over policy.

House of Commons: The lower and most powerful house of the British Parliament.

House of Lords: The upper and less powerful house of the British Parliament, filled largely through heredity.

House of Representatives: The lower house of the U.S. Congress, currently with 435 voting members elected by members of their districts for two-year terms.

Impeachment: The process, instituted by the House of Representatives, of bringing charges against an executive or judicial official. Charges are tried by the U.S. Senate where a two-thirds vote is required for a conviction. Treason, bribery, and other "high crimes and misdemeanors" are the constitutionally specified bases for impeachment. Conviction results in removal from office.

Implied Powers: Unspecified constitutional powers recognized by the necessary and proper clause of Article I, Section 8 as appropriate to carrying out the enumerated powers of Congress.

Impoundment: An executive practice, subsequently limited by law, of refusing to spend all the monies appropriated by Congress.

In Forma Pauperis Petition: A petition, like that filed in *Gideon v. Wainwright* (1963), that defendants, unable to afford attorneys, file on their own behalf.

Incompatibility Clause: The provision in Article I, Section 6 of the U.S. Constitution that prevents members of Congress from holding other simultaneous governmental offices.

Incorporation: The process by which most of the guarantees found in the Bill of Rights have been applied to the state governments via the due process clause of the Fourteenth Amendment.

Inferior Officers: Offices other than cabinet heads, judges, ambassadors and other constitutionally specified offices appointed by the president. Inferior officers may be appointed by the president, by courts of law, or by the heads of the departments.

Information: An alternative to grand jury indictments whereby a prosecutor presents information to a judge to establish that the state has sufficient evidence to proceed with a trial.

Inherent Powers: Powers, especially in the area of foreign affairs, thought to reside in the president simply by virtue of his office.

Interposition: The doctrine advanced in the Virginia and Kentucky Resolutions of 1798 whereby states had the right to interpose themselves against federal laws that they believed to be unconstitutional.

Interpretivists: Scholars and judges who emphasize adherence to the words of the Constitution and the intentions of its framers and ratifiers.

Item Veto: A veto, allowed in many states but not specifically provided for in the U.S. Constitution, whereby an executive may void individual items of a bill, especially those related to appropriations.

Jim Crow Laws: Laws, now illegal, that mandated racial segregation.

Judicial Activism: The view that the judicial branch should take a leading role in government.

Judicial Branch: The branch of government headed by the Supreme Court and responsible for interpreting the laws.

Judicial Restraint: The view that members of the judicial branch should be deferential to decisions made by the two elected branches of government.

Judicial Review: The power American courts exercise of reviewing executive and administrative actions, as well as state and federal laws, which come before them in the course of judicial decision-making, and deciding whether or not they are constitutional.

Jurisdiction: Areas in which courts or other bodies have authority to render decisions. U.S. courts exercise authority either based on the subject matter of the case or the parties to the suit. Jurisdiction of the courts may be further divided into original and appellate, the former dealing with cases heard for the first time, and the latter referring to cases heard on appeal.

Jus Sanguinis: A term meaning "law of the blood" that recognizes that persons born abroad to citizens of a nation may still themselves acquire such citizenship rights.

Jus Soli: A term meaning "law of the soil" that recognizes that those born within a nation are citizens thereof.

Justiciable: Considered capable of judicial resolution.

Lame Ducks: Elected officials who are finishing out their terms but already know that they will not be returning to office. The Twentieth Amendment shortened the period during which lame-duck presidents and members of Congress serve.

Legislative Branch: The lawmaking branch of government. In the United States, Congress has this authority; in Great Britain, the power resides in Parliament.

Legislative Courts: American courts created apart from the provisions of Article III and thus not subject to the same constitutional protections.

Legislative Veto: An extraconstitutional mechanism, invalidated by the U.S. Supreme Court in the *Chadha* case, in which Congress delegates powers to the president, with the proviso that one or both houses can subsequently invalidate his actions.

Lemon Test: A three-part test first fully formulated in *Lemon v. Kurtzman* (1971) to assess whether the establishment clause has been violated. The test, which the Supreme Court does not apply on a consistent basis, requires that legislation must: have a secular legislative purpose, neither advance nor inhibit religion, and avoid excessive entanglement with religion.

Letters of Marque And Reprisal: Authorizations used in colonial times and in early American history providing for free lance shipmen to attack the ships of enemy nations and share in the spoils.

Libel: The publication of false and damaging information about another. Although U.S. courts have ruled that such libel is not protected by the First Amendment, they have also made it difficult, especially for public figures, to prove accusations of libel.

Literacy Tests: Tests, now suspended by law, which were once a prerequisite for exercising the right to vote; such tests, combined with "understanding clauses," were often administered in a racially discriminatory fashion.

Madison, James: The Virginia delegate to the Constitutional Convention often designated both the "Father of the Constitution" and the "Father of the Bill of Rights." Madison appears to have been a major figure in the creation of the Virginia Plan and took the most extensive notes at the Constitutional Convention of 1787. He was one of three authors of *The Federalist Papers*, the leader of Congress who shepherded the Bill of Rights through the House of Representatives, and a leader, with Thomas Jefferson, of the Democratic-Republican Party.

Magna Carta: A Latin term meaning "great charter." This was a document wrested from King John of England by his noblemen in 1215 and signed at Runneymead. Often regarded as the fountainhead of English liberties, the document contained the principle of "no taxation without representation" which the American colonists would cite in the dispute with Great Britain that led to the Revolutionary War.

Marshall, John: The fourth, and arguably the greatest, chief justice of the United States. Marshall established the power of judicial review in *Marbury v. Madison* (1803), the doctrine of implied powers in *McCulloch v. Maryland*

(1819), and federal control over interstate commerce in *Gibbons v. Ogden* (1824). In his last major decision, *Barron v. Baltimore* (1833), Marshall decided that the Bill of Rights did not apply to the states.

Mayflower Compact: A charter of government drawn up by the New England pilgrims before embarking from their ship, the Mayflower. This charter served as a prototype for later constitutions and as a symbol of the colonists' commitment to self-government.

Miller Test: A three-part test formulated in *Miller v. California* (1973) for assessing whether works are obscene. Under this test, a work is considered obscene: if an average person, applying contemporary community standards, would find that the work, taken as a whole, appeals to a prurient (lustful) interest in sex; if it depicts or describes in a patently offensive way, sexual conduct specifically defined by law; and if the work lacks any serious literary, artistic, political, or scientific value.

Miranda Warnings: Statements required to be issued by police officers when arresting or cross-examining suspects. Such warnings, established in *Miranda v. Arizona* (1966), detail individual rights including the right to counsel and to remain silent.

Missouri Compromise: A law adopted by Congress in 1820 admitting Maine as a free state and Missouri as a slave state and seeking to draw a line in the territories north of which slavery would be excluded. The Supreme Court invalidated this compromise in the *Dred Scott* decision (1857).

Monarchy: Government by a single individual, usually a king or queen. In most modern democracies, this position is a largely symbolic one.

Natural Rights: Rights that individuals have by virtue of being human. The Declaration of Independence stated that such rights included "life, liberty, and the pursuit of happiness."

Naturalization: The process by which a person not born within a nation can become a citizen thereof. Article I, Section 8 vests this power in Congress.

New Jersey Plan: A plan introduced at the Constitutional Convention of 1787 by William Patterson of New Jersey. In contrast to the previously introduced Virginia Plan, the New Jersey plan called for equal state representation in a unicameral Congress.

Noninterpretivists: Scholars and judges who emphasize sources other than the language of the Constitution and the intent of the framers and ratifiers in interpreting the Constitution.

Northwest Ordinance of 1787: The law adopted during the Articles of Confederation specifying how the territory in the American West would be governed and outlawing slavery in this region.

Nullification: The doctrine, most forcefully advocated by South Carolina Senator John C. Calhoun, according to which states had the right to nullify, or void, federal laws that they believed to be unconstitutional.

One Person, One Vote: The principle, first articulated by the Supreme Court in *Gray v. Sanders* (1963), according to which legislative and congressional districts must have approximately equal numbers of constituents.

Original Jurisdiction: Refers to the first time a case is heard before any court. The fairly limited original jurisdiction of the Supreme Court is spelled out in Article III of the Constitution.

Overbreadth Doctrine: A doctrine, applied to free speech cases, in which courts strike down laws so overly broad that they sweep both protected and unprotected speech within their ambit.

Pardon and Reprieve Power: A power to mitigate punishment given to the president in Article II, Section 2 of the Constitution. This power includes that of granting general amnesties.

Parliament: The English legislature, composed of two houses, the House of Commons and the House of Lords. Under the theory of the British government, its parliament is sovereign.

Parliamentary Sovereignty: The doctrine, supported by the British in the dispute with the colonists, according to which the British Parliament had authority to make laws not only for Great Britain but also for the colonies. More generally, parliamentary sovereignty refers to the doctrine that there are no legal limits on what Parliament can do.

Per Curiam Opinion: An unsigned opinion issued on behalf of a court.

Peremptory Challenges: Dismissals of jurors during a voir dire examination for which no cause needs to be stated. Recent Supreme Court decisions have ruled that such dismissals may not be made on the basis of race or gender.

Petit Jury: A trial jury, typically consisting of twelve members of the community, which decides on a defendant's guilt or innocence and, in some cases, on an appropriate penalty.

Plea Bargains: Agreements in criminal cases in which prosecutors agree to seek a lesser charge in exchange for defendants' acknowledgment of guilt.

Pocket Veto: A veto exercised at the end of a congressional session, whereby a bill fails to become a law simply because the president pockets it.

Political Questions: Issues that the courts refuse to hear because they believe the resolution of such issues has been entrusted to other branches of government.

Poll Taxes: Taxes levied as a condition to voting. The Twenty-Fourth Amendment prohibited the payment of such poll taxes as a condition for voting in federal elections.

Power of Judgment: The only power Alexander Hamilton said that the judiciary would have.

Power of the Purse: The powers over taxing, borrowing, and spending allocated to Congress in Article I, Section 8 of the U.S. Constitution.

Power of the Sword: The power over the military allocated by the Constitution to the president.

Preamble to the Constitution: The opening paragraph that outlines the central purposes of the document.

Presentment Clause: The provision in Article I, Section 7 of the U.S. Constitution specifying that all laws must be presented to the president for his approval or veto.

President of the Senate: An office held by the U.S. vice president allowing him to preside and to cast tie-breaking votes.

Prior Restraint: The heart of freedom of the press in the United States is understood to rest in the strong presumption against any prior restraint of publication. Some such publications may subsequently be prosecuted, however, for example in cases where they are obscene or libelous.

Privacy Rights: Although not specifically mentioned in the Constitution, the Supreme Court has ruled in *Griswold v. Connecticut* (1965) and subsequent cases that such rights are protected by that document.

Privileges and Immunities Clause: The provisions in Article IV, Section 1 and in Section 1 of the Fourteenth Amendment, which provide that states must treat citizens of other states as they would their own.

Probable Cause: The standard of proof required before police officers can get search warrants.

Progressive Era: The time period early in the twentieth century during which there was a strong push for reform and democratization. Amendments 16 through 19 are associated with this period.

Publius: The pen name used by the three authors of *The Federalist Papers*, namely Alexander Hamilton, James Madison, and John Jay.

Pure Democracy: A government that operates like those of ancient Greece where citizens meet together in person to debate and resolve matters of public policy.

Ratification: Formal approval. The Constitution requires that treaties be ratified by two-thirds of the Senate and constitutional amendments by three-fourths of the state legislatures or conventions.

Reasonable Basis Test (Rational Basis Test): The standard courts use to evaluate classifications that are not tied to a suspect class, a fundamental right, or to gender. This is the Court's most deferential level of review.

Republican Government: A form of indirect, or representative, democracy, defended by James Madison and other American founders as superior to pure democracy.

Reserved Powers: Under the U.S. system, powers not expressly or implicitly delegated to the national government are reserved to the states. The Tenth Amendment is the clearest statement of this principle.

Rescission: The process of withdrawing approval. The Constitution is silent as to whether states can rescind proposed amendments that have not yet been approved by the necessary three-fourths majority of the states.

Resulting Powers: The sum of both the enumerated and implied powers of Congress.

Revolution: The act of changing government through violent means. In the Declaration of Independence, the Americans argued that such revolution could be justified when government did not secure individual rights and was unresponsive to the petitions of the people.

Riders: Amendments, not always germane, that legislators attach to bills in Congress.

Rights: Legitimate claims. Rights are historically divided into human rights, which apply to all persons, and civil rights, which extend only to citizens.

Rights of Men: Privileges, sometimes referred to as natural rights, to which human beings are entitled simply because they are human. The idea that governments had an obligation to protect such rights was prominent in the American struggle against the British.

Roll-Call Vote: A recorded vote in Congress.

Rule of Four: An informal rule utilized by the Supreme Court whereby it denies review to cases unless four or more justices agree that they want to hear them.

Salutary Neglect: The English policy, pursued prior to the French and Indian War, that allowed the American colonies to exercise a good deal of self government.

Search Warrant: A document specifying a place to be searched and a person or place to be seized. Under the Fourth Amendment, warrants cannot be issued unless police first establish probable cause.

Secession: The doctrine that argued that states had the right to withdraw from the Union without the consent of other states. The Civil War discredited this idea.

Selective Incorporation: The view that the due process clause of the Fourteenth Amendment was designed only to apply the most fundamental provisions of the Bill of Rights to the states. Justice Cardozo articulated this view in *Palko v. Connecticut* (1937).

Self-Incrimination: The act of testifying to crimes against one's self. The Fifth Amendment outlaws compulsion against self-incrimination in criminal cases.

Senate: The upper house of the U.S. congress, currently consisting of 100 members, two from each state. Since adoption of the Seventeenth

Amendment, members are elected directly by the people and serve for six-year terms.

Senatorial Courtesy: The practice whereby a senator from a president's party is permitted to block the nomination of a judge from the senator's state to whom the senator objects.

Seneca Falls Convention: A convention that met in New York in 1848 and issued a call for women's suffrage that eventually resulted in adoption of the Nineteenth Amendment (1920).

Separate but Equal: The principle, legitimating racial segregation, that is usually associated with the Supreme Court's decision in *Plessy v. Ferguson* (1896) but which was subsequently repudiated in *Brown v. Board of Education* (1954).

Separation of Church and State: A principle, not actually stated in the Constitution, but arguably consistent with the establishment clause of the First Amendment.

Separation of Powers: The principle of dividing government authority among different branches of government, in the United States, the legislative, executive, and judicial.

Shay's Rebellion: The revolt of debtors and taxpayers in Massachusetts in the winter of 1787 that convinced wavering states that the Articles of Confederation needed to be strengthened.

Shield Laws: Laws designed to shield reporters from grand jury inquiries about matters that they have discovered in their news-gathering capacities.

Social Contract Theorists: A group of philosophers, most notable of whom was the Englishman John Locke, who argued that governments were formed by consent in order to secure basic human rights. This idea is also embodied in the Declaration of Independence and the U.S. Constitution.

Sovereign: A word meaning supreme. The term sovereign is used to designate the person or agency of government with final ultimate authority. In the U.S. system, such sovereignty is difficult to locate.

Sovereign Immunity: The doctrine, somewhat affirmed by the Eleventh Amendment, that prohibits governments, as sovereign entities, from being sued without their consent.

Speech and Debate Clause: The provision in Article I, Section 6, whereby members of Congress are protected against prosecution for what they say within Congress.

Standing: The principle that requires that parties who bring cases to court must have a genuine stake in their outcome.

Stare Decisis: The doctrine, grounded in British common law, by which judges generally adhere to past precedents as a way of preserving legal stability and continuity.

State Action: The legal principle, forcefully articulated in the *Civil Rights Cases* of 1883, according to which discriminatory action is only illegal if engaged in by the state. Accordingly, purely private action is beyond the state's purview.

State of the Union Address: The president's annual message to Congress in January which, by modern practice, is delivered by the president in person.

Statutory Construction: The powers courts exercise of construing the meaning of laws and administrative rulings.

Stop and Frisk: Brief on-the-street searches, usually for weapons or contraband, sanctioned by the Supreme Court in *Terry v. Ohio* (1968).

Substantive Due Process: The idea that the due process clauses of the Fifth and Fourteenth Amendments do not simply limit the procedures governments may follow (procedural due process) but also the substance of such decisions.

Suffrage: The right to vote.

Supremacy Clause: The provision in Article VI of the Constitution (originating in the New Jersey Plan) that provides that the Constitution, U.S. laws, and treaties are the supreme law of the land.

Supreme Court: The highest court in the federal system and the only court mentioned by name in the U.S. Constitution. Under current law, the Court has nine members, eight associate justices and a chief.

Susan B. Anthony Amendment: Another name for the Nineteenth Amendment which granted women's suffrage. The name comes from one of the original and most consistent supporters of the amendment.

Suspect Classes: Groups, like racial minorities and aliens, to whom the Court has extended extra judicial scrutiny because of past use of such classifications in a discriminatory fashion.

Symbolic Speech: Communications other than through written or verbal words. The Court has extended protections to such speech through the First and Fourteenth Amendments.

Takings Clause: The provision found in the Fifth Amendment that forbids government from taking private property without providing just compensation.

Three-Fifths Clause: The provision in Article I, Section 2 of the U.S. Constitution specifying that slaves would be counted as three-fifths of a person for purposes of taxation and representation.

Titles of Nobility: Honors bestowed by foreign governments. Americans are forbidden by Article I, Section 9 from accepting such titles except with congressional permission.

Total Incorporation: The view that the Fourteenth Amendment intended to apply all the provisions in the Bill of Rights to the states. Prominent advocates of this view have included Justice John Marshall Harlan I and Justice Hugo Black.

Total Incorporation Plus: The view that the Fourteenth Amendment was designed to apply all the provisions of the Bill of Rights to the states but that it was not limited to this objective.

Treason: Defined by Article III, Section 3 of the Constitution as "levying War" or "adhering to their [the nation's] Enemies, giving them Aid and Comfort," this is one of three stated grounds for which public officers may be impeached and removed from office.

Treaties: Formal agreements with foreign nations negotiated by the president and requiring two-thirds majority approval by the Senate.

Unenumerated Rights: Rights that are not specifically listed in the Constitution but that may nonetheless deserve protection. The Ninth Amendment to the Constitution recognizes the existence of such rights.

Unicameralism: Provides for a single house of the legislative branch.

Unitary Government: A governmental system in which primary powers rest with the central government.

Unreasonable Searches and Seizures: Searches and seizures initiated without just cause or proper warrant procedures as specified in the Fourth Amendment.

Unwritten Constitution: A system of customs and usages that set the pattern for governmental operations but that are not collected together in a single written document. Under many such constitutions, the legislature is, at least in theory, sovereign.

Veto: A negative. Under the U.S. Constitution, if the president vetoes a bill, it does not become law unless subsequently readopted by a two-thirds majority of both houses of Congress.

Viability: The point at which a fetus can survive outside its mother's womb. In *Roe v. Wade* (1973), the Supreme Court used this point—then thought to be at the end of the second trimester of pregnancy—as the point at which a state could prohibit abortions, except when necessary to save the life or health of the mother.

Virginia and Kentucky Resolutions: Resolutions adopted by these two state legislatures in 1799 in opposition to the Alien and Sedition Acts of the previous year.

Virginia Plan: The first and most important plan introduced at the Constitutional Convention of 1787. The origin of such ideas as the separation of powers and bicameralism, the plan favored the larger states and called for a new national government much stronger than that under the Articles of Confederation.

Virtual Representation: The position advocated by the British in the dispute with the American colonies in which the British argued that, since members of Parliament represented all Englishmen, the colonists were virtually represented there and Parliament thus had authority over them.

Voir Dire: The name of the process by which a judge, and/or opposing counsel, ask questions of potential jurors in order to decide who shall be chosen to sit in on a trial and render a verdict.

Vote of No-Confidence: A mechanism employed in parliamentary governments by which the Parliament can bring down the elected government and trigger new elections by voting against a major initiative of the majority party or coalition.

War Powers Resolution of 1973: A law adopted over then President Nixon's veto, which was designed to provide for consultation between the president and Congress, notification of new troops deployments, and the termination of such new deployments after 90 days absent congressional approval.

Washington, George: The leader of American revolutionary forces in the war against England and subsequent first president of the new republic. Washington's decision to attend the Constitutional Convention of 1787, and his service as Chairman, contributed to the success of its deliberations.

White Primary: A primary, or nominating election, which was open only to white voters. The Supreme Court outlawed such primaries in *Smith v. Allwright* (1944).

Writ of Certiorari: Petitions by which cases are appealed to the U.S. Supreme Court. The Court has broad discretion over which of these petitions it will accept.

Writ of Habeas Corpus: A privilege upheld in Article I, Section 9, of the Constitution whereby defendants have the right to know what the charges against them are.

Writ of Mandamus: A judicial order requiring the performance of a ministerial act. An appeal for such a writ was at issue in *Marbury v. Madison* (1803).

Writs of Assistance: General warrants used by the British in colonial America and prohibited by the Fourth Amendment.

Written Constitution: A document, like that drawn up by the Constitutional Convention of 1787, which outlines the distribution of governmental powers and limits and which cannot be changed by ordinary legislative means.

Appendix

The Constitution of the United States

We the People of the United States, in Order to form a more perfect Union, establish Justice, insure domestic Tranquility, provide for the common defence, promote the general Welfare, and secure the Blessings of Liberty to ourselves and our Posterity, do ordain and establish this Constitution for the United States of America.

Article. I.

Section. 1. All legislative Powers herein granted shall be vested in a Congress of the United States, which shall consist of a Senate and House of Representatives.

Section. 2. The House of Representatives shall be composed of Members chosen every second Year by the People of the several States, and the Electors in each State shall have the Qualifications requisite for Electors of the most numerous Branch of the State Legislature.

No Person shall be a Representative who shall not have attained to the Age of twenty five Years, and been seven Years a Citizen of the United States, and who shall not, when elected, be an Inhabitant of that State in which he shall be chosen.

[Representatives and direct Taxes shall be apportioned among the several States which may be included within this Union, according to their respective Numbers, which shall be determined by adding to the whole Number of free Persons, including those bound to Service for a Term of Years, and excluding Indians not taxed, three fifths of all other Persons.]* The actual Enumeration shall be made within three Years after the first Meeting of the Congress of the United States, and within every subsequent Term of ten Years, in such Manner as they shall by Law direct. The number of Representatives shall not exceed one for every thirty Thousand, but each State shall have at Least one Representative; and until such enumeration shall be made, the State of New Hampshire shall be entitled to chuse three, Massachusetts eight, Rhode-Island and Providence Plantations one, Connecticut five, New-York six, New Jersey four, Pennsylvania eight, Delaware one, Maryland six, Virginia ten, North Carolina five, South Carolina five, and Georgia three.

When vacancies happen in the Representation from any State, the Executive Authority thereof shall issue Writs of Election to fill such Vacancies.

The House of Representatives shall chuse their Speaker and other Officers; and shall have the sole Power of Impeachment.

Section. 3. The Senate of the United States shall be composed of two Senators from each State, [chosen by the Legislature thereof,]* for six Years; and each Senator shall have one Vote.

Immediately after they shall be assembled in Consequence of the first Election, they shall be divided as equally as may be into three Classes. The Seats of the Senators of the first Class shall be vacated at the Expiration of the second Year, of the second Class at the Expiration of the fourth Year, and of the third Class at the Expiration of the sixth Year, so that one third may be chosen every second Year; [and if Vacancies happen by Resignation, or otherwise, during the Recess of the Legislature of any State, the Executive thereof may make temporary Appointments until the next

Meeting of the Legislature, which shall then fill such Vacancies.]*

No Person shall be a Senator who shall not have attained to the Age of thirty Years, and been nine Years a Citizen of the United States, and who shall not, when elected, be an Inhabitant of that State for which he shall be chosen.

The Vice President of the United States shall be President of the Senate, but shall have no Vote, unless they be equally divided.

The Senate shall chuse their other Officers, and also a President pro tempore, in the Absence of the Vice President, or when he shall exercise the Office of President of the United States.

The Senate shall have the sole Power to try all Impeachments. When sitting for that Purpose, they shall be on Oath or Affirmation. When the President of the United States is tried, the Chief Justice shall preside: And no Person shall be convicted without the Concurrence of two thirds of the Members present.

Judgment in Cases of Impeachment shall not extend further than to removal from Office, and disqualification to hold and enjoy any Office of honor, Trust or Profit under the United States: but the Party convicted shall nevertheless be liable and subject to Indictment, Trial, Judgment and Punishment, according to Law.

Section. 4. The Times, Places and Manner of holding Elections for Senators and Representatives, shall be prescribed in each State by the Legislature thereof; but the Congress may at any time by Law make or alter such Regulations, except as to the Places of chusing Senators.

The Congress shall assemble at least once in every Year, and such Meeting shall be [on the first Monday in December,]† unless they shall by Law appoint a different Day.

Section. 5. Each House shall be the Judge of the Elections, Returns and Qualifications of its own Members, and a Majority of each shall constitute a Quorum to do Business; but a smaller Number may adjourn from day to day, and may be authorized to compel the Attendance of absent Members, in such Manner, and under such Penalties as each House may provide.

Each House may determine the Rules of its Proceedings, punish its Members for disorderly Behaviour, and, with the Concurrence of two thirds, expel a Member.

Each House shall keep a Journal of its Proceedings, and from time to time publish the same, excepting such Parts as may in their Judgment require Secrecy; and the Yeas and Nays of the Members of either House on any question shall,

at the Desire of one fifth of those Present, be entered on the Journal.

Neither House, during the Session of Congress, shall, without the Consent of the other, adjourn for more than three days, nor to any other Place than that in which the two Houses shall be sitting.

Section. 6. The Senators and Representatives shall receive a Compensation for their Services, to be ascertained by Law, and paid out of the Treasury of the United States. They shall in all Cases, except Treason, Felony and Breach of the Peace, be privileged from Arrest during their Attendance at the Session of their respective Houses, and in going to and returning from the same; and for any Speech or Debate in either House, they shall not be questioned in any other Place.

No Senator or Representative shall, during the Time for which he was elected, be appointed to any civil Office under the Authority of the United States, which shall have been created, or the Emoluments whereof shall have been encreased during such time; and no Person holding any Office under the United States, shall be a Member of either House during his Continuance in Office.

Section. 7. All Bills for raising Revenue shall originate in the House of Representatives; but the Senate may propose or concur with Amendments as on other Bills.

Every Bill which shall have passed the House of Representatives and the Senate, shall, before it becomes a Law, be presented to the President of the United States; If he approve he shall sign it, but if not he shall return it, with his Objections to that House in which it shall have originated, who shall enter the Objections at large on their Journal, and proceed to reconsider it. If after such Reconsideration two thirds of that House shall agree to pass the Bill, it shall be sent, together with the Objections, to the other House, by which it shall likewise be reconsidered, and if approved by two thirds of that House, it shall become a Law. But in all such Cases the Votes of both Houses shall be determined by yeas and Nays, and the Names of the Persons voting for and against the Bill shall be entered on the Journal of each House respectively. If any Bill shall not be returned by the President within ten Days (Sundays excepted) after it shall have been presented to him, the Same shall be a Law, in like Manner as if he had signed it, unless the Congress by their Adjournment prevent its Return, in which Case it shall not be a Law.

Every Order, Resolution, or Vote to which the Concurrence of the Senate and House of

*Changed by the Seventeenth Amendment.

†Changed by section 2 of the Twentieth Amendment.

Representatives may be necessary (except on a question of Adjournment) shall be presented to the President of the United States; and before the Same shall take Effect, shall be approved by him, or being disapproved by him, shall be repassed by two thirds of the Senate and House of Representatives, according to the Rules and Limitations prescribed in the Case of a Bill.

Section. 8. The Congress shall have Power To lay and collect Taxes, Duties, Imposts and Excises, to pay the Debts and provide for the common Defence and general Welfare of the United States; but all Duties, Imposts and Excises shall be uniform throughout the United States;

To borrow Money on the credit of the United States;

To regulate Commerce with foreign Nations, and among the several States, and with the Indian Tribes;

To establish an uniform Rule of Naturalization, and uniform Laws on the subject of Bankruptcies throughout the United States;

To coin Money, regulate the Value thereof, and of foreign Coin, and fix the Standard of Weights and Measures;

To provide for the Punishment of counterfeiting the Securities and current Coin of the United States;

To establish Post Offices and post Roads;

To promote the Progress of Science and useful Arts, by securing for limited Times to Authors and Inventors the exclusive Right to their respective Writings and Discoveries;

To constitute Tribunals inferior to the supreme Court;

To define and punish Piracies and Felonies committed on the high Seas, and Offenses against the Law of Nations;

To declare War, grant Letters of Marque and Reprisal, and make Rules concerning Captures on Land and Water;

To raise and support Armies, but no Appropriation of Money to that Use shall be for a longer Term than two Years;

To provide and maintain a Navy;

To make Rules for the Government and Regulation of the land and naval Forces;

To provide for calling forth the Militia to execute the Laws of the Union, suppress Insurrections and repel Invasions;

To provide for organizing, arming, and disciplining, the Militia, and for governing such Part of them as may be employed in the Service of the United States, reserving to the States respectively, the Appointment of the Officers, and the Authority of training the Militia according to the discipline prescribed by Congress;

To exercise exclusive Legislation in all Cases whatsoever, over such District (not exceeding ten Miles square) as may, by Cession of particular States, and the Acceptance of Congress, become the Seat of the Government of the United States, and to exercise like Authority over all Places purchased by the Consent of the Legislature of the State in which the Same shall be, for the Erection of Forts, Magazines, Arsenals, dock-Yards and other needful Buildings;—And

To make all Laws which shall be necessary and proper for carrying into Execution the foregoing Powers, and all other Powers vested by this Constitution in the Government of the United States, or in any Department or Officer thereof.

Section. 9. The Migration or Importation of such Persons as any of the States now existing shall think proper to admit, shall not be prohibited by the Congress prior to the Year one thousand eight hundred and eight, but a Tax or duty may be imposed on such Importation, not exceeding ten dollars for each Person.

The Privilege of the Writ of Habeas Corpus shall not be suspended, unless when in Cases of Rebellion or Invasion the public Safety may require it.

No Bill of Attainder or ex post facto Law shall be passed.

[No Capitation, or other direct, Tax shall be laid, unless in Proportion to the Census or Enumeration herein before directed to be taken.]*

No Tax or Duty shall be laid on Articles exported from any State.

No Preference shall be given by any Regulation of Commerce or Revenue to the Ports of one State over those of another: nor shall Vessels bound to, or from, one State, be obliged to enter, clear, or pay Duties in another.

No Money shall be drawn from the Treasury, but in Consequence of Appropriations made by Law; and a regular Statement and Account of the Receipts and Expenditures of all public Money shall be published from time to time.

No Title of Nobility shall be granted by the United States: And no Person holding any Office of Profit or Trust under them, shall, without the Consent of the Congress, accept of any present, Emolument, Office, or Title, of any kind whatever, from any King, Prince, or foreign State.

Section. 10. No State shall enter into any Treaty, Alliance, or Confederation; grant Letters of Marque and Reprisal; coin Money; emit Bills of Credit; make any Thing but gold and silver Coin a Tender in Payment of Debts; pass any Bill of Attainder, ex post facto Law, or Law impairing the Obligation of Contracts, or grant any Title of Nobility.

No State shall, without the Consent of the Congress, lay any Imposts or Duties on Imports

---

*Changed by the Sixteenth Amendment.

or Exports, except what may be absolutely necessary for executing it's inspection Laws: and the net Produce of all Duties and Imposts, laid by any State on Imports or Exports, shall be for the Use of the Treasury of the United States; and all such Laws shall be subject to the Revision and Controul of the Congress.

No State shall, without the Consent of Congress, lay any Duty of Tonnage, keep Troops, or Ships of War in time of Peace, enter into any Agreement or Compact with another State, or with a foreign Power, or engage in War, unless actually invaded, or in such imminent Danger as will not admit of delay.

Article. II.

Section. 1. The executive Power shall be vested in a President of the United States of America. He shall hold his Office during the Term of four Years, and, together with the Vice President, chosen for the same Term, be elected, as follows

Each State shall appoint, in such Manner as the Legislature thereof may direct, a Number of Electors, equal to the whole Number of Senators and Representatives to which the State may be entitled in the Congress: but no Senator or Representative, or Person holding an Office of Trust or Profit under the United States, shall be appointed an Elector.

[The Electors shall meet in their respective States, and vote by Ballot for two Persons, of whom one at least shall not be an Inhabitant of the same State with themselves. And they shall make a List of all the Persons voted for, and of the Number of Votes for each; which List they shall sign and certify, and transmit sealed to the Seat of the Government of the United States, directed to the President of the Senate. The President of the Senate shall, in the Presence of the Senate and House of Representatives, open all the Certificates, and the Votes shall then be counted. The Person having the greatest Number of Votes shall be the President, if such Number be a Majority of the whole Number of Electors appointed; and if there be more than one who have such Majority, and have an equal Number of Votes, then the House of Representatives shall immediately chuse by Ballot one of them for President; and if no Person have a Majority, then from the five highest on the List the said House shall in like Manner chuse the President. But in chusing the President, the Votes shall be taken by States, the Representation from each State having one Vote; A quorum for this Purpose shall consist of a Member or Members from

two thirds of the States, and a Majority of all the States shall be necessary to a Choice. In every Case, after the Choice of the President, the Person having the greatest Number of Votes of the Electors shall be the Vice President. But if there should remain two or more who have equal Votes, the Senate shall chuse from them by Ballot the Vice President.]*

The Congress may determine the Time of chusing the Electors, and the Day on which they shall give their Votes; which Day shall be the same throughout the United States.

No Person except a natural born Citizen, or a Citizen of the United States, at the time of the Adoption of this Constitution, shall be eligible to the Office of the President; neither shall any person be eligible to that Office who shall not have attained to the Age of thirty five Years, and been fourteen Years a Resident within the United States.

[In Case of the Removal of the President from Office, or of his Death, Resignation, or Inability to discharge the Powers and Duties of the said Office, the Same shall devolve on the Vice President, and the Congress may by Law provide for the Case of Removal, Death, Resignation or Inability, both of the President and Vice President, declaring what Officer shall then act as President, and such Officer shall act accordingly, until the Disability be removed, or a President shall be elected.]†

The President shall, at stated Times, receive for his Services, a Compensation, which shall neither be increased nor diminished during the Period for which he shall have been elected, and he shall not receive within that Period any other Emolument from the United States, or any of them.

Before he enter on the Execution of his Office, he shall take the following Oath or Affirmation:—"I do solemnly swear (or affirm) that I will faithfully execute the Office of President of the United States, and will to the best of my Ability, preserve, protect and defend the Constitution of the United States."

Section. 2. The President shall be Commander in Chief of the Army and Navy of the United States, and of the Militia of the several States, when called into the actual Service of the United States; he may require the Opinion, in writing, of the principal Officer in each of the executive Departments, upon any Subject relating to the Duties of their respective Offices, and he shall have Power to grant Reprieves and Pardons for Offenses against the United States, except in Cases of Impeachment.

He shall have Power, by and with the Advice

*Changed by the Twelfth Amendment.
†Changed by the Twenty-Fifth Amendment.

and Consent of the Senate, to make Treaties, provided two thirds of the Senators present concur; and he shall nominate, and by and with the Advice and Consent of the Senate, shall appoint Ambassadors, other public Ministers and Consuls, Judges of the supreme Court, and all other Officers of the United States, whose Appointments are not herein otherwise provided for, and which shall be established by Law: but the Congress may by Law vest the Appointment of such inferior Officers, as they think proper, in the President alone, in the Courts of Law, or in the Heads of Departments.

The President shall have Power to fill up all Vacancies that may happen during the Recess of the Senate, by granting Commissions which shall expire at the End of their next Session.

Section. 3. He shall from time to time give to the Congress Information of the State of the Union, and recommend to their Consideration such Measures as he shall judge necessary and expedient; he may, on extraordinary Occasions, convene both Houses, or either of them, and in Case of Disagreement between them, with Respect to the Time of Adjournment, he may adjourn them to such Time as he shall think proper; he shall receive Ambassadors and other public Ministers; he shall take Care that the Laws be faithfully executed, and shall Commission all the Officers of the United States.

Section. 4. The President, Vice President and all civil Officers of the United States, shall be removed from Office on Impeachment for, and Conviction of, Treason, Bribery, or other high Crimes and Misdemeanors.

Article. III.

Section. 1. The judicial Power of the United States, shall be vested in one supreme Court, and in such inferior Courts as the Congress may from time to time ordain and establish. The Judges, both of the supreme and inferior Courts, shall hold their Offices during good Behaviour, and shall, at stated Times, receive for their Services, a Compensation, which shall not be diminished during their Continuance in Office.

Section. 2. The judicial Power shall extend to all Cases, in Law and Equity, arising under this Constitution, the Laws of the United States, and Treaties made, or which shall be made, under their Authority;—to all Cases affecting Ambassadors, other public Ministers and Consuls;—to all Cases of admiralty and maritime Jurisdiction;—to Controversies to which the United States shall be a Party;—to Controversies between two or more States; [between a State and Citizens of another

State;—]* between Citizens of different States— between Citizens of the same State claiming Lands under Grants of different States, [and between a State, or the Citizens thereof, and foreign States, Citizens or Subjects.]*

In all Cases affecting Ambassadors, other public Ministers and Consuls, and those in which a State shall be Party, the supreme Court shall have original Jurisdiction. In all the other Cases before mentioned, the supreme Court shall have appellate Jurisdiction, both as to Law and Fact, with such Exceptions, and under such Regulations as the Congress shall make.

The Trial of all Crimes, except in Cases of Impeachment; shall be by Jury; and such Trial shall be held in the State where the said Crimes shall have been committed; but when not committed within any State, the Trial shall be at such Place or Places as the Congress may by Law have directed.

Section. 3. Treason against the United States, shall consist only in levying War against them, or in adhering to their Enemies, giving them Aid and Comfort. No Person shall be convicted of Treason unless on the Testimony of two Witnesses to the same overt Act, or on Confession in open Court.

The Congress shall have Power to declare the Punishment of Treason, but no Attainder of Treason shall work Corruption of Blood, or Forfeiture except during the Life of the Person attainted.

Article. IV.

Section. 1. Full Faith and Credit shall be given in each State to the public Acts, Records, and judicial Proceedings of every other State; And the Congress may by general Laws prescribe the Manner in which such Acts, Records and Proceedings shall be proved, and the Effect thereof.

Section. 2. The Citizens of each State shall be entitled to all Privileges and Immunities of Citizens in the several States.

A Person charged in any State with Treason, Felony, or other Crime, who shall flee from Justice, and be found in another State, shall on Demand of the executive Authority of the State from which he fled, be delivered up, to be removed to the State having Jurisdiction of the Crime.

[No Person held to Service or Labour in one State, under the Laws thereof, escaping into another, shall, in Consequence of any Law or Regulation therein, be discharged from such Service or Labour, but shall be delivered up on Claim of the Party to whom such Service or Labour may be due.]†

---

*Changed by the Eleventh Amendment.

†Changed by the Thirteenth Amendment.

Section. 3. New States may be admitted by the Congress into this Union; but no new State shall be formed or erected within the Jurisdiction of any other State; nor any State be formed by the Junction of two or more States, or Parts of States, without the Consent of the Legislatures of the States concerned as well as of the Congress.

The Congress shall have Power to dispose of and make all needful Rules and Regulations respecting the Territory or other Property belonging to the United States; and nothing in this Constitution shall be so construed as to Prejudice any Claims of the United States, or of any particular State.

Section. 4. The United States shall guarantee to every State in this Union a Republican Form of Government, and shall protect each of them against Invasion; and on Application of the Legislature, or of the Executive (when the Legislature cannot be convened) against domestic Violence.

Article. V.

The Congress, whenever two thirds of both Houses shall deem it necessary, shall propose Amendments to this Constitution, or, on the Application of the Legislatures of two thirds of the several States, shall call a Convention for proposing Amendments, which, in either Case, shall be valid to all Intents and Purposes, as Part of this Constitution, when ratified by the Legislatures of three fourths of the several States, or by Conventions in three fourths thereof, as the one or the other Mode of Ratification may be proposed by the Congress; Provided that no Amendment which may be made prior to the Year One thousand eight hundred and eight shall in any Manner affect the first and fourth Clauses in the Ninth Section of the first Article; and that no State, without its Consent, shall be deprived of it's equal Suffrage in the Senate.

Article. VI.

All Debts contracted and Engagements entered into, before the Adoption of this Constitution, shall be as valid against the United States under this Constitution, as under the Confederation.

This Constitution, and the Laws of the United States which shall be made in Pursuance thereof; and all Treaties made, or which shall be made, under the Authority of the United States, shall be the supreme Law of the Land; and the Judges in every State shall be bound thereby, any Thing in the Constitution or Laws of any State to the Contrary notwithstanding.

The Senators and Representatives before mentioned, and the Members of the several State Legislatures, and all executive and judicial Officers, both of the United States and of the several States, shall be bound by Oath or Affirmation, to support this Constitution; but no religious Test shall ever be required as a Qualification to any Office or public Trust under the United States.

Article. VII.

The Ratification of the Conventions of nine States, shall be sufficient for the Establishment of this Constitution between the States so ratifying the Same.

done in Convention by the Unanimous Consent of the States present the Seventeenth Day of September in the Year of our Lord one thousand seven hundred and Eighty seven and of the Independence of the United States of America the Twelfth In Witness whereof We have hereunto subscribed our Names,

G? Washington—Presid!
and deputy from Virginia

New Hampshire	John Langdon
	Nicholas Gilman
Massachusetts	Nathaniel Gorham
	Rufus King
Connecticut	Wm. Saml. Johnson
	Roger Sherman
New York	Alexander Hamilton
New Jersey	Wil: Livingston
	David Brearley
	Wm. Paterson
	Jona: Dayton
Pennsylvania	B Franklin
	Thomas Mifflin
	Robt Morris
	Geo. Clymer
	Thos. FitzSimons
	Jared Ingersoll
	James Wilson
	Gouv Morris
Delaware	Geo: Read
	Gunning Bedford jun
	John Dickinson
	Richard Bassett
	Jaco: Broom
Maryland	James McHenry
	Dan of St Thos. Jenifer
	Danl Carroll
Virginia	John Blair—
	James Madison Jr.
North Carolina	Wm. Blount
	Richd. Dobbs Spaight
	Hu Williamson

South Carolina	J. Rutledge
	Charles Cotesworth Pinckney
	Charles Pinckney
	Pierce Butler
Georgia	William Few
	Abr Baldwin

In Convention Monday September 17th 1787.

Present

The States of

New Hampshire, Massachusetts, Connecticut, Mr. Hamilton from New York, New Jersey, Pennsylvania, Delaware, Maryland, Virginia, North Carolina, South Carolina and Georgia.

Resolved,

That the preceeding Constitution be laid before the United States in Congress assembled, and that it is the Opinion of this Convention, that it should afterwards be submitted to a Convention of Delegates, chosen in each State by the People thereof, under the Recommendation of its Legislature, for their Assent and Ratification; and that each Convention assenting to, and ratifying the Same, should give Notice thereof to the United States in Congress assembled. Resolved, That it is the Opinion of this Convention, that as soon as the Conventions of nine States shall have ratified this Constitution, the United States in Congress assembled should fix a Day on which Electors should be appointed by the States which shall have ratified the same, and a Day on which the Electors should assemble to vote for the President, and the Time and Place for commencing Proceedings under this Constitution.

That after such Publication the Electors should be appointed, and the Senators and Representatives elected: That the Electors should meet on the Day fixed for the Election of the President, and should transmit their Votes certified, signed, sealed and directed, as the Constitution requires, to the Secretary of the United States in Congress

assembled, that the Senators and Representatives should convene at the Time and Place assigned; that the Senators should appoint a President of the Senate, for the sole Purpose of receiving, opening and counting the Votes for President; and, that after he shall be chosen, the Congress, together with the President, should, without Delay, proceed to execute this Constitution.

By the unanimous Order of the Convention

G̱ WASHINGTON—Presiḏ

W. JACKSON Secretary.

AMENDMENTS TO THE CONSTITUTION OF THE UNITED STATES OF AMERICA

ARTICLES IN ADDITION TO, AND AMENDMENT OF, THE CONSTITUTION OF THE UNITED STATES OF AMERICA, PROPOSED BY CONGRESS, AND RATIFIED BY THE SEVERAL STATES, PURSUANT TO THE FIFTH ARTICLE OF THE ORIGINAL CONSTITUTION.

Amendment I.*

Congress shall make no law respecting an establishment of religion, or prohibiting the free exercise thereof; or abridging the freedom of speech, or of the press, or the right of the people peaceably to assemble, and to petition the Government for a redress of grievances.

*The first ten Amendments (Bill of Rights) were ratified effective December 15, 1791.

Amendment II.

A well regulated Militia, being necessary to the security of a free State, the right of the people to keep and bear Arms, shall not be infringed.

Amendment III.

No Soldier shall, in time of peace be quartered in any house, without the consent of the Owner, nor in time of war, but in a manner to be prescribed by law.

Amendment IV.

The right of the people to be secure in their persons, houses, papers, and effects, against unreasonable searches and seizures, shall not be violated, and no Warrants shall issue, but upon probable cause, supported by Oath or affirmation, and particularly describing the place to be searched, and the persons or things to be seized.

Amendment V.

No person shall be held to answer for a capital, or otherwise infamous crime, unless on a presentment or indictment of a Grand Jury, except in cases arising in the land or naval forces, or in the Militia, when in actual service in time of War or public danger; nor shall any person be subject for the same offence to be twice put in jeopardy of life or limb, nor shall be compelled in any criminal case to be a witness against himself, nor be deprived of life, liberty, or property, without due process of law; nor shall private property be taken for public use without just compensation.

Amendment VI.

In all criminal prosecutions, the accused shall enjoy the right to a speedy and public trial, by an impartial jury of the State and district wherein the crime shall have been committed; which district shall have been previously ascertained by law, and to be informed of the nature and cause of the accusation; to be confronted with the witnesses against him; to have compulsory process for obtaining witnesses in his favor, and to have the assistance of counsel for his defence.

Amendment VII.

In Suits at common law, where the value in controversy shall exceed twenty dollars, the right of trial by jury shall be preserved, and no fact tried by a jury shall be otherwise re-examined in any Court of the United States, than according to the rules of the common law.

Amendment VIII.

Excessive bail shall not be required, nor excessive fines imposed, nor cruel and unusual punishments inflicted.

Amendment IX.

The enumeration in the Constitution of certain rights shall not be construed to deny or disparage others retained by the people.

Amendment X.

The powers not delegated to the United States by the Constitution, nor prohibited by it to the States, are reserved to the States respectively, or to the people.

Amendment XI.*

The Judicial power of the United States shall not be construed to extend to any suit in law or equity, commenced or prosecuted against one of the United States by Citizens of another State, or by Citizens or Subjects of any Foreign State.

Amendment XII.**

The Electors shall meet in their respective states, and vote by ballot for President and Vice President, one of whom, at least, shall not be an inhabitant of the same state with themselves; they shall name in their ballots the person voted for as President, and in distinct ballots the person voted for as Vice-President, and they shall make distinct lists of all persons voted for as President, and of all persons voted for as Vice-President, and of the number of votes for each, which lists they shall

*The Eleventh Amendment was ratified February 7, 1795.

**The Twelfth Amendment as ratified June 15, 1804.

sign and certify, and transmit sealed to the seat of the government of the United States, directed to the President of the Senate;—The President of the Senate shall, in the presence of the Senate and House of Representatives, open all the certificates and the votes shall then be counted;—The person having the greatest number of votes for President, shall be the President, if such number be a majority of the whole number of Electors appointed; and if no person have such majority, then from the persons having the highest numbers not exceeding three on the list of those voted for as President, the House of Representatives shall choose immediately, by ballot, the President. But in choosing the President, the votes shall be taken by states, the representation from each state having one vote; a quorum for this purpose shall consist of a member or members from two-thirds of the states, and a majority of all the states shall be necessary to a choice. [And if the House of Representatives shall not choose a President whenever the right of choice shall devolve upon them, before the fourth day of March next following, then the Vice-President shall act as President, as in the case of the death or other constitutional disability of the President—-]† The person having the greatest number of votes as Vice-President, shall be the Vice-President, if such number be a majority of the whole number of Electors appointed, and if no person have a majority, then from the two highest numbers on the list, the Senate shall choose the Vice-President; a quorum for the purpose shall consist of two-thirds of the whole number of Senators, and a majority of the whole number shall be necessary to a choice. But no person constitutionally ineligible to the office of President shall be eligible to that of Vice-President of the United States.

Amendment XIII.*

Section 1. Neither slavery nor involuntary servitude, except as a punishment for crime whereof the party shall have been duly convicted, shall exist within the United States, or any place subject to their jurisdiction.

Section 2. Congress shall have power to enforce this article by appropriate legislation.

Amendment XIV.**

Section 1. All persons born or naturalized in the United States and subject to the jurisdiction

thereof, are citizens of the United States and of the State wherein they reside. No State shall make or enforce any law which shall abridge the privileges or immunities of citizens of the United States; nor shall any State deprive any person of life, liberty, or property, without due process of law; nor deny to any person within its jurisdiction the equal protection of the laws.

Section 2. Representatives shall be apportioned among the several States according to their respective numbers, counting the whole number of persons in each State, excluding Indians not taxed. But when the right to vote at any election for the choice of electors for President and Vice President of the United States, Representatives in Congress, the Executive and Judicial officers of a State, or the members of the Legislature thereof, is denied to any of the male inhabitants of such State, being twenty-one years of age, and citizens of the United States, or in any way abridged, except for participation in rebellion, or other crime, the basis of representation therein shall be reduced in the proportion which the number of such male citizens shall bear to the whole number of male citizens twenty-one years of age in such State.

Section 3. No person shall be a Senator or Representative in Congress, or elector of President and Vice President, or hold any office, civil or military, under the United States, or under any State, who, having previously taken an oath, as a member of Congress, or as an officer of the United States, or as a member of any State legislature, or as an executive or judicial officer of any State, to support the Constitution of the United States, shall have engaged in insurrection or rebellion against the same, or given aid or comfort to the enemies thereof. But Congress may by a vote of two-thirds of each House, remove such disability.

Section 4. The validity of the public debt of the United States, authorized by law, including debts incurred for payment of pensions and bounties for services in suppressing insurrection or rebellion, shall not be questioned. But neither the United States nor any State shall assume or pay any debt or obligation incurred in aid of insurrection or rebellion against the United States, or any claim for the loss or emancipation of any slave; but all such debts, obligations and claims shall be held illegal and void.

Section 5. The Congress shall have power to enforce, by appropriate legislation, the provisions of this article.

† Superseded by section 3 of the Twentieth Amendment.
*The Thirteenth Amendment was ratified December 6, 1865.
**The Fourteenth Amendment was ratified July 9, 1868.

Amendment XV.*

Section 1. The right of citizens of the United States to vote shall not be denied or abridged by the United States or by any State on account of race, color, or previous condition of servitude.

Section 2. The Congress shall have power to enforce this article by appropriate legislation.

Amendment XVI.**

The Congress shall have power to lay and collect taxes on incomes, from whatever source derived, without apportionment among the several States, and without regard to any census or enumeration.

Amendment XVII.***

The Senate of the United States shall be composed of two Senators from each State, elected by the people thereof, for six years; and each Senator shall have one vote. The electors in each State shall have the qualifications requisite for electors of the most numerous branch of the State legislatures.

When vacancies happen in the representation of any State in the Senate, the executive authority of such State shall issue writs of election to fill such vacancies: *Provided,* That the legislature of any State may empower the executive thereof to make temporary appointments until the people fill the vacancies by election as the legislature may direct.

This amendment shall not be so construed as to affect the election or term of any Senator chosen before it becomes valid as part of the Constitution.

Amendment XVIII.†

[**Section 1.** After one year from the ratification of this article the manufacture, sale, or transportation of intoxicating liquors within, the importation thereof into, or the exportation thereof from the United States and all territory subject to the jurisdiction thereof for beverage purposes is hereby prohibited.

Section 2. The Congress and the several States shall have concurrent power to enforce this article by appropriate legislation.

Section 3. This article shall be inoperative unless it shall have been ratified as an amendment to the Constitution by the legislatures of the several States, as provided in the Constitution, within seven years from the date of the submission hereof to the States by the Congress.]

Amendment XIX.*

The right of citizens of the United States to vote shall not be denied or abridged by the United States or by any State on account of sex.

Congress shall have power to enforce this article by appropriate legislation.

Amendment XX.**

Section 1. The terms of the President and Vice President shall end at noon on the 20th day of January, and the terms of Senators and Representatives at noon on the 3d day of January, of the years in which such terms would have ended if this article had not been ratified; and the terms of their successors shall then begin.

Section 2. The Congress shall assemble at least once in every year, and such meeting shall begin at noon on the 3d day of January, unless they shall by law appoint a different day.

Section 3. If, at the time fixed for the beginning of the term of the President, the President elect shall have died, the Vice President elect shall become President. If a President shall not have been chosen before the time fixed for the beginning of his term, or if the President elect shall have failed to qualify, then the Vice President elect shall act as President until a President shall have qualified; and the Congress may by law provide for the case wherein neither a President elect nor a Vice President elect shall have qualified, declaring who shall then act as President, or the manner in which one who is to act shall be selected, and such person shall act accordingly until a President or Vice President shall have qualified.

Section 4. The Congress may by law provide for the case of the death of any of the persons from whom the House of Representatives may choose a President whenever the right of choice shall have devolved upon them, and for the case of the death of any of the persons from whom the Senate may choose a Vice President whenever the right of choice shall have devolved upon them.

*The Fifteenth Amendment was ratified February 3, 1870.
**The Sixteenth Amendment was ratified February 3, 1913.
***The Seventeenth Amendment was ratified April 8, 1913.
† The Eighteenth Amendment was ratified January 16, 1919. It was repealed by the Twenty-First Amendment, December 5, 1933.

*The Nineteenth Amendment was ratified August 18, 1920.
**The Twentieth Amendment was ratified January 23, 1933.

Section 5. Sections 1 and 2 shall take effect on the 15th day of October following the ratification of this article.

Section 6. This article shall be inoperative unless it shall have been ratified as an amendment to the Constitution by the legislatures of three-fourths of the several States within seven years from the date of its submission.

Amendment XXI.*

Section 1. The eighteenth article of amendment to the Constitution of the United States is hereby repealed.

Section 2. The transportation or importation into any State, Territory, or possession of the United States for delivery or use therein of intoxicating liquors, in violation of the laws thereof, is hereby prohibited.

Section 3. This article shall be inoperative unless it shall have been ratified as an amendment to the Constitution by conventions in the several States, as provided in the Constitution, within seven years from the date of the submission hereof to the States by the Congress.

Amendment XXII**

Section 1. No person shall be elected to the office of the President more than twice, and no person who has held the office of President, or acted as President, for more than two years of a term to which some other person was elected President shall be elected to the office of the President more than once. But this Article shall not apply to any person holding the office of President when this Article was proposed by the Congress, and shall not prevent any person who may be holding the office of President, or acting as President, during the term within which this Article becomes operative from holding the office of President or acting as President during the remainder of such term.

Section 2. This article shall be inoperative unless it shall have been ratified as an amendment to the Constitution by the legislatures of three-fourths of the several States within seven years from the date of its submission to the States by the Congress.

Amendment XXIII.†

Section 1. The District constituting the seat of Government of the United States shall appoint in such manner as the Congress may direct:

A number of electors of President and Vice President equal to the whole number of Senators and Representatives in Congress to which the District would be entitled if it were a State, but in no event more than the least populous State; they shall be in addition to those appointed by the States, but they shall be considered, for the purposes of the election of President and Vice President, to be electors appointed by a State; and they shall meet in the District and perform such duties as provided by the twelfth article of amendment.

Section 2. The Congress shall have power to enforce this article by appropriate legislation.

Amendment XXIV.*

Section 1. The right of citizens of the United States to vote in any primary or other election for President or Vice President, for electors for President or Vice President, or for Senator or Representative in Congress, shall not be denied or abridged by the United States or any State by reason of failure to pay any poll tax or other tax.

Section 2. The Congress shall have power to enforce this article by appropriate legislation.

Amendment XXV.**

Section 1. In case of the removal of the President from office or of his death or resignation, the Vice President shall become President.

Section 2. Whenever there is a vacancy in the office of the Vice President, the President shall nominate a Vice President who shall take office upon confirmation by a majority vote of both Houses of Congress.

Section 3. Whenever the President transmits to the President pro tempore of the Senate and the Speaker of the House of Representatives his written declaration that he is unable to discharge the powers and duties of his office, and until he transmits to them a written declaration to the contrary, such powers and duties shall be discharged by the Vice President as Acting President.

Section 4. Whenever the Vice President and a majority of either the principal officers of the executive departments or of such other body as Congress may by law provide, transmit to the President pro tempore of the Senate and the Speaker of the House of Representatives their written

---

*The Twenty-First Amendment was ratified December 5, 1933.

**The Twenty-Second Amendment was ratified February 27, 1951.

†The Twenty-Third Amendment was ratified March 29, 1961.

*The Twenty-Fourth Amendment was ratified January 23, 1964.

**The Twenty-Fifth Amendment was ratified February 10, 1967.

declaration that the President is unable to discharge the powers and duties of his office, the Vice President shall immediately assume the powers and duties of the office as Acting President.

Thereafter, when the President transmits to the President pro tempore of the Senate and the Speaker of the House of Representatives his written declaration that no inability exists, he shall resume the powers and duties of his office unless the Vice President and a majority of either the principal officers of the executive department or of such other body as Congress may by law provide, transmit within four days to the President pro tempore of the Senate and the Speaker of the House of Representatives their written declaration that the President is unable to discharge the powers and duties of his office. Thereupon Congress shall decide the issue, assembling within forty-eight hours for that purpose if not in session. If the Congress, within twenty-one days after receipt of the latter written declaration, or, if Congress is not in session, within twenty-one days after Congress is required to assemble, determines by two-thirds vote of both Houses that the President is unable to discharge the powers and duties of his office, the Vice President shall continue to discharge the same as Acting President; otherwise, the President shall resume the powers and duties of his office.

Amendment XXVI*

Section 1. The right of citizens of the United States, who are eighteen years of age or older, to vote shall not be denied or abridged by the United States or by any State on account of age.

Section 2. The Congress shall have power to enforce this article by appropriate legislation.

Amendment XXVII.*

No law, varying the compensation for the services of the Senators and Representatives, shall take effect, until an election of Representatives shall have intervened.

*The Twenty-Sixth Amendment was ratified July 1, 1971.

*The Twenty-Seventh Amendment was ratified May 8, 1992.

Appendix

The Declaration of Independence*

In Congress, July 4, 1776, The unanimous Declaration of the thirteen united States of America,

When in the Course of human events, it becomes necessary for one people to dissolve the political bands which have connected them with another, and to assume among the Powers of the earth, the separate and equal station to which the Laws of Nature and of Nature's God entitle them, a decent respect to the opinions of mankind requires that they should declare the causes which impel them to the separation.

We hold these truths to be self-evident, that all men are created equal, that they are endowed by their Creator with certain unalienable Rights, that among these are Life, Liberty, and the pursuit of Happiness. That to secure these rights, Governments are instituted among Men, deriving their just powers from the consent of the governed, That whenever any Form of Government becomes destructive of these ends, it is the Right of the People to alter or to abolish it, and to institute new Government, laying its foundation on such principles and organizing its powers in such form, as to them shall seem most likely to effect their Safety and Happiness. Prudence,

---

*from *Documents of American History*, ed. by Henry Steele Commager (NY: Appleton-Century-Crofts, 8th edition, 1968).

indeed, will dictate that Governments long established should not be changed for light and transient causes; and accordingly all experience hath shown, that mankind are more disposed to suffer, while evils are sufferable, than to right themselves by abolishing the forms to which they are accustomed. But when a long train of abuses and usurpations, pursuing invariably the same Object evinces a design to reduce them under absolute Despotism, it is their right, it is their duty, to throw off such Government, and to provide new Guards for their future security.—Such has been the patient sufferance of these Colonies; and such is now the necessity which constrains them to alter their former Systems of Government. The history of the present King of Great Britain is a history of repeated injuries and usurpations, all having in direct object the establishment of an absolute Tyranny over these States. To prove this, let Facts be submitted to a candid world.

He has refused his Assent to Laws, the most wholesome and necessary for the public good.

He has forbidden his Governors to pass Laws of immediate and pressing importance, unless suspended in their operation till his Assent should be obtained; and, when so suspended, he has utterly neglected to attend to them.

He has refused to pass other Laws for the accommodation of large districts of people, unless those people would relinquish the right of Representation in the Legislature, a right inestimable to them and formidable to tyrants only.

He has called together legislative bodies at places unusual, uncomfortable, and distant from the depository of their Public Records, for the sole purpose of fatiguing them into compliance with his measures.

He has dissolved Representative Houses repeatedly, for opposing with manly firmness his invasions on the rights of the people.

He has refused for a long time, after such dissolutions, to cause others to be elected; whereby the Legislative Powers, incapable of Annihilation, have returned to the People at large for their exercise; the State remaining in the mean time exposed to all the dangers of invasion from without, and convulsions within.

He has endeavoured to prevent the population of these States; for that purpose obstructing the Laws of Naturalization of Foreigners; refusing to pass others to encourage their migrations hither, and raising the conditions of new Appropriations of Lands.

He has obstructed the Administration of Justice, by refusing his Assent to Laws for establishing Judiciary Powers.

He has made Judges dependent on his Will alone, for the tenure of their offices, and the amount and payment of their salaries.

He has erected a multitude of New Offices, and sent hither swarms of Officers to harass our People, and eat out their substance.

He has kept among us, in times of peace, Standing Armies without the Consent of our legislature.

He has affected to render the Military independent of and superior to the Civil Power.

He has combined with others to subject us to a jurisdiction foreign to our constitution, and unacknowledged by our laws; giving his Assent to their Acts of pretended legislation:

For quartering large bodies of armed troops among us:

For protecting them, by a mock Trial, from Punishment for any Murders which they should commit on the Inhabitants of these States:

For cutting off our Trade with all parts of the world:

For imposing taxes on us without our Consent:

For depriving us in many cases, of the benefits of Trial by Jury:

For transporting us beyond Seas to be tried for pretended offences:

For abolishing the free System of English Laws in a neighbouring Province, establishing therein an Arbitrary government, and enlarging its Boundaries so as to render it at once an example and fit instrument for introducing the same absolute rule into these Colonies:

For taking away our Charters, abolishing our most valuable Laws, and altering fundamentally the Forms of our Governments:

For suspending our own Legislature, and declaring themselves invested with Power to legislate for us in all cases whatsoever.

He has abdicated Government here, by declaring us out of his Protection and waging War against us.

He has plundered our seas, ravaged our Coasts, burnt our towns, and destroyed the lives of our people.

He is at this time transporting large armies of foreign mercenaries to compleat the works of death, desolation and tyranny, already begun with circumstances of Cruelty & perfidy scarcely paralleled in the most barbarous ages, and totally unworthy the Head of a civilized nation.

He has constrained our fellow Citizens taken Captive on the high Seas to bear Arms against their Country, to become the executioners of their friends and Brethren, or to fall themselves by their Hands.

He has excited domestic insurrections amongst us, and has endeavoured to bring on the inhabitants of our frontiers, the merciless Indian Savages, whose known rule of warfare, is an undistinguished destruction of all ages, sexes, and conditions.

In every stage of these Oppressions We have Petitioned for Redress in the most humble terms: Our repeated Petitions have been answered only by repeated injury. A Prince, whose character is thus marked by every act which may define a Tyrant, is unfit to be the ruler of a free People.

Nor have We been wanting in attention to our Brittish brethren. We have warned them from time to time of attempts by their legislature to extend an unwarrantable jurisdiction over us. We have reminded them of the circumstances of our emigration and settlement here. We have appealed to their native justice and magnanimity, and we have conjured them by the ties of our common kindred to disavow these usurpations, which, would inevitably interrupt our connections and correspondence. They too have been deaf to the voice of justice and of consanguinity. We must, therefore, acquiesce in the necessity, which denounces our Separation, and hold them, as we hold the rest of mankind, Enemies in War, in Peace Friends.

We, therefore, the Representatives of the united States of America, in General Congress, Assembled, appealing to the Supreme Judge of the world for the rectitude of our intentions, do, in the Name, and by Authority of the good People of these Colonies, solemnly publish and declare, That these United Colonies are, and of Right ought to be Free and Independent States; that they are Absolved from all Allegiance to the British Crown, and that all political connection between them and the State of Great Britain, is and ought to be totally dissolved; and that as Free and Independent States, they have full Power to levy War, conclude Peace, contract Alliances, establish Commerce, and to do all other Acts and Things which Independent States may of right do. And for the support of this Declaration, with a firm reliance on the Protection of Divine Providence, we mutually pledge to each other our Lives, our Fortunes and our sacred Honor.

JOHN HANCOCK.

New Hampshire
JOSIAH BARTLETT,
WM. WHIPPLE,
MATTHEW THORNTON.

Massachusetts Bay
SAML. ADAMS,
JOHN ADAMS,
ROBT. TREAT PAINE,
ELBRIDGE GERRY.

Rhode Island
STEP. HOPKINS,
WILLIAM ELLERY.

Connecticut
ROGER SHERMAN,
SAM'EL HUNTINGTON,
WM. WILLIAMS,
OLIVER WOLCOTT.

New York
WM. FLOYD,
PHIL. LIVINGSTON,
FRANS. LEWIS,
LEWIS MORRIS.

Pennsylvania
ROBT. MORRIS,
BENJAMIN RUSH,
BENJA. FRANKLIN,
JOHN MORTON,
GEO. CLYMER,
JAS. SMITH,
GEO. TAYLOR,
JAMES WILSON,
GEO. ROSS.

Delaware
CAESAR RODNEY,
GEO. READ,
THO. M'KEAN.

Georgia
BUTTON GWINNETT,
LYMAN HALL,
GEO. WALTON.

Maryland
SAMUEL CHASE,
WM. PACA,
THOS. STONE,
CHARLES CARROLL of
  Carrollton.

Virginia
GEORGE WYTHE,
RICHARD HENRY LEE,
TH. JEFFERSON,
BENJA. HARRISON,
THS. NELSON, JR.,
FRANCIS LIGHTFOOT LEE,
CARTER BRAXTON.

North Carolina
WM. HOOPER,
JOSEPH HEWES,
JOHN PENN.

South Carolina
EDWARD RUTLEDGE,
THOS. HEYWARD, JUNR.,
THOMAS LYNCH, JUNR.,
ARTHUR MIDDLETON.

New Jersey
RICHD. STOCKTON,
JNO. WITHERSPOON,
FRAS. HOPKINSON,
JOHN HART,
ABRA. CLARK.

Appendix

Articles of Confederation*

To all to whom these Presents shall come, we the undersigned Delegates of the States affixed to our names send greeting.

Whereas the Delegates of the United States of America in Congress assembled did on the fifteenth day of November in the Year of our Lord One Thousand Seven Hundred and Seventy seven, and in the Second Year of the Independence of America agree to certain articles of Confederation and perpetual Union between the States of Newhampshire, Massachusetts-bay, Rhodeisland and Providence Plantations, Connecticut, New York, New Jersey, Pennsylvania, Delaware, Maryland, Virginia, North-Carolina, South-Carolina and Georgia in the Words following, viz.

"Articles of Confederation and perpetual Union between the states of Newhampshire, Massachusetts-bay, Rhodeisland and Providence Plantations, Connecticut, New-York, New-Jersey, Pennsylvania, Delaware, Maryland, Virginia, North-Carolina, South-Carolina and Georgia.

Article I. The Stile of this confederacy shall be "The United States of America."

Article II. Each state retains its sovereignty, freedom and independence, and every Power, Jurisdiction and right, which is not by this

*Source: Thorpe, ed., 1 *Federal and State Constitutions* 9 (1909).

confederation expressly delegated to the United States, in Congress assembled.

Article III. The said states hereby severally enter into a firm league of friendship with each other, for their common defence, the security of their Liberties, and their mutual and general welfare, binding themselves to assist each other, against all force offered to, or attacks made upon them, or any of them, on account of religion, sovereignty, trade, or any other pretence whatever.

Article IV. The better to secure and perpetuate mutual friendship and intercourse among the people of the different states in this union, the free inhabitants of each of these states, paupers, vagabonds and fugitives from Justice excepted, shall be entitled to all privileges and immunities of free citizens in the several states; and the people of each state shall have free ingress and regress to and from any other state, and shall enjoy therein all the privileges of trade and commerce, subject to the same duties, impositions and restrictions as the inhabitants thereof respectively, provided that such restriction shall not extend so far as to prevent the removal of property imported into any state, to any other state of which the Owner is an inhabitant; provided also that no imposition, duties or restriction shall be laid by any state, on the property of the united states, or either of them.

If any Person guilty of, or charged with treason, felony, or other high misdemeanor in any state, shall flee from Justice, and be found in any of the united states, he shall upon demand of the Governor or executive power, of the state from which he fled, be delivered up and removed to the state having jurisdiction of his offence.

Full faith and credit shall be given in each of these states to the records, acts and judicial proceedings of the courts and magistrates of every other state.

Article V. For the more convenient management of the general interests of the united states, delegates shall be annually appointed in such manner as the legislature of each state shall direct, to meet in Congress on the first Monday in November, in every year, with a power reserved to each state, to recal its delegates, or any of them, at any time within the year, and to send others in their stead, for the remainder of the Year.

No state shall be represented in Congress by less than two, nor by more than seven Members; and no person shall be capable of being a delegate for more than three years in any term of six years; nor shall any person, being a delegate, be capable of holding any office under the united states, for which he, or another for his benefit receives any salary, fees or emolument of any kind.

Each state shall maintain its own delegates in a meeting of the states, and while they act as members of the committee of the states.

In determining questions in the united states, in Congress assembled, each state shall have one vote.

Freedom of speech and debate in Congress shall not be impeached or questioned in any Court, or place out of Congress, and the members of congress shall be protected in their persons from arrests and imprisonments, during the time of their going to and from, and attendance on congress, except for treason, felony, or breach of the peace.

Article VI. No state without the Consent of the united states in congress assembled, shall send any embassy to, or receive any embassy from, or enter into any conference, agreement, or alliance or treaty with any King, prince or state; nor shall any person holding any office of profit or trust under the united states, or any of them, accept of any present, emolument, office or title of any kind whatever from any king, prince or foreign state; nor shall the united states in congress assembled, or any of them, grant any title of nobility.

No two or more states shall enter into any treaty, confederation or alliance whatever between them, without the consent of the united states in congress assembled, specifying accurately the purposes for which the same is to be entered into, and how long it shall continue.

No state shall lay any imposts or duties, which may interfere with any stipulations in treaties, entered into by the united states in congress assembled, with any king, prince or state, in pursuance of any treaties already proposed by congress, to the courts of France and Spain.

No vessels of war shall be kept up in time of peace by any state, except such number only, as shall be deemed necessary by the united states in congress assembled, for the defence of such state, or its trade; nor shall any body of forces be kept up by any state, in time of peace, except such number only, as in the judgment of the united states, in congress assembled, shall be deemed requisite to garrison the forts necessary for the defence of such state; but every state shall always keep up a well regulated and disciplined militia, sufficiently armed and accoutred, and shall provide and constantly have ready for use, in public stores, a due number of field pieces and tents, and a proper quantity of arms, ammunition and camp equipage.

No state shall engage in any war without the consent of the united states in congress assembled, unless such state be actually invaded by enemies, or shall have received certain advice of a resolution being formed by some nation of Indians to invade such state, and the danger is so imminent as not to admit of a delay, till the united states in congress assembled can be consulted: nor shall any state grant commissions to any ships or vessels of war, nor letters of marque or reprisal, except it be after a declaration of war by the united states in congress assembled, and then only against the kingdom or state and the subjects thereof, against which war has been so declared, and under such regulations as shall be established by the united states in congress assembled, unless such state be infested by pirates, in which case vessels of war may be fitted out for that occasion, and kept so long as the danger shall continue, or until the united states in congress assembled shall determine otherwise.

Article VII. When land-forces are raised by any state for the common defence, all officers of or under the rank of colonel, shall be appointed by the legislature of each state respectively by whom such forces shall be raised, or in such manner as such state shall direct, and all vacancies shall be filled up by the state which first made the appointment.

Article VIII. All charges of war, and all other expences that shall be incurred for the common defence or general welfare, and allowed by the united states in congress assembled, shall be defrayed out of a common treasury, which shall be supplied by the several states, in proportion to the value of all land within each state, granted to or surveyed for any Person, as such land and the buildings and improvements thereon shall be estimated according to such mode as the united states in congress assembled, shall from time to time direct and appoint. The taxes for paying that proportion shall be laid and levied by the authority and direction of the legislatures of the several states within the time agreed upon by the united states in congress assembled.

Article IX. The united states in congress assembled, shall have the sole and exclusive right and power of determining on peace and war, except in the cases mentioned in the sixth article—of sending and receiving ambassadors—entering into treaties and alliances, provided that no treaty of commerce shall be made whereby the legislative power of the respective states shall be restrained from imposing such imposts and duties on foreigners, as their own people are subjected to, or from prohibiting the exportation or importation of any species of goods or commodities whatsoever—of establishing rules for deciding in all cases, what captures on land or water shall be legal, and in what manner prizes taken by land or naval forces in the service of the united states shall be divided or appropriated.—of granting letters of marque and reprisal in times of peace—appointing courts for the trial of piracies and felonies committed on the high seas and establishing courts for receiving and determining finally appeals in all cases of captures, provided that no member of congress shall be appointed a judge of any of the said courts.

The united states in congress assembled shall also be the last resort on appeal in all disputes and differences now subsisting or that hereafter may arise between two or more states concerning boundary, jurisdiction or any other cause whatever; which authority shall always be exercised in the manner following. Whenever the legislative or executive authority or lawful agent of any state in controversy with another shall present a petition to congress, stating the matter in question and praying for a hearing, notice thereof shall be given by order of congress to the legislative or executive authority of the other state in controversy, and a day assigned for the appearance of the parties by their lawful agents, who shall then be directed to appoint by joint consent, commissioners or judges to constitute a court for hearing and determining the matter in question: but if they cannot agree, congress shall name three persons out of each of the united states, and from the list of such persons each party shall alternately strike out one, the petitioners beginning, until the number shall be reduced to thirteen; and from that number nor less than seven, nor more than nine names as congress shall direct, shall in the presence of congress be drawn out by lot, and the persons whose names shall be so drawn or any five of them, shall be commissioners or judges, to hear and finally determine the controversy, so always as a major part of the judges who shall hear the cause shall agree in the determination: and if either party shall neglect to attend at the day appointed, without shewing reasons, which congress shall judge sufficient, or being present shall refuse to strike, the congress shall proceed to nominate three persons out of each state, and the secretary of congress shall strike in behalf of such party absent or refusing; and the judgment and sentence of the court to be appointed, in the manner before prescribed, shall be final and conclusive; and if any of the parties shall refuse to submit to the authority of such court, or to appear or defend their claim or cause, the court shall nevertheless proceed to pronounce sentence, or judgment, which shall in like manner be final and decisive, the judgment or sentence and other proceedings being in either case transmitted to congress, and lodged among the acts of congress for the security of the parties concerned: provided that every commissioner, before he sits in judgment, shall take an oath to be administered by one of the judges of the supreme or superior court of the state, where the cause shall be tried, "well and truly to hear and determine the matter in question, according to the best of his judgment, without favour, affection or hope of reward:" provided also that no state shall be deprived of territory for the benefit of the united states.

All controversies concerning the private right of soil claimed under different grants of two or more states, whose jurisdictions as they may respect such lands, and the states which passed such grants are adjusted, the said grants or either of them being at the same time claimed to have originated antecedent to such settlement of jurisdiction, shall on the petition of either party to the congress of the united states, be finally determined as near as may be in the same manner as is before prescribed for deciding disputes respecting territorial jurisdiction between different states.

The united states in congress assembled shall also have the sole and exclusive right and power of regulating the alloy and value of coin struck by their own authority, or by that of the respective states—fixing the standard of weights and measures throughout the united states.—regulating the trade and managing all affairs with the Indians, not members of any of the states, provided that the legislative right of any state within its own limits be not infringed or violated—establishing and regulating post-offices from one state to another, throughout all the united states, and exacting such postage on the papers passing thro' the same as may be requisite to defray the expences of the said office—appointing all officers of the land forces, in the service of the united states, excepting regimental officers.—appointing all the officers of the naval forces, and commissioning all officers whatever in the service of the united states—making rules for the government and regulation of the said land and naval forces, and directing their operations.

The united states in congress assembled shall have authority to appoint a committee, to sit in the recess of congress, to be denominated "a Committee of the States," and to consist of one delegate from each state; and to appoint such other committees and civil officers as may be necessary for managing the general affairs of the united states under their direction—to appoint one of their number to preside, provided that no person be allowed to serve in the office of president more than one year in any term of three years; to ascertain the necessary sums of Money to be raised for the service of the united states, and to appropriate and apply the same for defraying the public expences—to borrow money, or emit bills on the credit of the united states, transmitting every half year to the respective states an account of the sums of money so borrowed or emitted,—to build and equip a navy—to agree upon the number of land forces, and to make requisitions from each State for its quota, in proportion to the number of white inhabitants in such state; which requisition shall be binding, and thereupon the legislature of each state shall appoint the regimental officers, raise the men and cloath, arm and equip them in a soldier like manner, at the expence of the united states, and the officers and men so cloathed, armed and equipped shall march to the place appointed, and within the time agreed on by the united states in congress assembled: But if the united states in congress assembled shall, on consideration of circumstances judge proper that any state should not raise men, or should raise a smaller number than its quota, and that any other state should raise a greater number of men than the quota thereof, such extra number shall be raised, officered, cloathed, armed and equipped in the same manner as the quota of such state, unless the legislature of such state shall judge that such extra number cannot be safely spared out of the same, in which case they shall raise officer, cloath, arm and equip as many of such extra number as they judge can be safely spared. And the officers and men so cloathed, armed and equipped, shall march to the place appointed, and within the time agreed on by the united states in congress assembled.

The united states in congress assembled shall never engage in a war, nor grant letters of marque and reprisal in time of peace, nor enter into any treaties or alliances, nor coin money, nor regulate the value thereof, nor ascertain the sums and expenses necessary for the defence and welfare of the united states, or any of them, nor emit bills, nor borrow money on the credit of the united states, nor appropriate money, nor agree upon the number of vessels of war, to be built or purchased, or the number of land or sea forces to be raised, nor appoint a commander in chief of the army or navy, unless nine states assent to the same: nor shall a question on any other point, except for adjourning from day to day be determined, unless by the votes of a majority of the united states in congress assembled.

The congress of the united states shall have power to adjourn to any time within the year, and to any place within the united states, so that no period of adjournment be for a longer duration than the space of six Months, and shall publish the Journal of their proceedings monthly, except such parts thereof relating to treaties, alliances or military operations as in their judgment require secresy; and the yeas and nays of the delegates of each state on any question shall be entered on the Journal, when it is desired by any delegate; and the delegates of a state, or any of them, at his or their request shall be furnished with a transcript of the said Journal, except such parts as are above excepted, to lay before the legislatures of the several states.

Article X. The committee of the states, or any nine of them, shall be authorised to execute, in the recess of congress, such of the powers of congress as the united states in congress assembled, by the consent of nine states, shall from time to time think expedient to vest them with; provided that no power be delegated to the said committee, for the exercise of which, by the articles of confederation, the voice of nine states in the congress of the united states assembled is requisite.

Article XI. Canada acceding to this confederation, and joining in the measures of the united states, shall be admitted into, and entitled to all the advantages of this union: but no other colony shall be admitted into the same, unless such admission be agreed to by nine states.

Article XII. All bills of credit emitted, monies borrowed and debts contracted by, or under the authority of congress, before the assembling of the united states, in pursuance of the present confederation, shall be deemed and considered as a charge against the united states, for payment and satisfaction whereof the said united states, and the public faith are hereby solemnly pledged.

Article XIII. Every state shall abide by the determinations of the united states in congress assembled, on all questions which by this confederation are submitted to them. And the Articles of this confederation shall be inviolably observed by every state, and the union shall be perpetual; nor shall any alteration at any time hereafter be made in any of them; unless such alteration be agreed to in a congress of the united states, and be afterwards confirmed by the legislatures of every state.

And Whereas it hath pleased the Great Governor of the World to incline the hearts of the legislatures we respectively represent in congress, to approve of, and to authorize us to ratify the said articles of confederation and perpetual union. Know Ye that we the undersigned delegates, by virtue of the power and authority to us given for that purpose, do by these presents, in the name and in behalf of our respective constituents, full and entirely ratify and confirm each and every of the said articles of confederation and perpetual union, and all and singular the matters and things therein contained: And we do further solemnly plight and engage the faith of our respective constituents, that they shall abide by the determinations of the united states in congress assembled, on all questions, which by the said confederation are submitted to them. And that the articles thereof shall be inviolably observed by the states we respectively represent, and that the union shall be perpetual. In Witness whereof we have hereunto set our hands in Congress. Done at Philadelphia in the state of Pennsylvania the ninth Day of July in the Year of our Lord one Thousand seven Hundred and Seventy-eight, and in the third year of the independence of America.

On the part & behalf of the State of New Hampshire
JOSIAH BARTLETT
JOHN WENTWORTH Jun[r]
August 8th 1778

On the part and behalf of The State of Massachusetts Bay
JOHN HANCOCK
SAMUEL ADAMS
ELBRIDGE GERRY
FRANCIS DANA
JAMES LOVELL
SAMUEL HOLTEN

*On the part and behalf of the State of Rhode-Island and
Providence Plantations*
WILLIAM ELLERY
HENRY MARCHANT
JOHN COLLINS

On the part and behalf of the State of Connecticut
ROGER SHERMAN
SAMUEL HUNTINGTON
OLIVER WOLCOTT
TITUS HOSMER
ANDREW ADAMS

On the Part and Behalf of the State of New York
JA^S DUANE
FRA^S LEWIS
W^M DUER
GOUV MORRIS

On the Part and in Behalf of the State of New Jersey.
Novr 26, 1778.—
JNO WITHERSPOON
NATH^L SCUDDER

On the part and behalf of the State of Pennsylvania
ROB^T MORRIS
DANIEL ROBERDEAU
JON^A BAYARD SMITH.
WILLIAM CLINGAN
JOSEPH REED 22^d July 1778

On the part & behalf of the State of Delaware
THO M:KEAN Feby 12 1779
JOHN DICKINSON
May 5th 1779
NICHOLAS VAN DYKE,

On the part and behalf of the State of Maryland
JOHN HANSON
March 1 1781
DANIEL CARROLL d^o

On the Part and Behalf of the State of Virginia
RICHARD HENRY LEE
JOHN BANISTER
THOMAS ADAMS
JN^O HARVIE
FRANCIS LIGHTFOOT LEE

On the part and Behalf of the State of N⁰ Carolina
JOHN PENN July 21ˢᵗ 1778
CORNˢ HARNETT
JN⁰ WILLIAMS

On the part & behalf of the State of South-Carolina
HENRY LAURENS
WILLIAM HENRY DRAYTON
JN⁰ MATHEWS
RICHᴰ HUTSON
THOˢ HEYWARD Junʳ

On the part & behalf of the State of Georgia
JN⁰ WALTON 24ᵗʰ July 1778
EDWᴰ TELFAIR
EDWᴰ LANGWORTHY

Index

About the Author

JOHN R. VILE is Professor and Chair of Political Science at Middle Tennessee State University. He is the author of a number of works on the U.S. Constitution, including *Encyclopedia of Constitutional Amendments, Proposed Amendments, and Amending Issues, 1789–1995* (1996), *Constitutional Change in the United States* (Praeger, 1994), *Contemporary Questions Surrounding the Constitutional Amending Process* (Praeger, 1993), *The Constitutional Amending Process in American Political Thought* (Praeger, 1992), and *Rewriting the United States Constitution* (Praeger, 1991).